Walking in
THE ALPS

Walking in THE ALPS

Brian Spencer

HUNTER
PUBLISHING INC

British Library Cataloguing in Publication Data

Spencer, Brian, 1931-
Walking in the Alps
1. Walking — Alps (Europe)
2. Alps (Europe)
Description and travel — Guide-books
I. Title
796.5′22′094947 D823

Published in the UK by
Moorland Publishing Co Ltd,
8 Station Street,
Ashbourne, Derbyshire,
DE6 1DE England.
Tel: (0335) 44486

ISBN 0 86190 092 8 (paperback)
ISBN 0 86190 093 6 (hardback)

Published in the USA by
Hunter Publishing Inc,
300 Raritan Center Parkway,
CN94, Edison, NJ 08818

ISBN 0 935161 23 6 (paperback)

Printed in the UK by
Butler and Tanner Ltd,
Frome, Somerset.

Black and white photographs have been provided by:
The Swiss National Tourist Office, p 1, 2, 48, 54, 66, 84, 87, 96, 101, 103; The Austrian National Tourist Office p 107, 139, 143; Brian Spencer p 32, 33, 37, 113, 116, 120, 182, 184, 186; Gaetano Barone p 163, 166, 170; B. Nielson p 42; Fremdenvekehrsverband, Seefeld (Foto-Löbl) p 130; Neukirchen am Grossvenediger p 151, 154.

Colour photographs have been provided by:
R. Scholes (Zillertal to the Inn Valley, Col du Lauteret, Leukabad-Gemmi Pass, Argentière, Chamonix, Tuxertal above Lanersbach); Brian Spencer (The Dolomites, Mont Blanc range, Lac Chambon); Swiss Tourist Board (Kandersteg, Mayrhofen).

Half title page:
Walking through the woods in Switzerland

Frontispiece:
One of the well marked hiking trails in Switzerland

KEY TO SYMBOLS

ROAD (TUNNEL)	▬▬ ••••••
RIVER/STREAM	∼∼∼
RAILWAY	++++++++
TRAMWAY	┬┬┬┬┬┬┬┬
CABLE CAR/LIFT	○—○—○
TOWNS/VILLAGES	
BUILDINGS/FARM	■
LAKE	
WOOD	
GLACIER	
CHAPEL/CHURCH	
BRIDGE	
WATERMILL	
BUS STOP	H
VIEW POINT	△
HEIGHT (IN METRES)	(1509)
ROUTE OF WALK	— — —
(ALTERNATIVE ROUTE)	

Contents

Introduction 7

FRANCE

1. La Chaise Dieu (Auvergne-Massif Central) 13
2. Chamonix (Mont Blanc) 24
3. La Grave (Haute Alpes) 36

SWITZERLAND

1. Kandersteg (Bernese Oberland) 47
2. Zuos (Engadine) 60
3. Münster - (Obergoms) 71
4. Appenzell 83
5. Champex (Valais) 95

AUSTRIA

1. Damüls (Vorarlberg) 106
2. Haldensee (Tannheimertal) 115
3. Seefeld (Tyrol) 127
4. Mayrhofen (Zillertal) 138
5. Neukirchen (Grossvenediger) 150

ITALY

1. Courmayeur (Aosta Valley) 162
2. Corvara (Val Badia) 174
3. Belluno (Piave) 183

TEN RULES FOR MOUNTAIN WALKERS

1 Before starting out check your own physical condition and experience, that of your companions and in particular of your children. Sureness of step and freedom from vertigo are important prerequisites.

2 Plan every mountaineering tour in detail in advance. Maps, guides and information provided by Alpine clubs, local people, mountain guides and hut wardens will be of great assistance.

3 In the mountains you must have the appropriate equipment and clothing, above all strong, high-ankle shoes or boots with soles which do not slip. Since the weather can often change suddenly it is vital to take with you protection against rain and cold.

4 For safety's sake and in case of emergency always leave notice of your route and destination in the log books in the huts, in restaurants and inns or with friends. The expected time of your return is vital.

5 Adjust your speed always to your abilities and those of your companions. Walking too fast will inevitably lead to early exhaustion.

6 Never leave the marked path and always concentrate, for even in easy terrain you can have a fall. In particular walking on steep grass banks, especially if they are wet, on steep snow slopes or on glaciers is always difficult and dangerous.

7 Never dislodge stones through careless walking. They can seriously endanger other walkers. Always pass as quickly as possible areas where there may be danger of falling stones.

8 Turn back in good time. This is not a sign of weakness but of sensible and safe planning. This may be necessary if the weather changes, mist comes down or the path becomes difficult or obstructed.

9 Remain calm if an accident happens. Try to obtain assistance by the means at your disposal, such as calling, or waving with clothing. An injured person should, if possible, remain at the place of the accident in a clearly visible position.

10 Keep mountain areas tidy. Take litter with you and help us keep our mountains free of rubbish.

USEFUL ADDRESSES

Austrian National Tourist Office,
30 St George St,
London W1

Austrian National Tourist Office,
500 5th Avenue,
New York

French Government Tourist Office,
178 Piccadilly,
London W1

Gîtes de France (Booking service for rented accommodation),
178 Piccadilly,
London W1V 0PQ

French Government Tourist Office,
610 5th Avenue,
New York

Italian State Tourist Department
(ENIT), 1 Princes Street,
London W1

Italian State Tourist Department
(ENIT), 630 5th Avenue,
New York

Swiss National Tourist Office,
Swiss Centre,
1 New Coventry Street,
London W1V 3HG

Swiss National Tourist Office,
608 5th Avenue,
New York

Introduction

WHAT THIS GUIDE IS ALL ABOUT

The huge swathe of towering snow-clad summits and glaciers in the middle of Europe is not only the realm of the mountain climber who is at home on rock and ice; the secluded valleys beneath the peaks make a unique holiday area for all who wish to enjoy mountain scenery without too much effort. This guide is, therefore, about those places where mountain walking is comparatively easy, but at the same time the walks described are set in beautiful surroundings.

The sixteen 'centres' in the guide have been carefully chosen for their scenic qualities. None are quite as remote as might be expected and travel to and from them, whether it be by road, rail or air is relatively easy. All centres offer in their own individual ways a chance to follow well maintained and easily graded footpaths through some of the best mountain scenery in Europe. Each centre differs from its neighbour, even though they might be on opposite sides of the same mountain range, so that the walking is of an entirely different flavour, centre by centre. Some walks are more strenuous than others, but all are well within the capabilities of the average walker. European weather patterns often give better weather in Central France when the Alps may be enduring a spell of prolonged rain; for this reason la Chaise-Dieu has been included. Although not strictly an alpine area, it is a hilly region that is worth exploring for its delightful high level moorland and forest walks.

Every centre has plenty of alternative diversions to offer for rest days and for that reason alone they are interesting places to visit. Some are near ancient cities or attractive lakes, most are in areas which pride themselves on their cuisine, and all can offer a completely relaxed holiday amidst spectacular scenery.

Each of the four countries covered by this guide is divided into various centres which are described in turn, together with details of how to get there and what to do if you do not wish to walk on any particular day. Each centre has a full range of accommodation, from, in some cases, three- and four-star hotels to excellent camp sites.

As well as the walks themselves there is useful information and local addresses so that the potential visitor has the most enjoyable holiday possible.

ABOUT THE WALKS

Seven walks are described for each centre. They start with the easiest and progress to the hardest, but all should be suitable for even the most inexperienced hill walker. Seven walks only have been chosen deliberately as most visitors on a holiday of say 10-14 days duration will want time off to do other things, but also there is always enough scope around each centre for individual exploration over many days.

The description of each walk begins with a list of the major features or places seen or visited along the route, together with a grading of the walk, the time required and distance covered. Details of the walk itself follow and finally there is a note of highlights of the route or anything special or dangerous to look out for.

The first walk is usually ideal for the beginning of a holiday and is designed to both show the delights of the area and to loosen up tired limbs after a long journey.

HOW THE WALKS ARE GRADED

Each walk is graded from easy to difficult and the time to do the walk is also quoted. *Easy* means that the walk is mostly along level grassy paths, while *difficult* means that the track is rough and steep and often tiring. Most paths are signposted and waymarked, usually with coded paint splashes which vary from area to area, but in patterns which are usually obvious at the start of each path. The time quoted in the description of each walk is more important than distance and is a fair average of the time spent actually walking, but it does not include time taken for eating meals or admiring the view.

There will be slight variations in the degree of difficulty from area to area, but none should be beyond the limits of anyone who is used to hill walking in Britain.

HOW THE WALKS ARE DESCRIBED

This guide is not intended to be carried in the hand and therefore, for clarity, descriptions are kept to an absolute minimum. Almost all the walks are along well marked paths and it should be a simple matter to follow the signs once the beginning of the path has been located.

Descriptions are intended to be used in conjunction with the map of the area and are of the major features shown on the map. Directions are always given as facing the feature and place names are spelt as given on the map. In certain instances where the featured name includes its descriptions, such as lake, river, pass, etc, its English translation will also be given to help with identification. Where there is any appreciable change in altitude, the heights of important features such as summits, passes, path junctions, etc, are shown in metres. If a change in altitude coincides with a very short horizontal distance this can only indicate a steep climb and allowances both in time and ability of the party should be made on those sections.

MAPS

The map or maps mentioned in the introduction to each area are those which have been found to be the most accurate and useful. Route descriptions are based on these maps and their use is therefore strongly recommended.

Maps can usually be bought in the area, but if they are acquired beforehand they can often add to the greater anticipation and better planning of a holiday. All the maps mentioned can be bought from specialist map shops such as:

Edward Stanford Limited,
12-14 Long Acre,
London WC2

Rand McNally Map Store
10 E. 53rd Street
New York, New York

Swiss maps are also available through the Swiss Tourist Office in London or New York.

HINTS ON CLOTHING

In the mountains, weather conditions can change dramatically, so the prudent walker must go prepared for anything between hot sun and cold rain or even snow. Fortunately in the Alps, the weather is more predictable than say on the Scottish hills and is certainly warmer, even in winter. Clothing should therefore be lightweight, warm and windproof. Ideally one should wear, depending on the day or altitude, either shorts or breeches and a medium weight shirt with sleeves. Boots are the most comfortable footwear in the mountains and certainly the safest on rough or rocky tracks. Woollen socks prevent rubbing and blisters. A rucksack which fits snugly and high up on your back is the best type; inside it you should carry a spare pullover and a windproof anorak with hood, or a cagoule which would also serve as a waterproof. Sun glasses and some form of skin lotion are essential on walks which are close to snow or bare rock. Take a small first aid kit for cuts and bruises and also spare food such as chocolate. A whistle and torch are handy in case of emergencies. A map and compass are essential if you intend moving over tracks where you might be unsure of the route.

PREPARING FOR THE WALKS

1 *At home*

It helps if you walk regularly, but no large scale keep-fit sessions are necessary.

2 *Before setting out:*

Check the route.

Check the local weather forecast (usually available from tourist information centres).

Make sure that you have enough time to complete the planned walk.

Tell someone where you are going and what time to expect you back.

Make a note of the telephone number of your hotel or camp site, so that you can get a message back if you are delayed.

REMEMBER Mountain Rescue in most alpine areas can be a very expensive item, so do not allow anything to happen where you might cause unnecessary concern to others and a large bill to yourself!

3 *Weather*

Weather in the Alps is fairly settled, but sudden changes can occur. Check the local forecast before hand. Snow should not normally be encountered on any of the walks in this guide. On no account should you try to climb any slopes covered by early or late falls of snow without adequate equipment, such as ice axes and compass and have the knowledge and skills required in their use.

LONG DISTANCE WALKS

Long distance mountain walks pass through several of the centres covered by this guide. All are hard walks, but again are within the capabilities of fit and ambitious walkers. Accommodation which can be found at easy intervals along the route is mostly simple and ranges from mountain huts to dormitories attached to hotels. It is not advisable to try to book more than a day in advance, so parties and even individuals must be prepared to rough it now and then. However, no one will be turned away on arrival at a mountain hut or similar remote accommodation, even if it appears to be already full.

The main long distance routes which pass through this guide are:

Tour of Mont Blanc (Chamonix, Champex, Courmayeur Sections)
As the title suggests this route is around Mont Blanc and follows well signposted footpaths over high and usually snow-free passes from France to Switzerland, into Italy and back to France. The walk may be done in any direction and has several interesting variants. Highly recommended for its constantly changing views of the peaks and glaciers around Mont Blanc.

Grande Randonnée 54 (la Grave Section)
A high level route through the Écrins National Park in some of France's most remote and unspoilt alpine scenery.

Grande Randonnée 3 (la Chaise Dieu Section)
Follows the Loire Valley through the Auvergne region.

Grande Randonnée 4 (la Chaise Dieu Section)
Crosses a chain of extinct volcanos around le Puy in the central Auvergne.

AUSTRIAN HIKING BOOT SCHEME

A light hearted scheme designed to encourage family walking in Austria. To qualify you must collect a series of 'Hiking Boot' stamps from huts and restaurants and mark them on a special card, which is available from local tourist offices throughout Austria. When a total of 15 hours walking has been completed you will then be able to claim the special 'Hiking Boot' badge.

THE BEST TIME TO GO TO THE ALPS

This depends on what you want from an alpine holiday. If you like to see the alpine flowers, then June and July are the best months. If you want clear views and do not mind lower temperatures, especially early in the day, then September would be suitable. July and August are the hottest months, but are sometimes prone to thunderstorms, and are also the most popular months.

HOW TO MAKE YOUR MONEY GO FURTHER

Switzerland: The Swiss have enjoyed a lower rate of inflation than the rest of Europe and with the stable Swiss Franc, prices are often cheaper than visitors expect.

One of the best bargains in Switzerland and which gives scope to explore their unique railway system, is the Swiss Holiday Card which gives greatly reduced fares on the Swiss transport system. Several variations of this scheme are available and up to date details are obtainable from the Swiss National Tourist Offices, or the Swiss Federal Railway Information Offices.

Austria: The Austrian Federal Railways have a ticket which enables those under 23 to travel anywhere in Austria at reduced rates.

In value for money, Austria comes next to Switzerland for price stability. Food, drink and accommodation are reasonably priced, but consumer goods, especially if imported, can be expensive.

France and Italy: Buy a Runabout (Carnet) bus ticket if you intend using local buses more than a couple of times during your stay. These are usually sold by the driver or at local depots and make a considerable overall saving.

Prices of most commodities in France tend to be on a par with those in the UK and America but Italy with its rampant inflation often alarms visitors, especially those on a self catering holiday. However, some items like wine or speciality foods can be very cheap and climbing boots and other footwear are often sold at bargain prices.

Post Buses are found in most alpine countries, they are reasonably priced and run regular services to some of the most remote villages.

Alpine Club Huts: If you intend using the huts more than once or twice it helps to be a member of one of the recognised alpine clubs. All huts have two scales of charges, for members and non members, and all acknowledge each other club's membership. In the UK the Austrian Alpine Club is the easiest to join, their address is:

Austrian Alpine Club,
13 Longcroft House, Fretherne Road,
Welwyn Garden City,
Herts AL8 6PQ

Insurance Always remember to take out holiday insurance both for medical cover as well as for theft and other contingencies. It is worth bearing in mind that mountain rescue is not a voluntary service in the Alps and especially in France where it can be very expensive, so make sure you have adequate cover if you intend venturing onto more difficult terrain.

Specialist Insurance cover can be obtained in the UK through:

West Mercia Insurance Services,
High Street, Wombourne,
Wolverhampton WV5 9DN

France

LA CHAISE-DIEU

(Auvergne - Massif Central)

Recommended Map:
Institute Geographique National,
Carte Touristique
Sheet 50 : (1:100,00)
St Etienne - le Puy

HOW TO GET THERE

Road: (1) South by A7 to Lyon, A47 to St Etienne and Firminy. N88 to le Puy. D906 north to la Chaise-Dieu. (2) N444 to Clermont-Ferrand, N9 and N102 to Brioude, then D588 east to la Chaise-Dieu. (3) From the east : Via Lyon then St Etienne, Firminy and le Puy.
Rail: Clermont-Ferrand or le Puy with local bus connections.
NB The line which passes through le Chaise-Dieu is now goods only.
Air: Nearest airport : Clermont-Ferrand with connections by rail and local bus services.

THE AREA

When the weather in the High Alps is fine it can be glorious, but when it breaks it can be infuriating, especially to the walker who has spent months of anticipatory planning only to find that once the rain starts it never knows when to stop. This then is the prime reason for including the Auvergne and la Chaise-Dieu as the centre of a walking area in a guide primarily intended for alpine centres. The advantages are several; firstly the weather, if as we have said the weather remains bad in the high mountains, the Auvergne which is considerably lower is often fine and sunny, for its weather patterns seem to differ against those further east. Secondly, the Auvergne and in particular the country around la Chaise-Dieu has some little known but excellent walking. Thirdly and perhaps most important is the simple fact that this is an area of beautiful countryside, the people are very friendly and hospitable and

THINGS TO DO AND PLACES TO VISIT AROUND LA CHAISE-DIEU

Folklorique Events:
Local song and dance concerts arranged throughout summer and winter seasons.

Abbey
Church dedicated to St Robert in fourteenth century.
Dance Macabre. Mural 85ft long; fifteenth century.
Tapesteries; sixteenth century.
Organ loft.
Salle de l'Echo.

Cycling
Cycle hire from Syndicat d'Initiative (rue St Martin).

Bathing
Plan d'Eau 1½km north-east on D906. Etang du Breuil 1½km east in forest.

Boating
Plan d'Eau.

Tennis
Plan d'Eau.

the hoteliers take great pride in their cuisine. The region of the Auvergne has been designated a conservation park covering a variety of mountain masses (Monts Dôme, Dore and Chantal), and lakes which fill ancient volcanic craters. It is an area for quiet strolling and nature study.

The ancient abbey town of la Chaise-Dieu sits astride one of the many steep sided forest covered ridges, which, with their attendant deep gorges and twisting rivers, are a feature of the Masif Central. La Chaise-Dieu is in the department of Haute-Loire, one of the four departments of the Auvergne. 'Recent' geological activity has shaped much of this region and the legacy of ancient volcanos can be seen, especially near the city of le Puy which is completely encircled by extinct volcano craters and their stumps. These stumps, or more correctly the cores of volcanos which being made of harder rock, remained after the soft outer areas were worn away, are a feature of the landscape around le Puy. Over the centuries after man came to the region they became venerated and are now capped by monasteries or religious statues of huge proportions.

La Chaise-Dieu (the Seat of God) is dominated by its ancient abbey which was dedicated to St Robert in the fourteenth century and contains the celebrated 'Danse Macabre', an 85ft mural which indicates that no matter what ones station is in life, then death is the final leveller of us all. Other features are the beautiful Flemish tapestries and the massive organ loft which is the central pivot of an annual festival of French music. Nearby is a room with strange acoustic qualities, known as the Salle de l'Echo, where the gentlest whispered remark in the corners of the room can be clearly heard opposite.

La Chaise Dieu

Houses cluster around the walls of the abbey for in the Middle Ages la Chaise-Dieu was the scene of much religious strife and the town was fortified with a wall, parts of which can still be seen to this day. Small comfortable family-run hotels are found in and around la Chaise-Dieu and are mostly unpretentious, but all offer a competively high standard of Auvergnat cooking. Based on farm house cuisine, the regional specialities are such mouth watering dishes as coq au vin, leg of mutton brayaude or delicious pastries filled with local fruits. Crystallised fruits and jams are other specialities and all deserve mention, also the excellent wines from the Upper Loire as well as spirits made from local wild fruits. Above all the Auvergne is famous for its cheeses such as Saint Nectaire or the pungently flavoured Gaperon.

Life in nearby villages is leisurely and takes its pace from the plodding oxen which are still used on some of the small farms, where boggy ground makes the use of tractors impractical. Traditional crafts such as lace making still goes on in the area and on warm summer evenings one can still see groups of women sitting in the open air with the special lace making cushions on their knees, deftly twisting lace bobbins to and fro, while managing to keep a constant chatter amongst themselves. Not only do old ladies make lace, but it is pleasing to see that traditions are being kept alive by young girls. Folk dancing is still very popular and la Chaise-Dieu has an active folk song and dance society which arranges concerts at intervals throughout the year.

Almost every town in the region has its interesting feature; volcanic remains are not only seen as the strange stumps around le Puy, but basaltic dykes and columns shaped like organ pipes outcrop in various places. Castles such as the one at Polignac on the road from Chaise-

Dieu to le Puy took advantage of the natural rock defences left by a volcano. Chateaux slumber in quiet rural settings and above all is a certain relaxed timelessness which seems to lure the tourist into gentle inactivity. Robert Louis Stevenson fell under the charm of the area

FURTHER INFORMATION

Interesting towns nearby

Ambert
28km north. Paper mill and museum of Richard de Bas. Restaurants.

Brioude
33km west. Old streets and houses. Lafayette was born nearby.

Clermont-Ferrand
95km north-west. Chief town of the Auvergne. Eleventh-twelfth century church. Petrifying springs. Headquarters of the Michelin Company.

Le Puy
38km south. A town encircled by extinct volcanos. Romanesque cathedral. Lace museum. Shops and restaurants.

Gorges de l'Allier
35km south-west. 18 miles of splendid gorge scenery up and downstream of Monistrol d'Allier.

Zoo
Ambert.

Accommodation
Small hotels and pensions details from:
Bureau d'Accueil,
la Chaise-Dieu.
Holiday villages at la Monadiere, la Chapel-Geneste. Tel: 00 02 40. (8km north-west of la Chaise-Dieu).

Rented accommodation: Contact either:
Gîtes de France, London.
or
Bureau d'Accueil, la Chaise-Dieu.

Camp Sites

La Chaise-Dieu
Les Sapins — lieu-dit St Jean (1km from town centre).

le Puy — Municipal site.

Tourist Information
Bureau d'Accueil et
d'Information Touristique,
Rue St Martin,
43160 la Chaise-Dieu,
Auvergne.

Comité Regional de Tourisme,
45 Avenue Julien, BP 395,
53011 Clermont-Ferrand.
Tel: (73) 930403

Cycle Hire
Enquire at Bureau d'Accueil.

Fishing
Trout. Rivers and lakes.
Salmon. River Allier. Most fishing is without the need of a permit, but check locally to see if the waters are private.

Museums
Aurillac. Castle and museum of volcanology.
Ambert. Paper making.
Montloçon. Fairground equipment.
Mouline (Allier). Folk museum.
le Puy. Lace making.
Volvic. Lava quarry and volcano museum.
Thiers. Knife making.
Chavagne. Country life.

when he travelled south from le Puy with his donkey Modestine, a journey which was recounted in his *Travels with a Donkey*. This book sums up well the delights of the Auvergne and nearby Cévennes regions.

Walking, horse riding, cycling and cross country skiing in winter are all well catered for around la Chaise-Dieu. There are over 600 miles of waymarked footpaths and two long distance routes and their variants, (Grandes-Randonnées, usually signified by the initials GR) pass through the Auvergne. The GR3 is along the Loire Valley and GR4 crosses the long chain of volcanos. Three-figure numbers, ie GR412, signify variations from the main routes. Public transport in the form of local bus services tends to be along main roads, but it is efficient and can be used for extended itineries.

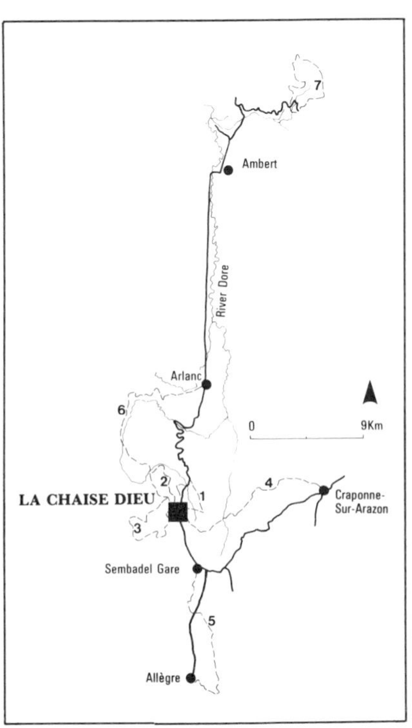

THE WALKS

All the walks in this area are on easy terrain and some are waymarked.
However as most of the walking is in forest care should be taken not to stray from the route. If in doubt retrace your steps.

In summer vipers are likely to be encountered in dry sunny places, so take care if walking through undergrowth! Snakes do not usually bite unless provoked in some way, ie tormented or accidentally trodden on. If bitten seek immediate medical attention.

ROUTE 1

Etang du Breuil, les Guillaumanches, Plan d'Eau, Baffour

7½km (4½ miles). 2 hours. Easy. Forest roads and quiet villages.

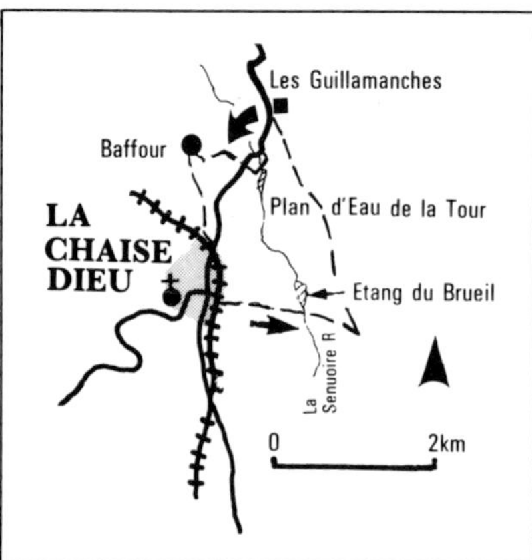

Walk eastwards from the abbey of la Chaise-Dieu and cross the main road. Pass a farmhouse and go along the track under the railway. Almost immediately beyond the railway there is a junction of four roads, continue ahead and downhill past a man-made lake, the Etang du Brueil. Climb gently uphill to a crossroads and turn left; walk along a track beneath pine trees, over another crossroads and continue as far as the main road by the farm of les Guillaumanches. Turn left and pass the recreation area by the lake of Plan d'Eau de la Tour and after about 100m, turn right to the village of Baffour and left along the lane back to la Chaise-Dieu.

Mostly road walking but traffic free, apart from the main road.

ROUTE 3

La Pénide, Lachaux, Lavese, Montrecoux, Connangles, Arfeuilles

14km (8½ miles). 4 hours. Easy/Moderate. Meadowland and the interesting ruins of a mill at Lachaux.

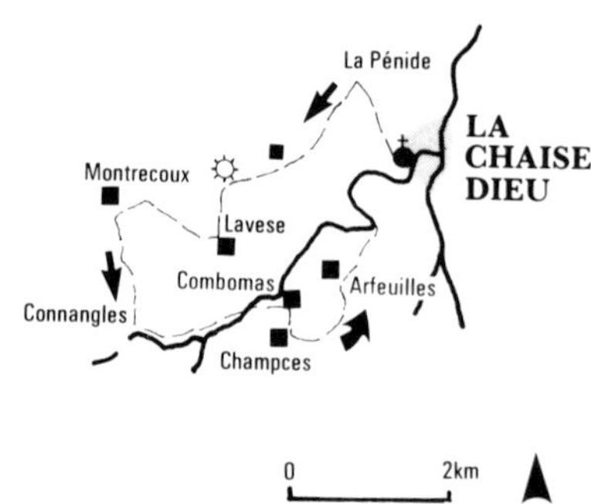

ROUTE 2

La Pénide, Bois de Mozun, la Chapelle Geneste

9km ($5\frac{1}{2}$ miles). 3 hours. Easy. Delightful rural scenery.

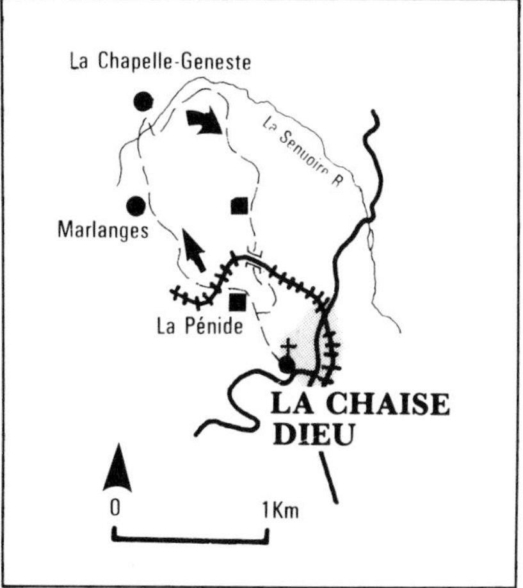

Walk out of la Chaise-Dieu by the lane which leads downhill, away from the market square and in front of the abbey. By the last houses on the lane turn right on to a path across some fields to the group of houses known as la Pénide. Cross the main road and turn left over the railway line on to a cart track signposted GR412, then forward into the forest. Pass above and to the right of the village of Marlanges and join the road over the river Senouire and then climb uphill to the pretty village of la Chapelle-Geneste. Walk back downhill in the direction of Marlanges and beyond the river turn left along a farm track. Beyond the farm buildings the track continues as a well defined footpath through the forest to a farm house. Ignore the lane to the left (to Baffour), but walk across the fields to the railway line. Go under the railway bridge and join the road, turning left into la Chaise-Dieu.

Leave la Chaise-Dieu by the track to la Pénide as walk 2. Turn left at the road and walk downhill for about one kilometre then left along the lane to Lachaux. Beyond the houses a rough path crosses marshy ground and a stream to a ruined mill. Beyond the mill follow a gradually improving track to the farm of Lavese. The track turns sharply to the right here. After about 100m look out for a path on the right. Follow this over a series of meadows and through woodland to the road at Montrecoux. Turn left along the road to the village of Connangles. Pass through the village by road and turn left again, gradually moving downhill to cross a stream (this is the same one which was crossed before the mill), and right at a group of houses (Combomas), then left at another group (Champces) where a path leads through the forest to the hamlet of Arfeuilles. A good track leaves Arfeuilles to join the road back to la Chaise-Dieu.

In wet weather the track from Laschaux to the mill can be very muddy but it is safe.

ROUTE 4

Dom du Breuil, les Brayes, Bonneval, Beaumont, St Victor-sur-Aurlanc, Cheyrac, Craponne-sur-Arzon

18km (11 miles). 5 hours. Moderate.
Forest, with a steep valley leading to farmland.

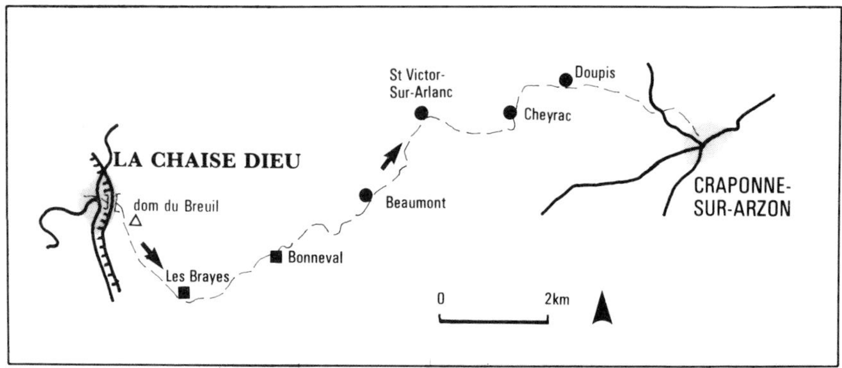

Cross the main road and go under the railway bridge as in walk 1, but turn right at the road junction then left and uphill to the viewpoint of Dom du Breuil. A path leads downhill and across a stream to the road by the farm of les Brayes. Go behind the farm and cross a field (there is no path so do not walk on any growing crops), then downhill through a small wood to a road. Turn left and go down a steep hill along the road to Bonneval where there is a restaurant. Continue downhill along a wide track and over the river. By a road junction look out for a path climbing uphill through the forest and signposted to Beaumont. Enter the village and turn left in the village square and follow a well defined field path to St Victor-sur-Aurlanc. Turn right in front of the church and follow the road to Cheyrac. Go left in the centre of the village for a path to Doupis and then right to join the road into Craponne-sur-Arzon.

Careful map reading will be necessary on this walk and also transport back from Craponne. Buses running to Bellevue le Montagne should connect with a bus back to la Chaise-Dieu, but check beforehand.

ROUTE 5

Allégre, Mont Bar, Bréchignac, lac de Malguet, Sembadel Gare

14km ($8\frac{1}{2}$ miles). 4/5 hours.
Moderate.
A walk through an area of ancient volcanic activity.

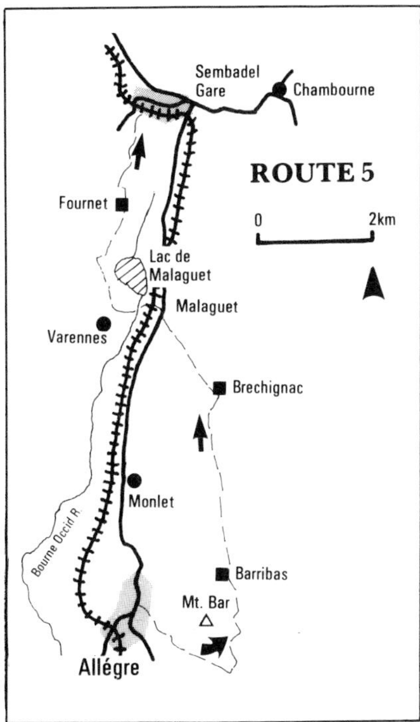

Either take the local bus or arrange transport to Allégre. From the town centre of Allégre walk uphill in an easterly direction to the outskirts. Turn right on a path which follows the contours across the slopes of Mont Bar and is signposted GR40 and GR41. On the far side of the mountain turn left where the path joins the road between Céaux d'Allégre and Moulet. Walk uphill along the road and across the small col which is directly ahead. Continue along the road and go through the village of Barribas. Ignore the first path on the right, but where the road turns sharply to the left continue ahead on a path through meadow and woodland. Cross a minor road and follow another path into the forest to Bréchignac. Turn left in the village and then right from the square along the country road to Malaguet. Cross the main road and walk down to the lake and turn left to Varennes. Turn right just before entering the village on a path which begins at the church. Follow this path above the lake to Fournet and join the road to Sembadel Gare to catch a bus back home.

Mont Bar and lac de Malaguet are both tangible reminders of the volcanic activity which once affected this area.

ROUTE 6

La Chapelle-Geneste, St Alyre d'Arlanc, Aubapeyre, Besse, la Sagne, Capartel, Arlanc

20km (12½ miles). 6 hours. Moderate.
Along a section of the GR412 long distance footpath above steep gorges.

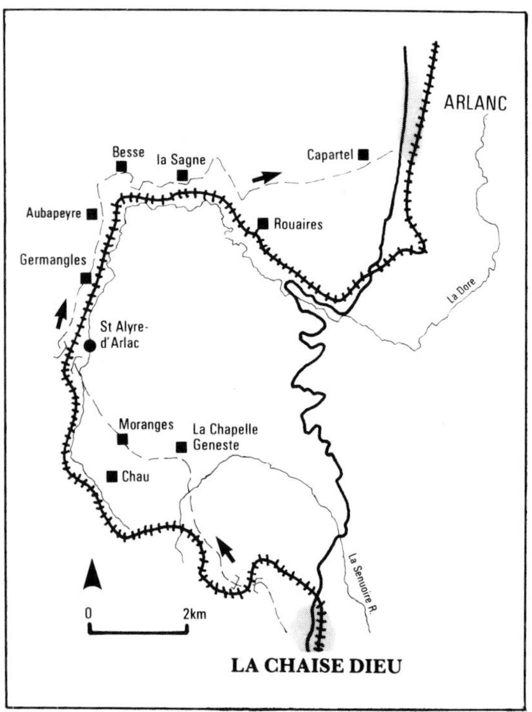

Follow route 2 by GR412 (signposted) to la Chapelle-Geneste and turn left opposite the church. Turn left at the cross roads then right at the junction with the lane down to the hamlet of Chau. Leave this lane before entering the village and cross several fields to join the road at Moragnes. Turn left along the road into the small town of St Alyre D'Arlanc. Walk through the town and look out for the GR412 signposts at the start of a lane on the right. Follow this route through Germangles and eventually on a path to Aubapeyre. Leave the GR412 here and follow the path ahead to Besse then right along the road to la Sagne. There is a small hill ahead; follow the lane which turns slightly to the left around the hill and as far as a junction with a road from Rouaries. Turn left at this junction and after about ¼km turn right on a path through about 1km of forest to Capartel and on to Arlanc where buses run back to la Chaise-Dieu.

Check the bus timetable before embarking on this walk — it is a long uphill road from Arlanc back to la Chaise-Dieu.

ROUTE 7

Perrier, Plateau Pégrol (1,486m), Jasserie de la Croix de Fossat, le Puy

12km (7 miles). 4/5 hours. Moderate.
High level walking across moorland.

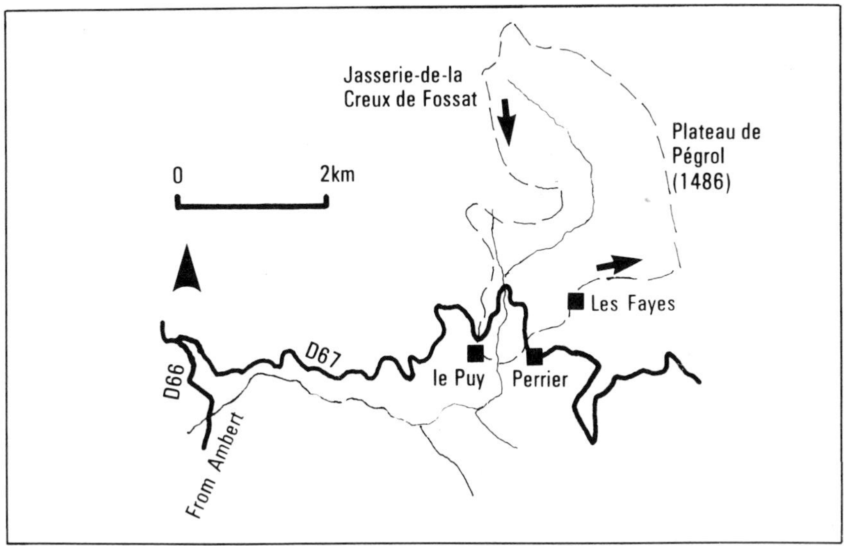

Drive to Ambert and take the D66 road and then D67 (the col des Supeyres road), to Perrier which is about half way up the steep zig-zags on the climb to the col. Leave your car where it will not inconvenience anyone and walk beyond the village to a forest track on the left. Follow this for about 200m and turn right along a path which climbs steeply uphill past the group of hill farms called les Fayes. At the top of the hill the Plateau de Pégrol opens out to the left and right. Continue forwards to a junction with another path and turn left across the plateau. The path swings round to the left and excellent views open up on either side. Walk gently downhill on this path and look out for a group of farm buildings away to the left in a depression below the level of the plateau. This is the Jasserie de la Croix de Fossat. Turn left behind the farm buildings and walk down a steep hill to the forest ahead. Turn right and follow an easier path to more farmsteads and then again downhill to the road at le Puy. Walk left uphill along the road and back to the car.

There is some steep up and down hill walking on this route, but the views are delightful. This walk can be included with a visit to Ambert and the old paper mill and museum of Richard de Bas.

The le Puy mentioned here is only a farmhouse and is not the le Puy of volcanic fame which is a much larger place.

CHAMONIX

(Mont Blanc)

Recommended Map:
Didier and Richard (1:50,000)
Sheet 8
Massifs du Mont Blanc

HOW TO GET THERE

Road: The 'Autoroute Blanche' connects Chamonix to the European Motorway system and the Mont Blanc Tunnel enables direct access to and from Italy (Aosta Valley). Regular long distance coach services from Grenoble, Annecy, Geneva, Aosta and Milan.
Rail: Chamonix is on the St Gervais-Martigny (Switzerland) Line. Connections with the main lines of both the French and Swiss Railways.
Air: International airports at Geneva (connection by bus or rail) and Lyon (connection by rail).

THE AREA

Chamonix can undoubtably claim to be the most dramatically situated of all of Europe's mountain holiday resorts. On one side is Mont Blanc with its attendant glaciers, the highest point in Europe at 4,807m (15,781ft), and on the other side the Aiguille Rouge chain forms a natural and easily accessible viewing balcony. Glaciers dominate the town and are only held in check by a breathtaking ridge which starts from Mont Blanc's summit and runs as a series of needle sharp towers almost to the outskirts of Chamonix. The most famous of all these towers is the Aiguille du Midi, which is so steep sided that it is almost unbelievable to find a cable car running to its summit.

The group of mountains including Mont Blanc form a narrow chain running roughly north-east from the Col de la Seigne (2,542m) to Mont Dolent (3,823m) and make a natural frontier between France and Italy. Beyond Mont Dolent the ridge turns north and the land to the east belongs to Switzerland. The mountain slope on the French side is nominally easier than that descending to Italy and as a result the French glaciers are longer. Peaks such as the Grandes Jorasses, and the subsidiary ridge which includes the Aiguille du Midi, rise in awesome stature above the eternal snows.

Mountaineers and seekers of mountain relaxation discovered the beauties of the Chamonix valley many years ago. The first recorded interest in Mont Blanc was in the early 1700s, when Horace Benedict de Saussure, a Swiss who devoted himself to the study of glaciers, offered a reward for the first person to find a route to the top of the mountain. The prize was won in 1786 by Dr Paccard, a local doctor who was guided by Jacques Dalmat; from all accounts the real credit went to the guide who virtually dragged the doctor up the final stages of the climb. Countless numbers have climbed the mountain since then, but probably no expedition has ever bettered the luxury of that made in 1851 by a certain Albert Smith who together with four companions, twenty guides and numerous porters took with them over a hundred bottles of wine, twenty loaves, eight legs of mutton, six pieces of veal, a side of beef and forty chickens, with a vast quantity of cheese, chocolate and fruit!

Today's visitors find the ascent much less arduous and are helped by a tramway from le Fayet as far as the Hotel Nid d'Aigle, then by cable car to the Refuge du Goûter. Afterwards the climb is literally a treadmill across the Dome du Goûter with the Refuge Vallot hut in case of bad weather. As a mountain climb Mont Blanc is easy, but it is not for the inexperienced and ill equipped as it is mostly on snow and ice. In addition the altitude creates its own problems once climbers are above 10,000ft.

With the opening of the motorway system linked to the Mont Blanc tunnel, travel into the region of Chamonix became very easy indeed and as a result there has been a considerable growth of tourism. Mostly this is in the Nant Valley to the south-east of Chamonix around les Contamines-Montjoie, which is rapidly becoming a major ski resort. Fortunately Chamonix, despite its popularity, has retained a tasteful, almost Edwardian, atmosphere. Mechanical aids to reach the high ridges and glaciers have long been a feature of these mountains and began with the tramway to the Mer de Glace above Chamonix. At one time the upper station of le Montenvers was well above the terminal section of the glacier, but now, with the dramatic shrinking of alpine glaciers, it is rapidly being left behind. Cable cars and chair lifts abound and make it possible for valley based walkers to visit high level paths without the need to waste energy in climbing the lower slopes. With the ambitious system of lifts from Chamonix via the Aiguille du Midi and across the Glacier du Géant to Entrèves in Italy, all the year round skiing is now possible below the Col du Géant. The Névé de l'Index above la Flégère also offers summer snow and again access is by cable car, in this case the lower station is a little to the north-east of the town at les Praz. A word of warning though to anyone with a heart condition or breathing difficulty — the summit of the Aiguille du Midi

Mont Blanc and the Chamonix valley

is 3,842m (12,606ft), and the sudden change of altitude from Chamonix at 1,039m (3,409ft) can sometimes cause distress.

Entertainment other than walking is varied and ranges from dances and functions held at the highly select casino to cinemas and night-clubs. Musical weeks are popular and are rapidly becoming part of Europe's concert diary. The Festival of Mountain Guides which takes place in mid August, is now an established feature with parades and demonstrations of rock climbing skills. At Merlet there is a small zoological garden with examples of alpine animals in their natural surroundings. Early mountaineering expeditions are commemorated in a museum which has some interesting relics; possibly they look crude when compared with modern climbing equipment, but they still helped their users to make some dramatic first ascents. There is a large modern swimming pool where on a hot clear day the lazy mountaineer can float in one of the outside pools and gaze up to the high summits. Indoor skating, tennis and golf are all catered for with the most up to

THINGS TO DO AND PLACES TO VISIT AROUND CHAMONIX

Swimming Pool
North of the town centre.

Tennis
Near swimming pool, Tel: 53 11 57

Golf
18-hole. Les Praz. Tel: 53 06 28

Horse Riding
Les Bossons.

Indoor Ice Skating
Near swimming pool.

Summer Skiing
Névé de l'Index.
Col du Géant (for instruction telephone 53 22 57).

Coach Excursions
Enquire at the tourist office.

Zoo
Merlet above Montquart. Collection of alpine animals in natural surroundings.

date facilities. Equestrian training is available at les Bossons beneath the Glacier des Bossons, but there are no facilities for pony trekking.

Anyone who wants to develop their mountaineering ability can enrole on one of the many courses run by the Chamonix Climbing School. French is the standard language used at the school and anyone taking part in one of the courses must first be proficient in the language. Training is available up to 'guides standard' — the Chamonix guides being some of the most famous in the alps. Two guiding services are available, the Company of Mountain Guides and

FURTHER INFORMATION

Interesting towns nearby:

Geneva
Switzerland. 70km north-west. On Lake Geneva (Lac Leman). Shops, lake cruising, gardens, restaurants.

St Gervais les Bains
16km west. Attractive small spa town.

Les Contamines-Montjoie
24km south-west. Popular ski resort. Shops, Roman Bridge, Restaurants and Cafes.

Mountain tramways
Mer de Glace (Chamonix to Montenvers)
le Fayet to Nid d'Aigle Restaurant.

Camp Sites
Nineteen private campsites in the Chamonix valley. (Camping is only allowed on approved sites).

Accommodation
Hotel Booking Service. Tel: 53 23 33
Daily Hotel Reservations. Tel: 53 00 24
Furnished Accommodation. Tel: 53 00 24

Tourist Information
Office du Tourism,
Place de l'Église,
Chamonix.
Tel: 53 00 24

Cable Car Ascents
Montenvers - Mer de Glace
Chamonix - Plan de l'Aiguille
Plan de l'Aiguille - Aiguille du Midi
Aiguille du Midi - Helbronner
Chamonix - Brévent
Les Praz - La Flégère
La Flégère - L'Index
Les Houches - Belle Vue
Col de Voza - Prarion
Les Houches - Prarion
Argentière - Lognan
Lognan - Grandes Montets
Les Bossons - Bossons Glacier*
Le Tour - Charmillon
Charmillon - Col de Balme
Chamonix - Les Planards*
* = chair lifts

Mountain Guides
Company of Mountain Guides. Tel: 53 00 88
High Mountain Office. Tel: 53 22 08
Mont Blanc Independant Guide Association. Tel: 53 27 05
Club Alpin Français (Membership & Insurance). Tel: 53 16 03

Mountain Rescue
Society Chamoniarde de Secours en Montagne,
Place du Mont Blanc,
Chamonix.
Tel: 53 16 89

Mont Blanc Independant Guide Association, both offer tours and courses to very high standards.

Accommodation around the Chamonix valley ranges from simple rented rooms to the highest class of hotels. One useful feature which is standard in all hotels is that of issuing to anyone wishing to be away from the hotel at lunchtime, or any other meal, vouchers in lieu of meals. The vouchers may be used in any other hotel or restaurant in the area including mountain restaurants.

Public transport is excellent. Buses run between most of the surrounding villages. It is usual to obtain a weekly ticket (carnet) which covers the whole valley and is a useful saving on transport costs.

THE WALKS

All footpaths encountered on the walks described in this section are well maintained and clearly marked and should present no difficulties to the fit walker and mountaineer, but adequate clothing and boots are required, especially on the higher routes.

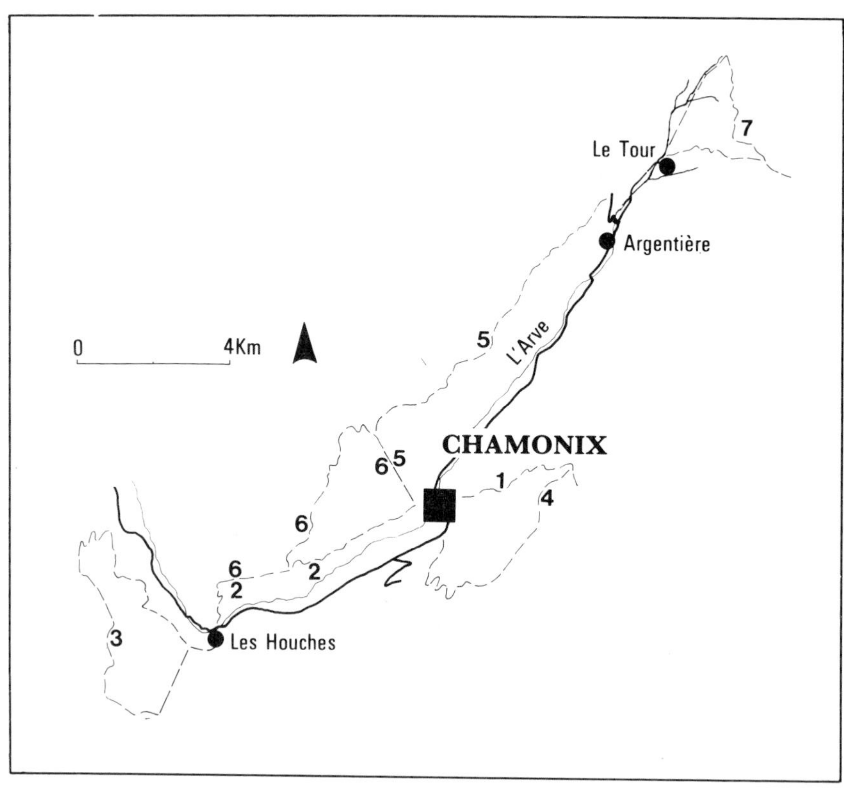

ROUTE 1

Montenvers, Mer de Glace, les Bois, Chamonix

6½km (4 miles). 2 hours. Easy.
A downhill walk from Europe's largest glacier.

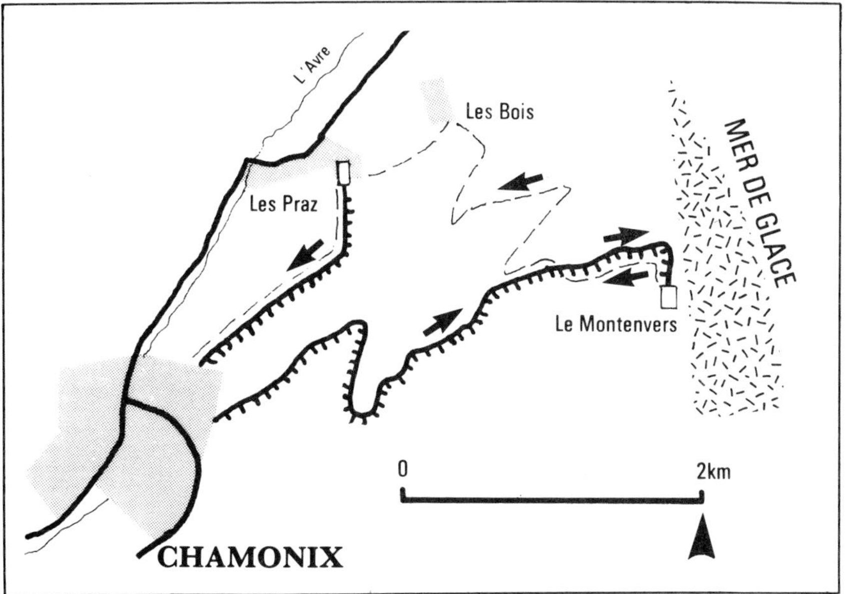

Take the Mer de Glace tramway (opposite the mainline railway station) to the upper station of le Montenvers, then visit the Mer de Glace glacier either on foot or by using the cable car from the hotel to the side of the glacier. The walk from the glacier starts by the Montenvers hotel and follows the tram track for a little way into a forest. Look out for a junction of paths before a small hut. Turn right at the junction and zig-zag downhill to the village of les Bois and turn left along the edge of the forest to les Praz Station. Continue to a junction with another path and turn left, then right after about 100m and enter Chamonix by the sports ground and swimming pool.

This is an easy introduction to the area and gives the visitor a close look at a major glacier.

ROUTE 2

Les Houches, le Coupeau, Merlet, Les Epinettes, les Moussoux, Chamonix

9km ($5\frac{1}{2}$ miles). 4/5 hours. Easy.
A gentle climb taking in an alpine zoo.

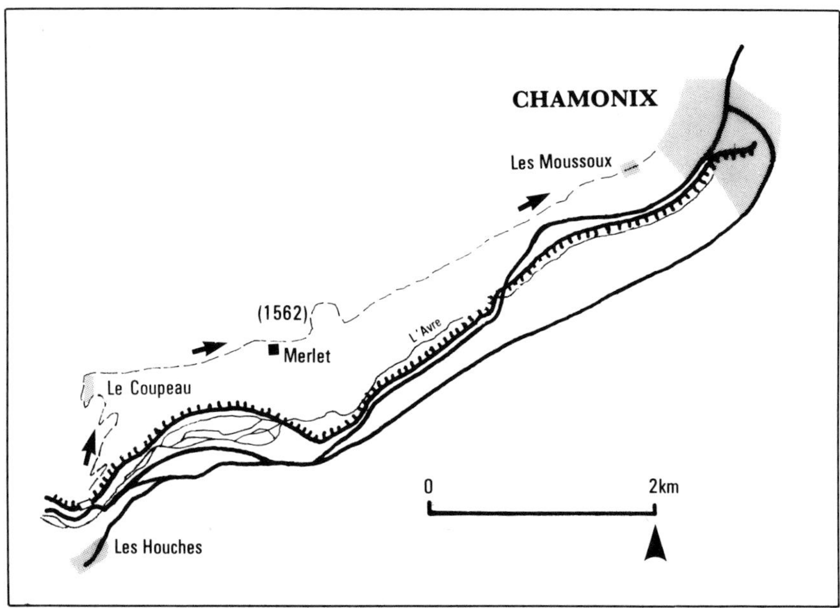

Take the train to les Houches station and from there walk up the road to le Coupeau. Turn right in the village and continue as far as Merlet (signposted). After visiting the alpine zoo follow the path on the right beyond the zoo, ignoring the main path (uphill). Start to descend through the forest across the hillside, ignoring paths to the right or left, and enter Chamonix by way of les Moussoux.

The alpine zoo is an interesting highlight to this walk.

ROUTE 3

Les Houches, Bellevue, Col de Voza, Col de la Forcle, Mont Barrel, Vaudagné, les Chauvants

10km (6 miles). 5 hours. Easy/Moderate.
Forest walking beneath Mount Prarion and through quiet alpine villages.

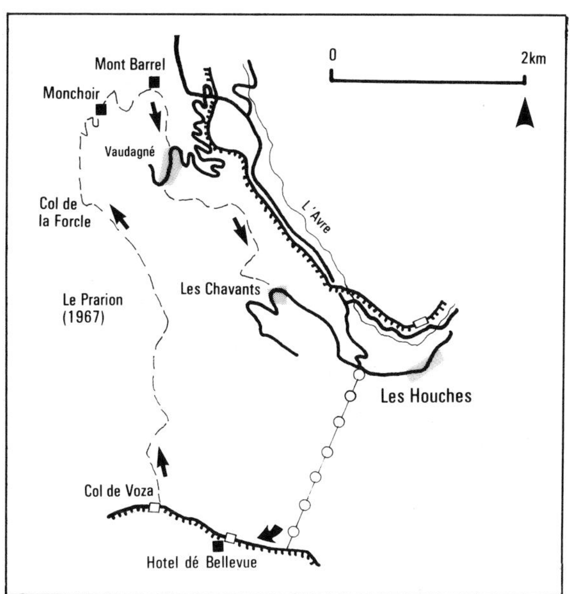

Use the cable car to get from les Houches to Bellevue. Walk along the Mont Blanc tramway as far as Col de Voza and turn right, then immediately left at the top of a ski lift. Walk through forest beneath Mount Prarion, at first slowly loosing height, and then uphill to the Col de la Forcle. Turn right downhill past the farms of Monchon and Mont Barrel. Turn right at the latter and continue downhill to Vaudagné. Above the church in Vaudagné another path crosses the valley; follow this through more forest and follow the contour round the hillside to les Chauvants and les Houches.

This is a forest walk which is ideal for a hot sunny day. Clearings allow views of the surrounding peaks.

ROUTE 4

Le Montenvers, Sentier Henry Vallon, Hotel Plan de l'Aigle, Cascade de Blatière

10km (6 miles). 5/6 hours. Moderate.

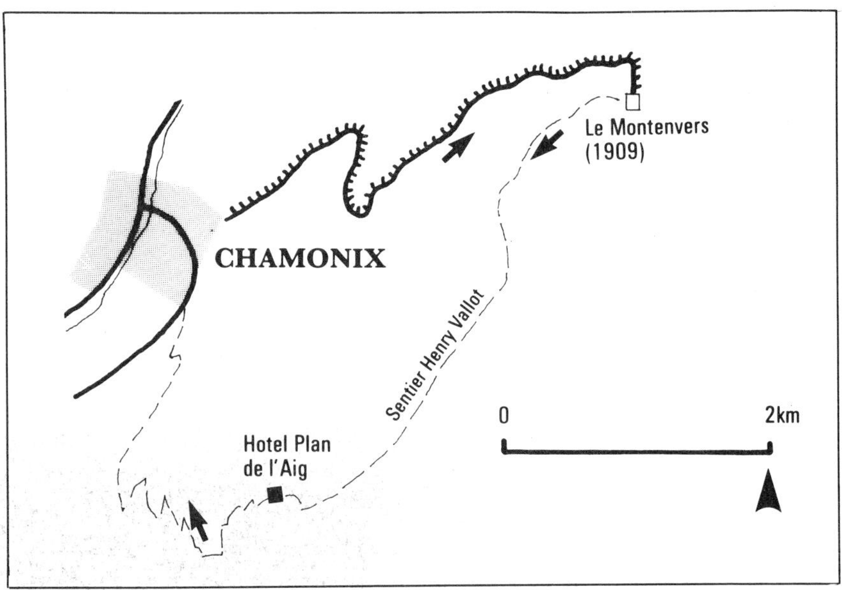

Take route 1 as far as le Montenvers and follow the signposted path known as the 'Sentier Henry Vallon', which follows the contours of the hillside on a dramatic route beneath the Aiguille ridge, as far as the Hotel Plan de l'Aigle. Continue forwards on a steep path which zig zags downhill into the forest. As the angle of descent eases the path makes a wide sweep to the right; continue along this and into Chamonix.

The Sentier Henry Vallon is one of the finest scenic paths in the Alps.

Primula minima – *one of the flowers of the alps*

Argentière, Chamonix

Chamonix

Lac Chambon, La Grave

Col du Lauteret, La Grave

ROUTE 5

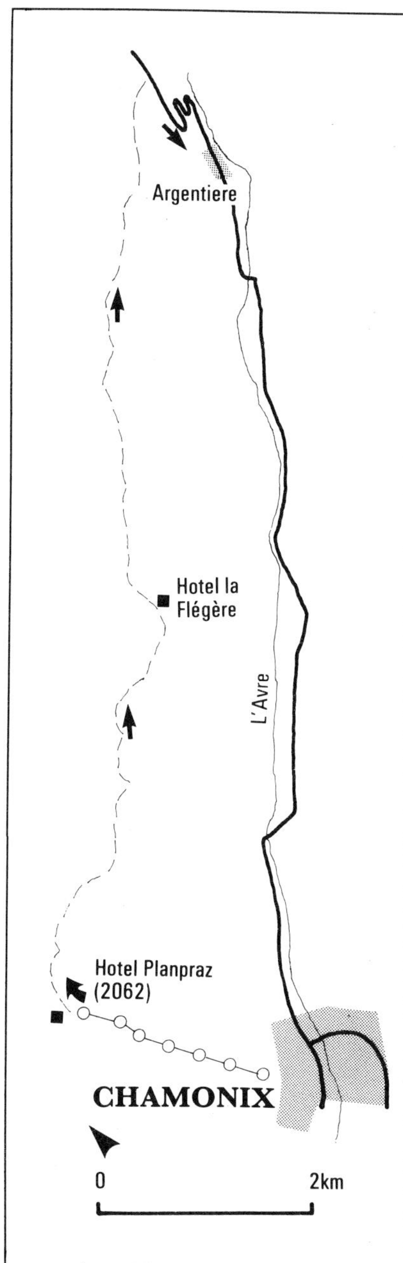

Planpraz, Belvedère path, la Flégère, Argentière

9km ($5\frac{1}{2}$ miles). 5/6 hours. Moderate.

This is the most famous walk in the Chamonix area and follows the Belvedère balcony with its unrivalled views of the Aiguille du Midi ridge, the Mer de Glace and the summit of Mont Blanc. The path is a section of the Tour of Mont Blanc long distance walk.

From Chamonix take the Planpraz cable car and walk on to the hotel. Turn right along the path marked TMB (Tour of Mont Blanc); this easy path is cut into the hillside and follows the contours to Hotel la Flégère and has the best views of the whole walk. Walk a little way uphill from the hotel following the TMB signs and gradually descend to the road above Argentière village.

Without doubt this is the finest walk in the area, so remember to carry a camera!

Argentière

ROUTE 6

Planpraz (2,062m), le Brévent summit (2,524m), Merlet, les Houches

9km ($5\frac{1}{2}$ miles). 6 hours. Moderate/Difficult.
The route climbs a mountain peak and descends a rocky ridge by an excellent and well marked footpath. There are views of the Mont Blanc range to the south and the Aiguilles Rouges to the north.

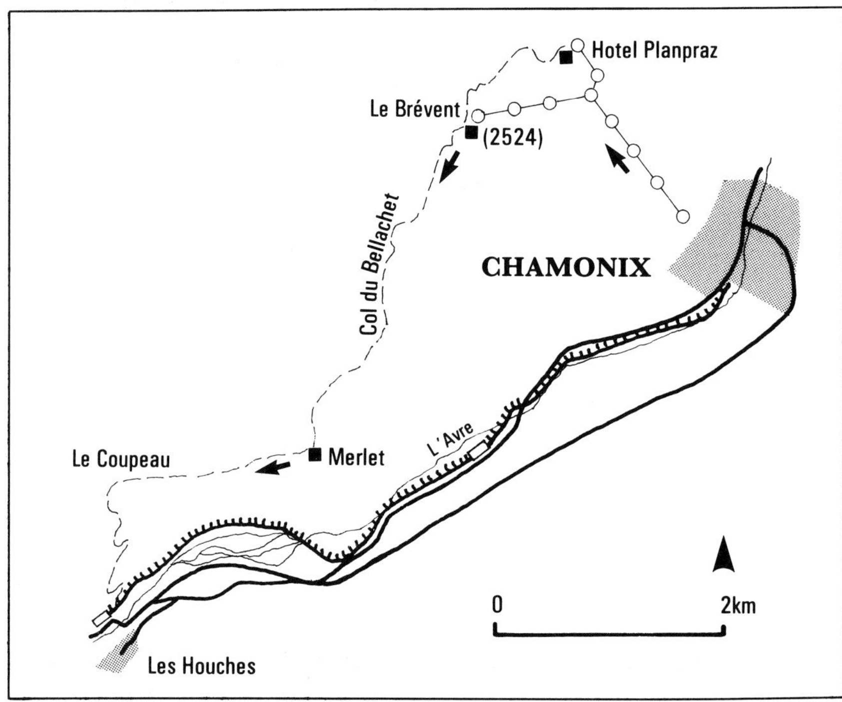

Take the Planpraz cable car as walk 5 but follow the path to the left above the hotel (again marked TMB), climbing gradually to the col du Brévent then on to the summit ridge of the Brévent itself. (This fairly steep section can be avoided by using a cable car from Planpraz to le Brévent.) There is a restaurant and a viewing platform on the summit.

Descend a steep path with care, again following the TMB signs, down the ridge to the Col du Bellachet and beyond, eventually reaching Merlet and its alpine zoo. Easy walking along a wide track leads to le Coupeau and eventually the station and main road opposite les Houches.

NB This walk can be extended by following route 2 from Merlet but it involves an extra 5km (3 miles) or $1\frac{1}{2}$ hours of walking.

Le Brévent is an attractive peak and reaching its summit on foot will give any walker a certain satisfaction.

ROUTE 7

Le Tour, Col de Balme (2,204m), lac de Charamillon, Refuge Albert 1st (2,702m), Glacier du Tour

8km (5 miles). 6/7 hours. Difficult.
A walk beneath towering peaks to an alpine hut and close to the dramatic formations at the end of a steep glacier.

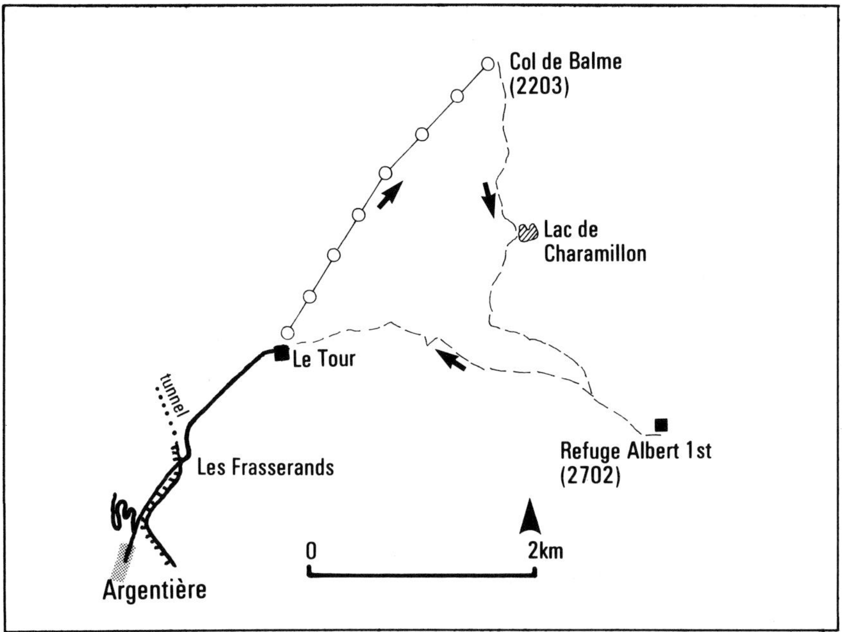

Le Tour is at the end of the side road which starts at the bottom of the hairpin bends near Argentière. From le Tour take the gondola lift to Charamillon and then Col de Balme (2,203m). Turn right away from the col along a path signposted to lac de Charamillon (2,271m). After about ½ hour of easy climbing the angle of ascent steepens, but the path is well defined all the way to the Refuge Albert 1st (2,702m). This hut is perched above the Glacier du Tour and makes an excellent vantage point for viewing the glacier and the peaks at its head. To descend retrace the route uphill as far as the junction of paths above the glacier's side moraine. Do not turn right, but keep straight ahead on scree and moraine which has been dumped by the glacier over the centuries. This is a very steep section and care must be taken on loose rock. Ignore any paths to the right and after some very steep downhill walking reach le Tour and Argentière.

On no account should this walk be undertaken by anyone not wearing strong boots. It is a hard walk, but very rewarding as it comes close to the crevasses and ice towers of the lower reaches of the Glacier du Tour.

LA GRAVE
(Hautes-Alpes)

Recommended Map:
Didier and Richard
Sheet 6 : (1:50,000)
Massifs Ecrins, Haut Dauphiné

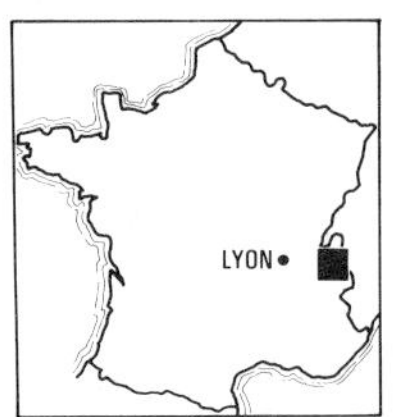

HOW TO GET THERE

Road: (1) South by Autoroute du Soleil (A7) to Lyon, E13 to Bourgoin, then routes 85 and 75 to Grenoble and 91 (Briançon road) to la Grave.
(2) North by A7 to Valence. 92 and 75 to Grenoble, then as above.
(3) From the east (Italy), via Briançon then 91 west.
Rail: Via Grenoble, Briançon or Geneva, then long distance bus (Grenoble/Briançon service, twice daily).
Air: Geneva - bus via Annecy and Grenoble.
Gap - rail and bus via Briançon. Grenoble (via Paris) - bus.
Lyons - rail and bus via Grenoble.

THE AREA

The Ecrins National Park is set in the most northerly part of Dauphiné and contains some of the finest alpine scenery in France. It is completely free of any habitation and is a natural sanctuary for alpine flora and fauna. Alpine animals such as the chamois and marmot are almost tame as a result of the lack of interference from man either as a hunter or farmer.

No roads cross any part of the Ecrins National Park so visitors must find accommodation outside its boundaries, although exceptions have been made to allow mountaineers access for the use of mountain huts. Fortunately the park is surrounded by good roads and la Grave is ideally situated on the Grenoble to Briançon road and is an excellent base from which to explore the northern limits of the park.

La Grave is built on a ledge above the Romanche river; to the north are a series of grassy hills with an average height of about 2,500m (8,200ft). To the south, and immediately across the Romanche valley, rises the snowy majesty of la Meije, 3,983m (13,068ft). The transition between mountain types is made more dramatic by the close proximity of glaciers to la Grave. These glaciers seem almost to dominate the village and when the wind is from the south they can bring a chill to the brightest day. No one who stays at la Grave can fail to be impressed by the stark beauty of the snow and the greens and blues of the ice falls.

La Meije from Lac Noir

Man first came to live in this area during the Middle Ages and early settlers built farmsteads and later villages on a series of natural terraces above the Upper Romanche. With high mountains on either hand they found sanctuary in times of religious persecution. These villages today are in decline as farming communities, but most of the old buildings are being preserved as the second homes of people from the industrial cities of Grenoble and Lyon. A number of houses are available to let and details of these will be found in literature published by the Gîtes de France organisation.

Accommodation in la Grave tends to be simple but good. Hotels are old fashioned, comfortable and family-run offering good French cuisine. They range from the two star Castillan and la Meijette to the simple l'Auberge Ensoleillée in les Terrasses, which seems to be very popular with families, or even the Au Vieux Guide which has dormitory accommodation and is used by mountaineers.

Evening entertainment has to be mostly selfmade, although there are occasional films shown on local subjects. These are organised by the Association of Mountain Guides and it must be stressed that they are only occasional and the language used is naturally French.

The Briançon road from Grenoble which climbs a series of valley steps as far as la Grave, makes one final rise of almost 600m to cross the

THINGS TO DO AND PLACES TO VISIT AROUND LA GRAVE

Fifteenth-century church
Chapel of the Penitents and graves of British climbers killed on la Meije.

Chapel de Nôtre Dame de Bon Secours
Tiny chapel by the top of a dramatic waterfall above les Fréaux.

La Meije Glacier Cable Car
From village to the high glaciers.

Col du Lautaret
Alpine garden with a comprehensive collection of local plants; managed by the University of Grenoble.

Panorama Plaque
On the Signal de la Grave summit. Names all the surrounding peaks in view.

Col du Lautaret before descending the Durance valley. From this col another road climbs ever higher across the Col du Galibier, which is often blocked by snow until late spring. This road is used by the famous Tour de France cycle race and it is not unknown for the road to be still blocked until a day or so before the race when it takes heroic efforts to clear away enough snow to allow the race and its attendant vehicles to pass through. Often the road is blocked again after the race and it is some time before it can be completely free for normal traffic.

On top of the Col du Lautaret the University of Grenoble have built an alpine garden, stocked with examples of most of the plants which grow in the area.

An important feature of la Grave, or at least to lovers of l'escargots (edible snails), are the large numbers of these special molluscs which are found in abundance in the damp vegetation of the lower valleys. These are so highly esteemed locally that frequently one will see notices on private property forbidding the gathering of snails.

For really good walkers who can cope with a number of very stiff uphill paths or like some rock scrambling, the long distance path GR54, is an exciting challenge. This route, which passes through la Grave, is around the mountain of la Meije and numerous other high peaks. Accommodation is in the well spaced system of French Alpine Club huts and simple dormitory accommodation found in the valleys.

Two mountain huts, the Refuge de l'Alpe du Villard d'Arene and the Refuge Chancel are both accessible to walkers staying in la Grave. It is not necessary to be a member of the Club Alpin Français if you are only calling in for refreshment, but it is advisable to join the association if you plan to stay overnight.

La Grave has a single cable car system which can be used to gain closer views of the glaciers and ridges on the north face of la Meije.

Long distance bus routes pass through la Grave and the service is infrequent and expensive, but it is useful to find the times of buses and use them to avoid, say, climbing the road to the top of the Col du Lautaret. Taxis or a mini coach are available however, and even if you have your own transport they should be considered on walks such as those which start at a higher village and yet do not return to the same place at the end of the day.

Downhill skiing is a winter-only sport in the area, but the glaciers are climbed in summer by ski mountaineers; this is a highly specialised and tough sport requiring tremendous skill and stamina.

Further down the valley and mercifully hidden by the west ridge of la Meije is the purpose built ski village of les Deux Alpes. Ski lifts festoon the mountain sides and apartment blocks line the valley bottom. Not everyone's idea of a tasteful development, but certainly it meets a demand.

Mountain walking, as distinct from mountaineering, around la Grave is easy and everywhere the views are delightful. Usually the foreground is filled with colourful alpine flowers just made to enhance a photograph.

FURTHER INFORMATION

Interesting towns nearby

Grenoble
65km north-west. Old town, art galleries, museums, shops, cobbled squares.

Voiron
24km north of Grenoble. Distilleries and cellars of green and yellow Chartreuse.

Briançon
39km south-east. Fortress town commanding the road into northern Italy. Old town with stepped streets, shops, restaurants. Highest city in France.

la Bérarde
On the south side of la Meije. Scenic mountain village.

Camp Site
Below village at L'Hermitage au Grand Clot. (Tel: 80 05 33).

Cable Car Ascent
la Meije glaciers. From west end of village.

Accommodation
Two-star hotels to dormitory accommodation, also numerous rented houses available.

Tourist Information
Syndicat d'Initiative de la Meije, 05320 La Grave (Hautes Alpes).

THE WALKS

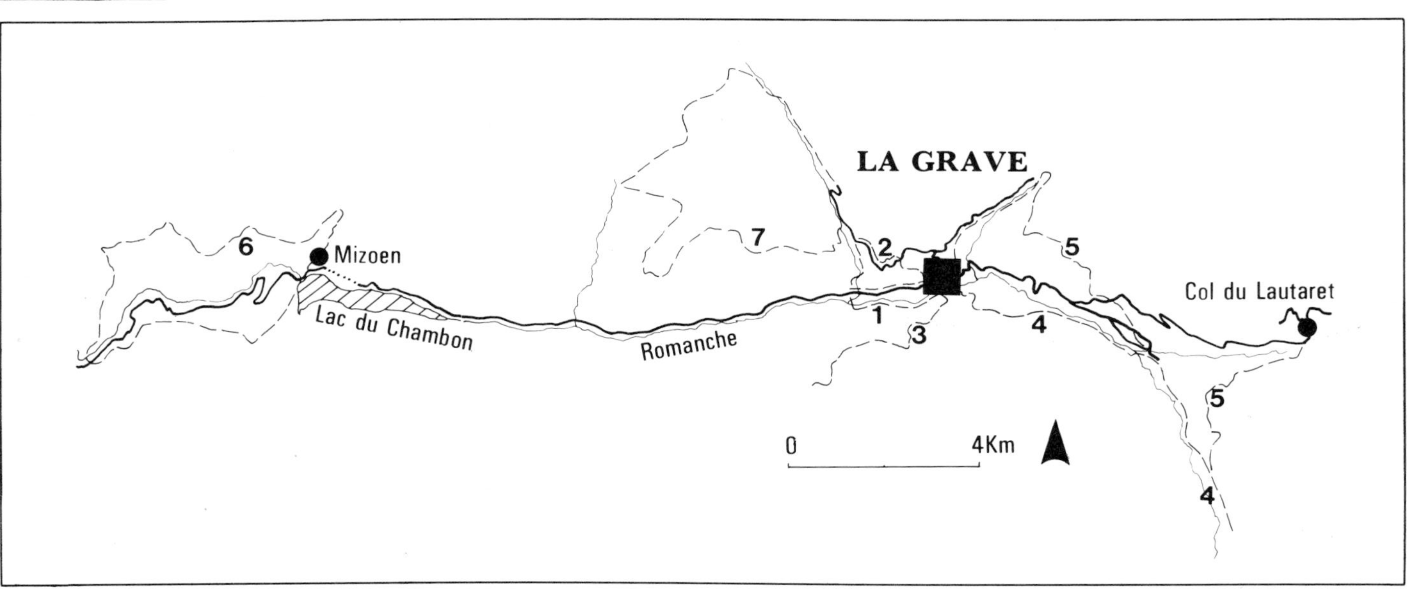
LA GRAVE
Mizoen
Lac du Chambon
Romanche
Col du Lautaret
0
4Km
1
2
3
4
4
5
5
6
7

ROUTE 1

L'Hermitage au Grand Clot, les Fréaux

6km (4 miles). 2 hours. Easy. Pleasant valley walking after a long journey.

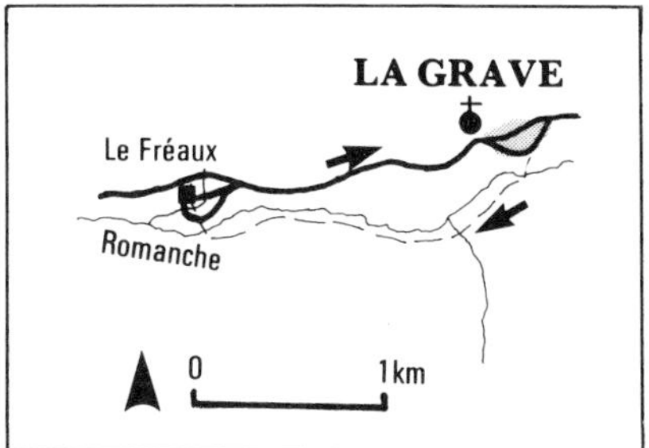

Follow the narrow lane from the tourist information office down to and across the river. Turn right before the campsite and walk downstream along the old roadway. When the outskirts of les Fréaux come into view turn right over a bridge and then pass a couple of farms before entering the main part of les Fréaux. Return to la Grave along the road.

This is an interesting introduction to the masses of flowers, both alpine and woodland, which are found in the area around la Grave.

ROUTE 2

La Grave, les Terrasses, le Chazelet, Chapel de Nôtre Dame de Bon Secours, Pucelle Waterfall, les Fréaux

8km (5 miles). 3/4 hours. Moderate.

Walk uphill past the fifteenth-century church of la Grave and on to the narrow lane which leads to a well marked path climbing steeply up the hillside to les Terrasses. Turn left along the hill road to le Chazelet. Left onto a path which is indistinct at the start, then across meadows and downhill towards an outcrop of rocks. At the bottom of the rocks is the chapel of Nôtre Dame de Bon Secours. Pass round the front of the chapel and go down a steeply zig-zagging path towards the Pucelle waterfall. Cross the fields beneath the fall and enter les Fréaux. Return to la Grave by following walk 1 in a reverse direction, ie follow the old road on the far bank of the river.

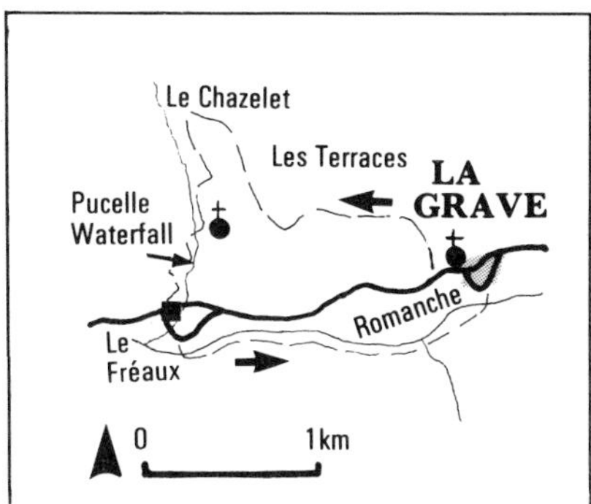

The tricky part of this walk is finding the path to the chapel and the secret is to keep about two-thirds of the way down the slope from the road, but do not go down to the stream. After the chapel, the waterfall is worth a slight deviation away from the main path.

ROUTE 3

Lac de Puy Vachier, Refuge Chancel

10km (6 miles). 5/6 hours. Easy/Moderate.
Straightforward climbing on an easy track to a mountain hut.

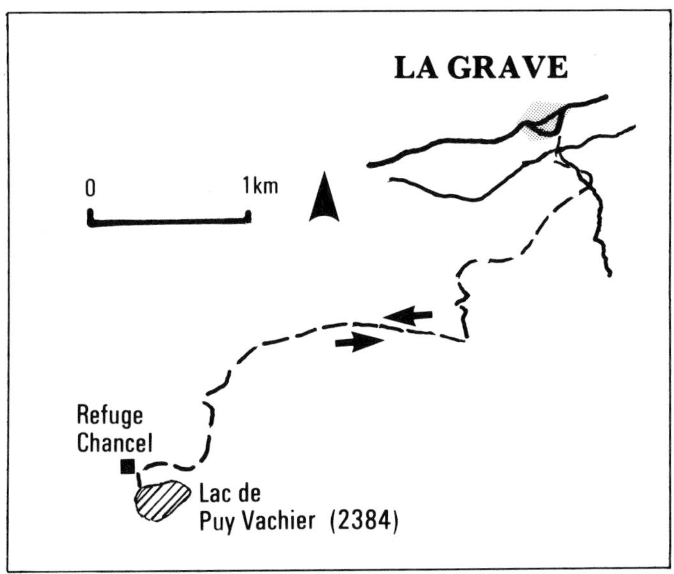

Take the path which crosses the valley beneath la Grave and simply follow the signposted track which climbs through the forest of Bois des Fréaux and on to open mountainside to the lac de Puy Vachier and the Refuge Chancel. Return in the reverse direction.

It is steep but rewarding climb to the hut. Nearby are often found clumps of a compact blue flower known as King of the Alps *(eritrichium nanum),* which is one of the most beautiful of all mountain flowers.

La Grave and La Meije

ROUTE 4

Romanche Valley, les Crevasses, le Plan de l'Alpe, Refuge de l'Alpe du Villar d'Arene

19km (12 miles). 6 hours. Easy/Moderate.
A walk beside a mountain torrent.

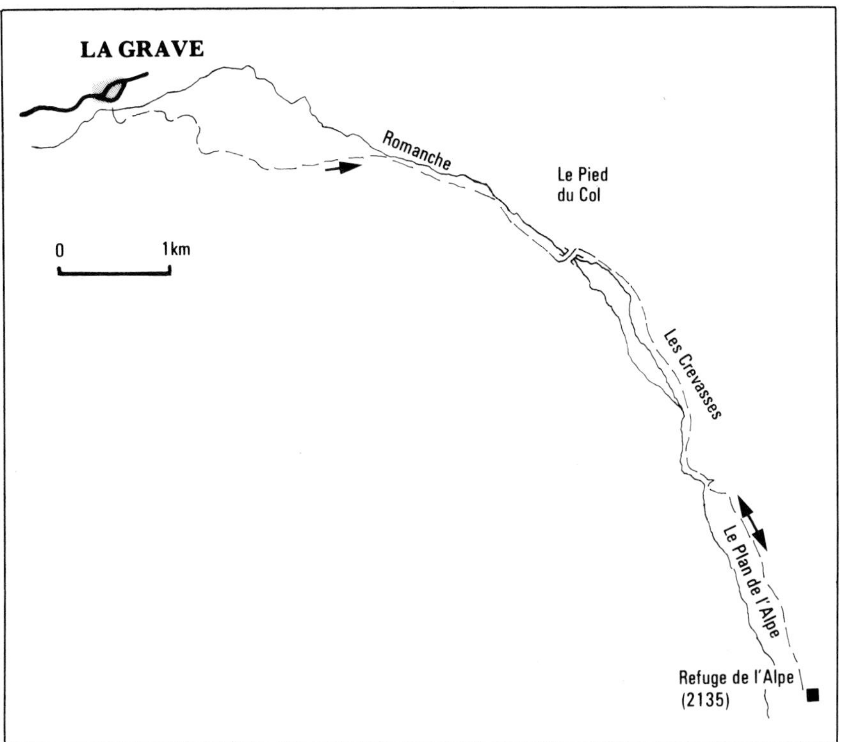

Cross the river below la Grave and turn left to climb the route of the old forest road. Beyond the end of the road a path leads into the forest and back down to the river. Cross over the river on a plank bridge beneath le Pied du Col and turn right to follow the river upstream all the way past the rock formations of les Crevasses and climb to le Plan de l'Alpe and eventually reach the Refuge de l'Alpe du Villard d'Arene. Return by the same route.

If necessary the walk can be shortened by starting and finishing at le Pied du Col. The mountain hut at l'Alpe du Villar d'Arene is an ideal lunch stop as an alternative to an outdoor picnic.

ROUTE 5

Col du Lautaret, le Rivier Blanc, Plan de l'Alpe, Arsine, les Cours, Crête de Puy Golèfre, Valfroids, Pramailler, les Hières, la Grave

16km (10 miles). 6/7 hours. Moderate.

A hill and valley walk with considerable variations of terrain and one which visits charming old-world villages.

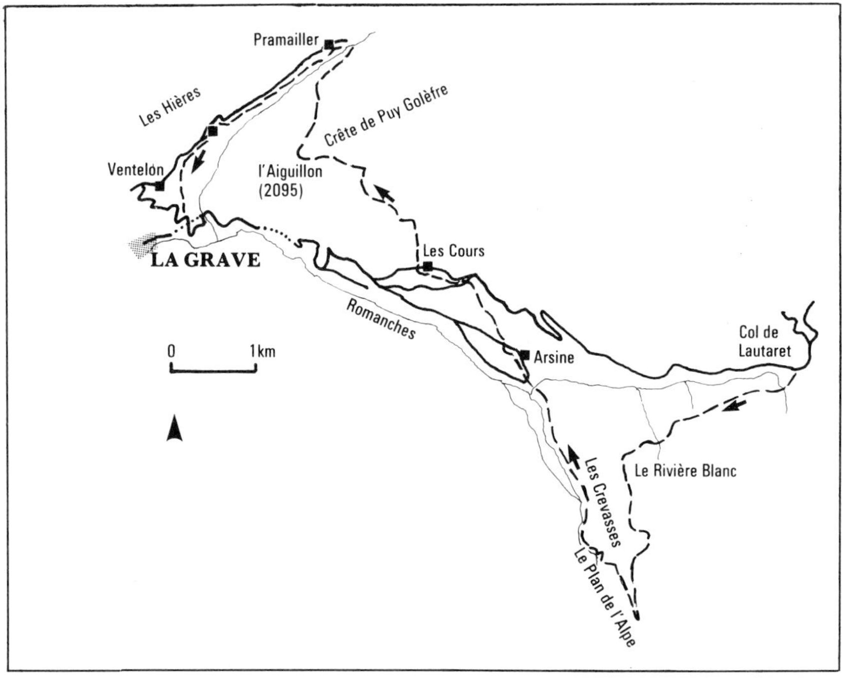

Go by bus or taxi to the top of the Col du Lautaret and after viewing the alpine garden walk back along the la Grave road a little way and turn left along the path which follows the contours of the hillside of le Rivier Blanc. Keep above les Crevasses and eventually join the River Romanche at the Plan de l'Alpe. Turn right and walk downstream as far as the track which leads up to the hamlet of Arsine. Walk through the village towards, and then across, the road into les Cours. Go through les Cours village and turn right along an indistinct path which aims towards the ridge of the Crête de Puy Golèfre. Cross the ridge slightly to the right of l'Aiguillon (2,095m). Slant to the right on a feint path which goes down the steep grassy hillside into Valfroids. Cross the river beyond Pramailler and turn left along the road to les Hières and la Grave, avoiding the steep section of road walking by taking the path downhill from Ventelon.

Take extra care when dropping downhill on the grassy slopes to Pramailler, especially in wet weather.

ROUTE 6

Lac de Chambon, Mizoen, le Puys, les Cours, Gorges de l'Infernet, Bons, Les Granges

17km (10½ miles). 8 hours. Moderate/Difficult.
Steep hill walking amongst aromatic flowers.

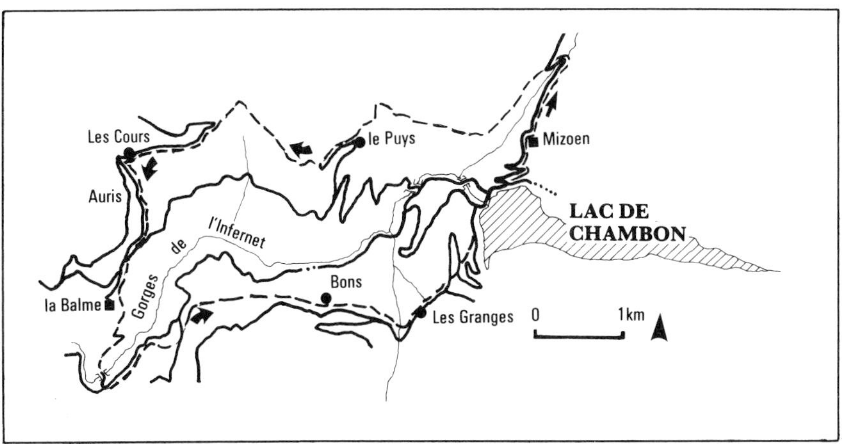

Starting from the dam of lac de Chambon, turn right and walk up the road to Mizoen. Continue beyond the village for a little over 1km and leave the road by turning left at the second hairpin bend above the river. Join a path through sparse woodland and out on to a dry rocky hillside covered with sweet smelling aromatic plants. The track follows the contours of the hill as far as le Puys. Ignore a roadway on the left and continue around the mountain past an old mine entrance, eventually joining a road. Turn left at the road and walk down to les Cours. Follow the road to go below the village, keeping left at every downhill junction as far as le Balme. Continue from the village and walk down the steep track into the Gorges de l'Infernet. Climb up to the main road and turn left, when after about ¾km a path leads off to the right to Bons and then by easy road to les Granges and path back to lac Chambon.

On a hot day the scent of lavender on the hillside before le Puys can be almost overpowering.

Take care on the rocky sections when walking downhill on the steep section below la Balme to the Gorges de l'Infernet.

ROUTE 7

Le Chazelet, les Plagues, Plateau d'en Paris, lac Noir, Cime du Rachas, Chalets Aubert, Baraque de la Buffe, Valley of the Gâ, Rivet du Pied

26km (16 miles). 8/9 hours. Moderate/Difficult.
Hard walking in hilly country, but with unrivalled views.

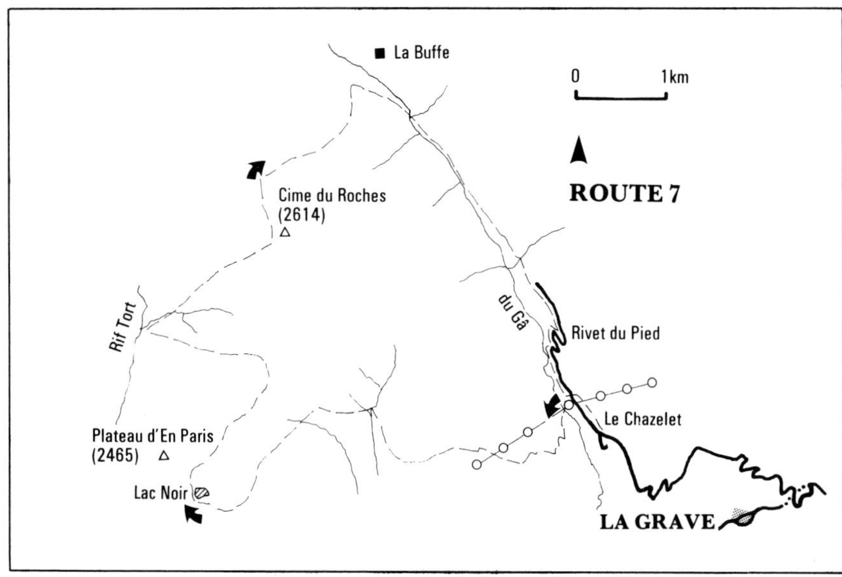

Walk (or drive) to le Chazelet and walk on beneath the ski tow below les Plagues. Turn left to cross the valley, then climb steeply up to the Plateau d'en Paris. Turn left from the main path and follow the track around the plateau passing the beautiful pool of lac Noir. Turn left and rejoin the main path for about $1\frac{1}{2}$km. Just before the col of Rif Tort turn right and climb steeply to the top of Cime du Roches. Turn left along the summit ridge and gradually lose height all the way down to the main (Gâ) valley which is on the right. Join the stream below the army post of Baraque de la Buffe and turn right to follow the river downstream into Rivet du Pied and le Chazelet.

This is a hard walk which may be made easier by the use of transport to le Chazelet, but the views from Plateau d'en Paris and Cime du Raches make any effort worthwhile.

NB Military firing practice sometimes takes place in the upper Gâ valley, so look out for warning notices.

Switzerland

KANDERSTEG

(Bernese Oberland)

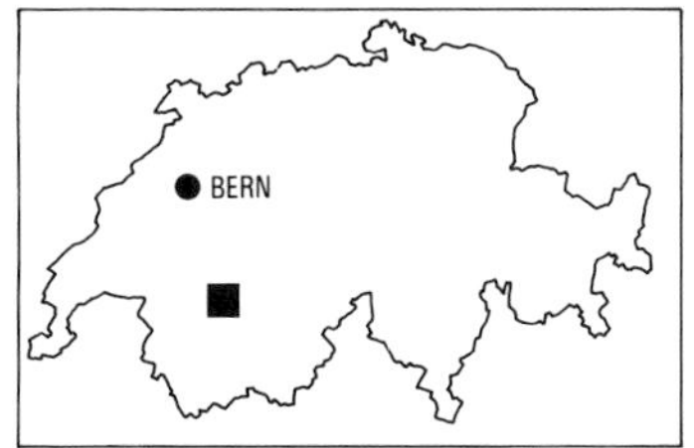

Recommended Map:
Landeskarte der Schweiz
(1:50,000 series)
Sheet 263 - Wildstrubel and
Sheet 264 - Jungfrau

HOW TO GET THERE

Road: (1) South by the European motorway system through Basel to Bern, then Thun to Spiez and south by valley road to Kandersteg (25km). (2) Via the Zürich/Geneva road to Bern and then as above.
Rail: Main line to Bern with regular connections to Kandersteg.
Air: International airports at Zürich, Bern and Geneva all have rail links to Kandersteg.
Main Language: German.

THE AREA

A motorist travelling to Kandersteg might, from the volume of traffic, think that he is entering an extremely busy town, for surely the road ends here? He can be forgiven for that thought, as the greatest volume of traffic intends travelling beyond Kandersteg — and its immediate destination is the railway. Regular loads of cars are attached to trains which travel on the Lötschberg line to Brig, or even beyond to Domodossola in Italy through the Simplon tunnel. The Lötschberg tunnel cuts out a tremendous mileage by going beneath a mountain range which includes such giants as the Jungfrau and Eiger. Further south the Simplon tunnel is an all-weather route avoiding the Simplon Pass.

Once the visitor has arrived in Kandersteg and turned his back on the station he finds himself in a walker's paradise where there are unlimited tracks, ridges and peaks to suit the tastes of all mountain lovers. Kandersteg itself is situated on a plateau almost at the head of

Hiking trail to the Oeschinensee above the Kandersteg/Bernese Oberland

the Kander valley; far from being shut in by the surrounding peaks it enjoys the maximum hours of sunshine and has the added advantage that the mountains hold back some of the more unpleasant aspects of the weather.

Being situated at 1,176m (about 3,850ft) the relatively flat area around Kandersteg gives anyone who finds uphill walking difficult the opportunity to enjoy high mountain scenery without undue effort. A chairlift will carry them up to the famous Oeschinen Lake which is set in a dramatic ampitheatre of crags and peaks and yet is so easily accessible. A mile or so up the valley from Kandersteg is the start of the Stock/Sunnbühl cable car which lifts the visitor up to the Sunnbühl, a basin high above the Kander valley which enjoys even more sunshine than the main valley.

The Oeschinen Lake is supposed to feed one of Kandertal's natural wonders, the Blausee or Blue Lake, near Mitholz down the valley from Kandersteg. This small lake is hidden in the depths of a pine forest and is a most beautiful and impressive sight, with unbelievably deep blue colouring. Much controversy surrounds the cause of this colouring, locally it is thought to be caused by chemical action deep in the earth between the Oeschinen lake and the Blausee. More prosaic thinking puts the reason firmly on algae, but whatever the reason, Blausee is a most beautiful lake and has the added attraction of being the home of fine trout. The water is crystal clear and not only can trout be seen, but also the remains of ancient trees whose fossilized remains litter the lake bed, together with algae and other water plants.

More energetic mountain walkers will find ample scope for their activities in this area, some of the walks described in this section are quite ambitious and require the use of Alpine Club huts which are strategically sited throughout the local mountains. By using Kandersteg as a base, several long distance tours lasting several days length are possible, or alternatively a short drive to one of the many high level cableways will give easy access to much higher altitudes. For the less energetic there are over 350km of well marked walking paths to choose from and flower lovers will find ample scope from the vast variety of alpine flowers found in the surrounding area of Kandersteg — there are twenty-six different kinds of orchids, but naturally all are protected and photography is the only approved method of collecting examples.

Lauterbrunnen and Grindelwald are easily reached by rail or road and from them a whole exciting range of cableways or mountain railways lead to the Schilthorn or the Jungfraujoch. As the higher

THINGS TO DO AROUND KANDERSTEG

Swimming
Heated indoor pools:
Royal-Bellevue Hotel.
Victoria and Ritter Hotel.
Blümisalp Hotel.
Alfa-Soliel Hotel.
Heated outdoor pool:
Royal-Bellevue Hotel.

Lake-bathing
Oeschinensee.
Blausee.

Ice Skating, Curling and Ice Hockey
Skating Rink near railway station.

Fishing
River Kander. Oeschinensee and Blausee lakes. Check locally for permits. (Mainly trout).

Horse Riding School
Royal-Bellevue Hotel.

Golf
18-hole course. Interlaken - Par 72.

Tennis
Royal-Bellevue Hotel.
Victoria and Ritter Hotel.
Schweizerhof Hotel.

Bowling Alleys
Blümisalp Hotel.
Zur Post Hotel.

Cable Ascents
Kandersteg - Oeschinensee (Chair)
Stock (Kandersteg) - Sunnbühl (Cabin)
Lauterbrunnen - Schilthorn 'Piz Gloria' (Cabin)

Mountain Railways
Grindelwald - Jungfraujoch.

Keep Fit Course
In forest beyond the Catholic Church.

Lake Cruises
Lakes Thun and Brienz.

stations and summits are mainly situated in the regions of permanent snow and ice, they are normally out of bounds to the average walker as starting places for mountain tours. However, they are places where one can visit in safety and really be on the top of the world. The Schilthorn is reached by using the mountain railway from Lauterbrunnen to Mürren, followed by the longest cableway in Europe. The Schilthorn (2,970m) has been renamed 'Piz Gloria' since it was used as the setting for the James Bond film *On Her Majesty's Secret Service.* The summit restaurant revolves on its axis once every 50 minutes to give an all-weather panoramic view (fog permitting). First one sees the Swiss lowlands in the north and the smooth lines of the Jura, and then the Black Forest; gradually the scene changes as the Alpine giants appear: first the Eiger, then Mönch followed by the Jungfrau and in the far western distance the Mont Blanc group completes the circle. The summit ridge of the Schilthorn is wide enough and reasonably snow-free to allow access to the walker, in fact there is a good path all the way from the summit to Mürren. However it is a high mountain and care must be taken by anyone even following the well signposted routes.

Kandersteg offers a wide range of amenities, the thirty-one hotels in the area range in quality from the five-star Royal-Bellevue to various special establishments which can offer dormitory accommodation to groups or individuals on tour. Similar to youth hostels, the latter are very clean, comfortable and above all inexpensive. Restaurants abound and the standard of catering is extremely high. Local facilities range from an all the year round skating rink where the Scottish sport of curling (a kind of bowls on ice) takes place and is quite a spectator sport locally, to tennis, minigolf, fishing, bathing, dancing, boating and horse riding instruction.

The craft of ivory carving is carried out locally. Beautifully carved pieces made from walrus or elephant ivory are offered for sale in local speciality shops.

If you speak reasonable German do not be too surprised if you cannot understand the local inhabitant's conversation, for their language, while being based on German, is 'Schwyzerdütch' and sounds quite difficult to the ears of even the best German speakers.

Finally some of the walks suggest that you will be away from 'base' for a night, and so before setting out make enquiries about conditions likely to be encountered and also make sure that the huts are open and not likely to be crowded.

FURTHER INFORMATION

Interesting towns nearby

Bern
70km north-west. Seat of government for the Swiss Confederation of the amalgamation of twenty-three uniquely different cantons. The name means 'bear', and this animal features on the city's coat of arms and a live bear lives in the city bear pit beneath the Nydegg Bridge. The city fathers confidently give 1191 as the founding date of their city, but no doubt it was built on earlier foundations. Major attractions to Bern are its arcades of shops and fountains, but perhaps the most famous is the Zytgloggeturm — a clock tower built in 1530 with various mechanically operated puppet figures which appear on the hour.

Interlaken
45km north north-east. Literally 'between two lakes' and is a useful starting point for cruises on Lake Thun and Lake Brienz. Beautiful formal gardens. Edwardian atmosphere. Casino. Open air concerts. Shops. Restaurants.

Grindelwald
75km north-east. Mountain resort. Start of mountain railway to Kleine Scheidegg and the Jungfraujoch.

Lauterbrunnen
55km north-east. Mountain resort. Start of mountain railway and cable car ascent of the Schilthorn.

Adelboden
25km west. Small resort in the next valley to the Kandertal. Useful base for further exploration of the surrounding mountains. Hotels, shops, restaurants. Camp site.

Mountain Railways

Jungfraujoch. Start from Interlaken East Station for Wengen and Kleine Scheidegg. Change trains for the Jungfraujoch. The train climbs in a series of loops inside the Eiger and Mönch mountains where viewing holes give views of the famous North Wall and several glaciers. Return to Kleine Scheidegg and then take a train to Grindelwald and onward to Interlaken. Although this is an expensive trip it is well worth the money for the fabulous mountain scenery.

Cable Ascents

Lauterbrunnen-Schilthorn.
Tel: 036552141
Kandersteg - Oeschinensee.
Tel: 033751234
Stock-Sunnbühl.
Tel: 033751234

Camp Sites

Filfalle ½km south of Kandersteg (Official camp site of the Boy Scouts Association).

Rendezvous Camp Site. On forest edge close by the Oeschinensee chair lift.

Accommodation

Up-to-date details are always available from the tourist office.

Tourist Office

Verkehrsbüro Kandersteg,
CH 3718 Kandersteg.
Tel: (033) 75 1234

THE WALKS

As Kandersteg is on the edge of two maps (Wildstrubel - Sheet 263 and Jungfrau - Sheet 264), some of the walks will require the use of both sheets. The appropriate map or maps is mentioned in the description of each walk.

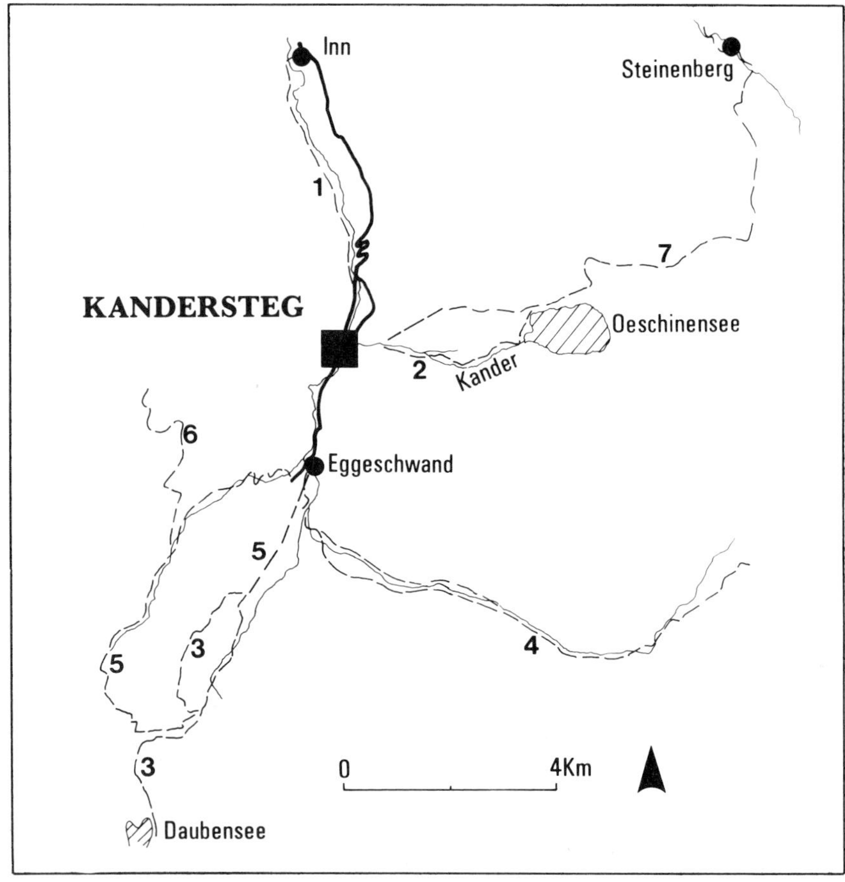

ROUTE 1

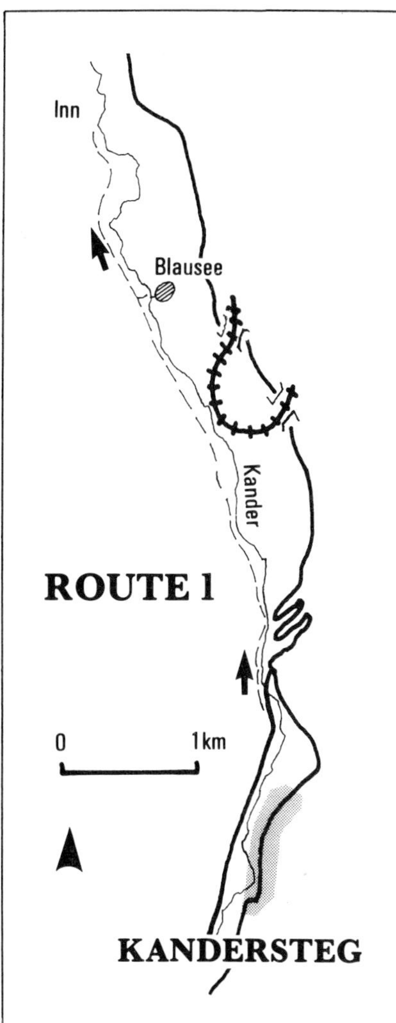

Kandersteg, Kandertal, Blausee, Inn

7km ($4\frac{1}{4}$ miles). 2 hours. Easy.
(Wildstrubel Map)
A gentle meadow walk with stretches of pine wood and an idyllic lake.

From Kandersteg station walk down the main road for a little way and just before it crosses the river turn left on to a side road and then right on a signposted path which follows the west bank of the Kander river downstream through woodland and meadows. Look out for a signpost marked 'Blausee' and turn right and cross the river by a bridge to reach this lake, where there are refreshments, bathing, etc.

Retrace your steps back across the river and turn right, first by the river and then through meadows along the edge of a pine forest as far as the village of Inn. Return by local transport.

The highlight of this introductory walk to the area is undoubtably the beautifully coloured Blausee (Blue Lake). The walk can be extended downstream as far as the walker's energies allow beyond Inn. The path on the west side of the Kandertal keeps parallel to both the main road and railway line so public transport is never far away.

ROUTE 2

Oeschinenholz, Oeschinensee, Oeschinental

7km ($4\frac{1}{4}$ miles). 3 hours. Easy.
(Wildstrubel and Jungfrau maps)
Easy walking to a high alpine lake.

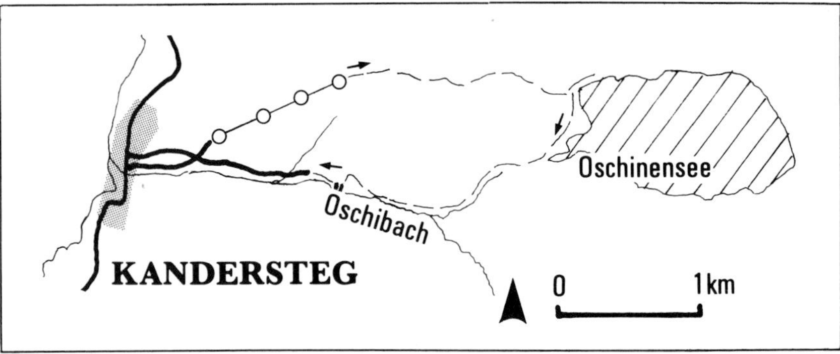

Take the chairlift to the Oeschinenholz plateau and following signposts walk down to the lake (Oeschinensee) where one may explore its banks and nearby pine forests, or swim and sail. Return downstream by valley path on either side of the Oeschinenbach through the pine forest.

Probably this walk is best reserved for a rest day when the sun is really hot.

Chairlift over the mountain meadows

ROUTE 3

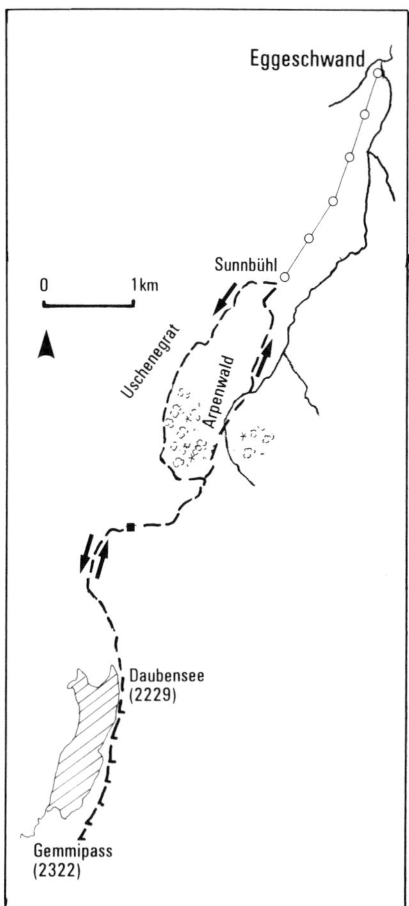

Egge-Stock Cable Car, Sunnbühl Chair Lift, Sunnbühl Valley, Arpenwald, Daubensee

10km ($6\frac{1}{4}$ miles). 4/5 hours.
Easy/Moderate.
(Wildstrubel Map)

Climb into the high Sunnbühl valley by using the Stock cable car from Eggeschwand followed by the chair-lift to Sunnbühl. Turn right away from the restaurant at Sunnbühl and follow the path which climbs beneath the crags of Uschenegrat to the small pine forest ahead (marked Arpenwald on the map). Walk round the west side of Arpenwald to re-join the main valley path. Turn right uphill past the Schwarenbach restaurant and eventually reach the lake (Daubensee). Return by the main path all the way to the upper station of the Sunnbühl chairlift.

As the name suggests, Sunnbühl is a natural suntrap. The setting is truly alpine and yet the climbing negligible. A strong party may wish to continue above Daubensee as far as the summit of the Gemmi Pass where refreshments are available. Another alternative would be to walk back to Eggeschwand, all the way downhill by the path on the west side of the valley beyond both the chairlift and cable car.

ROUTE 4

Gasterntal, Selden, Kander Glacier

20/25km ($12\frac{1}{2}/15\frac{1}{2}$ miles). 7/9 hours. Moderate.
(Wildstrubel and Jungfrau maps)
A valley walk beneath towering peaks to the Kander Glacier.

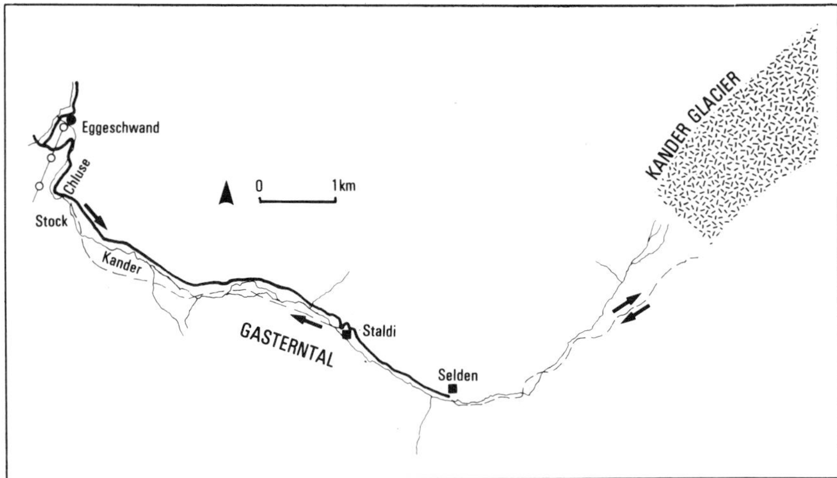

Either walk or take the bus to Eggeschwand. Walk on beyond the cable car lower station by the mountain road as far as a 'T' junction. Turn left and follow this rough road beneath the crags of Stock and into the valley of the Gasterntal. Continue along the road as far as Selden (refreshments available), where the road ends. Beyond the hut a track climbs steadily onwards and uphill as far as the bottom end of the Kander glacier and it will depend largely on the ability of the party how far you climb towards the glacier. **However, on no account should you attempt to climb on it without proper equipment. Also beware of rocks falling from the lower section.**

Return by the same route, but turn left and cross the river below the hairpin bend near Staldi to follow a path on the south side of the river as far as the gorge of Chluse, where the road is rejoined.

This walk will take you right into the heart of the high Alps and gives the opportunity of viewing a glacier at close quarters. Do not on any account try any ice climbing on the glacier without proper equipment or supervision.

ROUTE 5

Egge (1,265m), Alpbachtal, Uschene, Balme, Uf der Egge, Schwarzgräth (2,383m), Schwarenbach, Sunnbühl

14½km (8¾ miles). 7/8 hours. Moderate/Difficult.
(Wildstrubel Map)
Gradually climbing through a high valley with alpine farms to a dramatic col followed by an easy downhill walk.

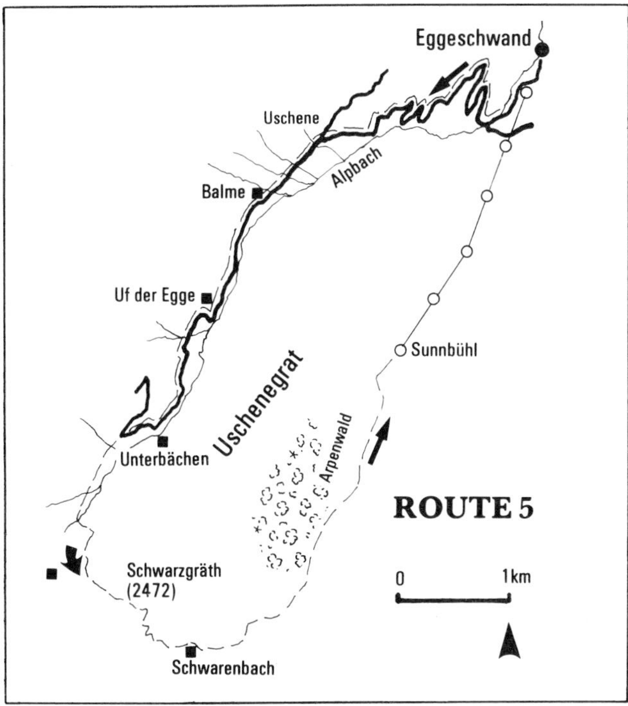

Start at Eggeschwand as walk 4 but turn right at the 'T' junction. Climb this high level road up into the Alpbach valley to another 'T' junction at Uschene. Turn left here and continue up the Alpbachtal passing the summer farm settlements of Balme and Uf der Egge, to a little way beyond the Unterbächen farms where the road turns sharply right. Turn left at this point away from the road and climb up the steep mountain side until a small chalet is reached at a junction of three paths. Turn left away from the chalet and climb the last steep section to the col at Schwarzgräth. Go downhill now, passing two small lakes into the Sunnbühl valley. Turn left at Schwarenbach and follow the path to the chairlift as in route 3.

The climb up to Schwarzgräth is very steep, but the view from the col is marvellous.

ROUTE 6

Egge (1,265m), Alpbachtal, Uschene (1,595m), Alpschele, Bunderschrinde, (2,385m), Bunderspitz (2,546m)

13km (8 miles). 9/10 hours. Difficult.
(Wildstrubel map)
A mountain climb.

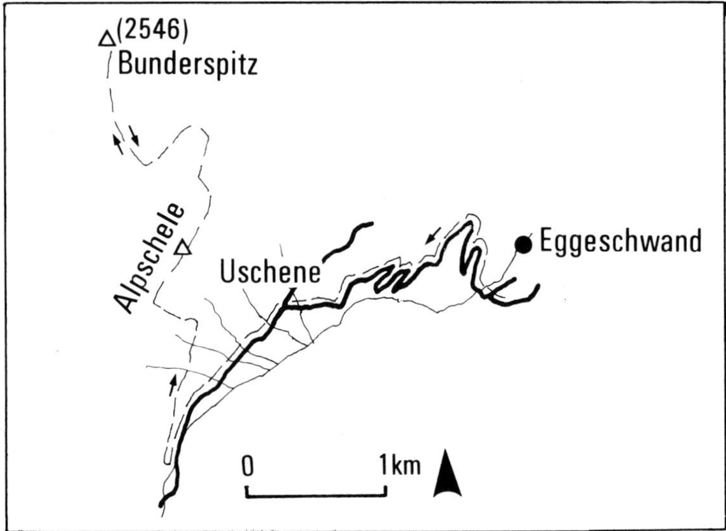

Follow the same route as walk 5 into the Alpbachtal as far as Uschene. At the second stream beyond the 'T' junction turn right and take the path which follows the stream up a steep hill before traversing beneath the wall of crags ahead. The path climbs through a natural gap in the rocks and then turns right along their crest to a group of old farm buildings at Alpschele. Take the lefthand and upper of the two paths beyond the farm and climb to the col of Bunderschrinde. Turn right at the col to follow the steep path which leads uphill to the summit of the Bunderspitz. Return by the same route.

Turn back if snow conditions are met unless you have an ice axe and know how to use it — this is a very steep climb and it is wise to be cautious.

ROUTE 7

Oeschinensee (1,578), Bergli, Blümisalphütte (2,837m), Schnattwäng, Gamchibach River, Griesalp (1,407m)

13km (8 miles). 9 hours. Difficult.
(Jungfrau Map)
A climb into high mountain and glacier country, visiting an alpine club hut along the way.

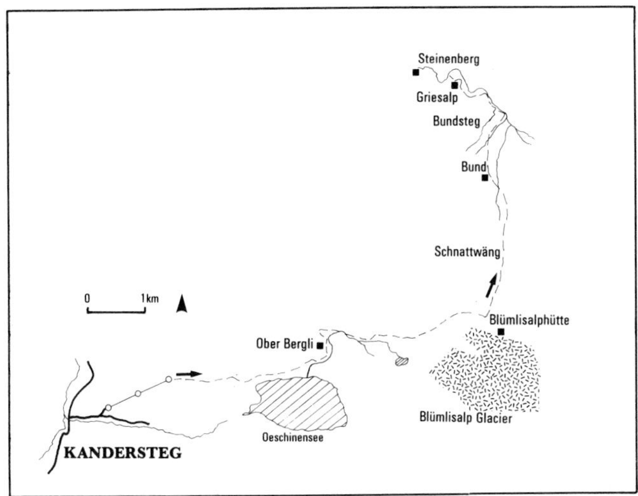

Take the chairlift to Oeschinensee and follow the path signposted to Blümisalp through pine forest and in and out of rocky crags to the old farmstead of Ober Bergli. Turn right away from the farm buildings to climb a scree slope beneath the Blümisalp glacier. At the col ahead either turn right if visiting the Blümisalphütte, or left (retrace your steps to this point from the hut) and down a moraine at the side of a small glacier. The path works its way through some very rough ground below the glacier and great care must be taken to follow the route markers on prominent rocks. Gradually the going gets easier but is still on a steep path through the area marked Schnattwäng until Bund is reached. Below the farm buildings a zig-zag path leads through alpine pasture then pine forest to Bundsteg and the Gamchibach river. Continue down the valley to Griesalp and the road.

To return either arrange for a local taxi or catch the post bus, unless you have been able to have transport sent round from Kandersteg.

This is another tough climb, which must be abandoned if snow conditions are met.

A stay at the Blumisalphütte will make the walk into two short days and leave more time to admire the scenery and the wealth of alpine flowers on either side of the col. Also allow time to work out variations on either side of the route.

ZUOZ
Engadine (Grisons)

Recommended Map:
Landeskarte der Schweiz
Sheet 258 (1:50,000) - Bergün
Sheet 268 (1:50,000) - Julierpass

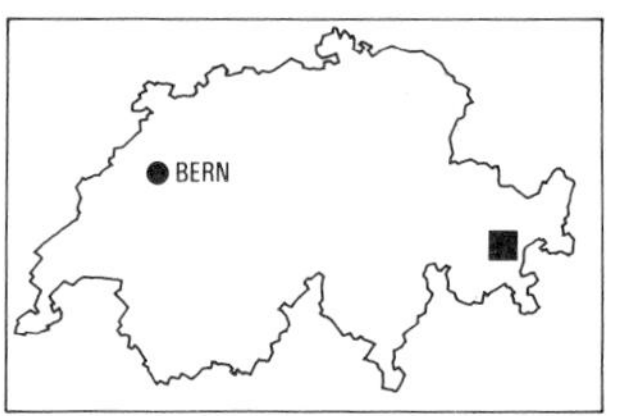

HOW TO GET THERE

Road: (1) South by the European motorway system to Zürich, then road 3 south-east to Chur and St Moritz. Road 27 north-east to Zuoz.
(2) From Northern Italy over the Maloja Pass (road 3) to St Moritz and road 27 to Zuoz.
Rail: Main line services via Zürich and Chur, then branch line via Bever to Zuoz.
Air: International airport at Zürich. Connections by rail. Airstrip for local traffic at Samedan, 11½km from Zuoz.
Main language: German.

THE AREA

To most people the Upper Engadine is probably thought of as the winter playground of the rich and famous, for the best known resorts of this valley are certainly St Moritz and its neighbour Pontresina. This may be true of those towns, but the rest of the area comprises of farming villages where accommodation of a more modest kind may be found. The mountains are, in summer, an exciting preserve for the walker, mountaineer and wildlife admirer. Zuoz is one of those villages where the true character of the Engadine, and especially its architecture, have been preserved. Some of its buildings go back to the Middle Ages and the local people speak the ancient language known as Romansch.

Zuoz is situated on the River Inn and is surrounded by picturesque meadows, large forests and majestic mountains in close proximity to the Swiss National Park. It is an ideal base for mountain walking or for studying such alpine animals as the ibex, chamois, marmot and deer. Eagles and other mountain birds are frequently seen on the heights and the whole region abounds in alpine flowers, many of which are rare and therefore protected.

One of the unique features of the Engadine is that despite being remote and surrounded by high snowclad peaks, the valley bottom is remarkably flat and broad. Steep glaciers flow northwards from the Swiss-Italian border into narrow side valleys, which in their turn give out onto the flat main valley. Above St Moritz are three lakes, the

Segl, Silvaplana and Murezzan. Below them the valley is kept fertile by the River Inn, which in its spring floods brings down fresh soil. Zuoz and its neighbours are sited above the flood plain and are on the northern side of the valley to catch the maximum sunshine. Beyond the Engadine, the Inn continues as one of Europe's major rivers, passing through Austria to eventually join the Danube on its way to the Black Sea.

The Engadine has been settled for at least 3,000 years and its waters have always had a certain theraputic value, a feature noted first by the Romans and later by royalty. The first recorded visit of a nobleman was that of the Duke of Parma in the late seventeenth century when he brought a retinue of twenty-five to sample waters once described as 'puckering the lips and tongue like vinegar and [is] like champagne to the nose'. Development of the large hotels and the making of St Moritz and Pontresina started in the late nineteenth century with the building of the Cresta toboggan run. The Winter Olympics of 1928 and 1948 and the development of superb wintersports facilities finally set the seal on these two places, which then became the winter mecca for film stars and royalty alike.

Entry into the Engadine is exciting whether it is by road over the Julier or Maloja Passes, or by air to land at the tiny airstrip below Samedan. Few will doubt though, that the very best way to come to the Engadine is by rail. This is the famous narrow gauge Rhætian line which climbs 405m (1,329ft) from the village of Bergun in the Albula valley to the summit of the line in 6km (4 miles), by a complex series of loops and short tunnels where the passenger often becomes disoriented and has the distinct feeling of travelling backwards! On the far side of the valley the Bernina Railway follows the route of the old post road across the Tirano Pass into Italy.

A wide range of facilities is offered in the area, from guided mountain walks to open air swimming, golf, sailing and riding. Glaciers above Pontresina can be viewed at close quarters from safe footpaths. Well placed lifts and cable railways take much of the more strenuous effort out of mountain climbing.

As the Engadine is close to both the German speaking part of Switzerland and also to Italy, the cuisine reflects both influences.

Walking ranges from easy valley strolls, to safe mountain tracks or serious snow and rock work. The Engadine's scenery has always been popular with film makers and mountain photographers, who have not been slow to exploit the breathtaking vistas which opens up constantly as the walker traverses well maintained high level paths.

THINGS TO DO AROUND ZUOZ

National Park
Access from S-chanf (2km north-east). Alpine Wildlife. Tours. Information centre.

Sailing
Lakes Segl and Silvaplana, above St Moritz.

Tennis and Squash
Courts at Zuoz and most other local towns and villages.

Golf
Samedan, 18-holes, par 70. Open June-October.

Fishing
River and lake permits from Hotel Eden, St Moritz. Tel: 082/3 34 04.

Cycle Hire
From Tourist Office, Zuoz.

Village Tours
Wednesday 16.00hrs throughout the year.

Horse drawn carriages
Into National Park. Minimum six persons. From Zuoz Tourist Office.

Dances
Most local hotels hold informal functions throughout the summer and winter seasons.

Cable Ascents
St Moritz-Piz Nair (from Corviglia mountain railway to upper station).
Bernina-Diavolezza Glacier.
Silvaplana-Munt Arlas.

Mountain Railways
Punt Muragl-Muottas Muragl.
St Moritz-Corviglia (for Piz Nair).

Railways
Rhætian-(via Albula Tunnel to Chur).
Bernina-(via Tirano Pass to Italy).

Museums
St Moritz. Displays show over 3,000 years of Engadine life.

Cresta Run
World famous toboggan run.

Accessible Glaciers
Val Roseg.
Morterasch.
Diavolezza.

FURTHER INFORMATION

Interesting towns nearby

St Moritz
16km south-west. Internationally famous ski resort. Shops, hotels, restaurants. Roman site. Church built in 1573. Museum.

Pontresina
18km south. Ski resort. Access to nearby glacier scenery. Shops, hotels, restaurants.

Accommodation
Everything from rented rooms to five-star hotels available in the area.

Camp Sites
Maloja
Sils
Silvaplana
St Moritz
Pontresina
Madulain

Tourist Office
Verkehrsbüro CH7424 Zuoz.
Tel: 082/7 1510
Telex: 74410

THE WALKS

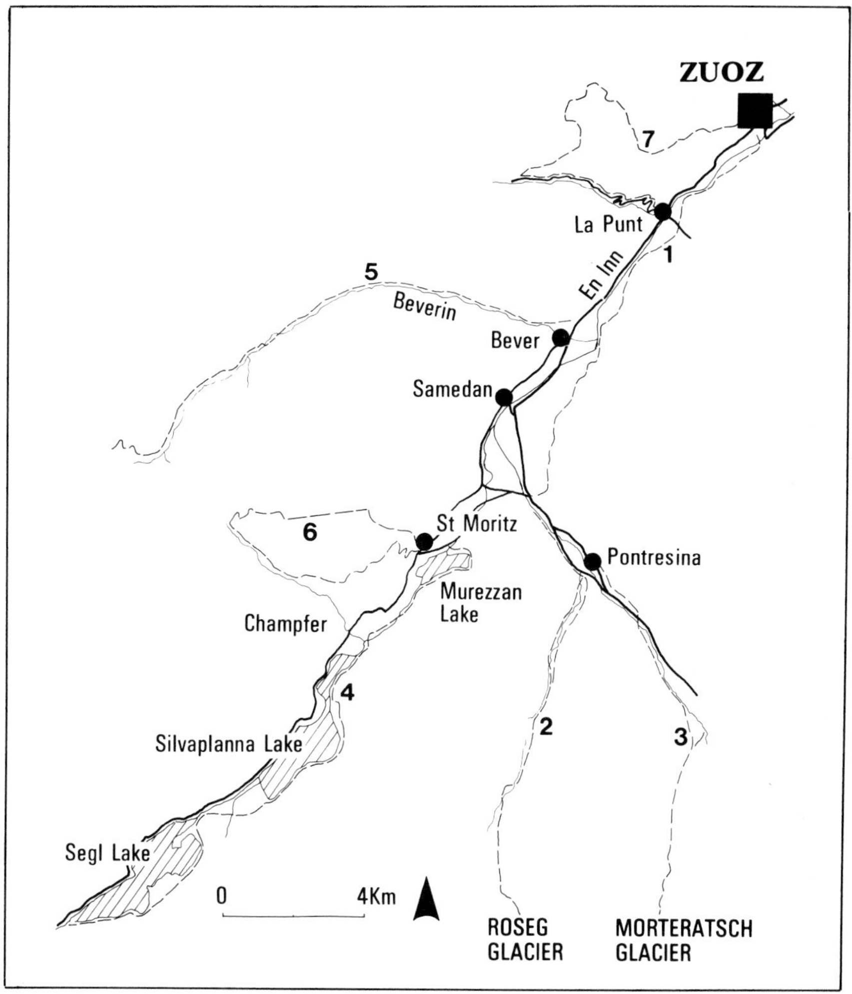
ZUOZ
7
La Punt
1
En Inn
5
Beverin
Bever
Samedan
St Moritz
6
Pontresina
Murezzan
Lake
Champfer
4
Silvaplanna Lake
2
3
Segl Lake
0
4Km
ROSEG
GLACIER
MORTERATSCH
GLACIER

ROUTE 1

Resgia, Chamues-ch, Champesch, Chuoz, Punt Muragl

14km ($8\frac{1}{2}$ miles). 4/5 hours. Easy.
Maps: Sheet 258 and 268
A valley and forest walk with distant views of the peaks of the western Engadine.

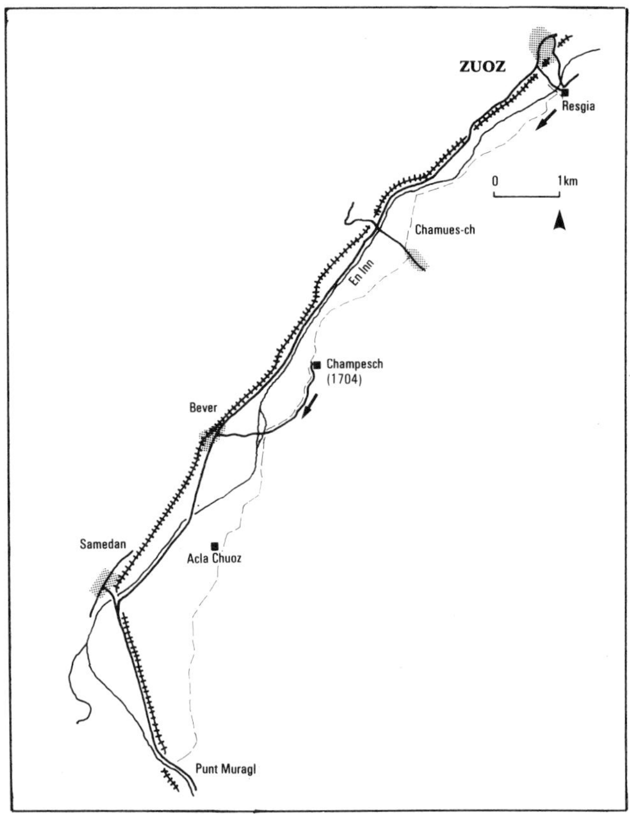

Cross the River Inn below Zuoz by the old bridge and at the farm house opposite (Resgia) turn right and follow the signposted track through farmland to where, opposite Madulain, a path leads to Chamues-ch. In the centre of the village a path aims slightly uphill towards the forest, but not into it. Follow this to the farm community of Champesch. Take the farm road to Bever as far as the swampy area just before the river. Turn left here on to a track which climbs into forest above Chuoz. Continue along this and above the airfield as far as Punt Muragl. Return by train to Zuos.

The views of distant peaks seen through forest clearings should soon remove any travel weariness.

Leukabad-Gemmi Pass, Kandersteg

Kandersteg

ROUTE 2

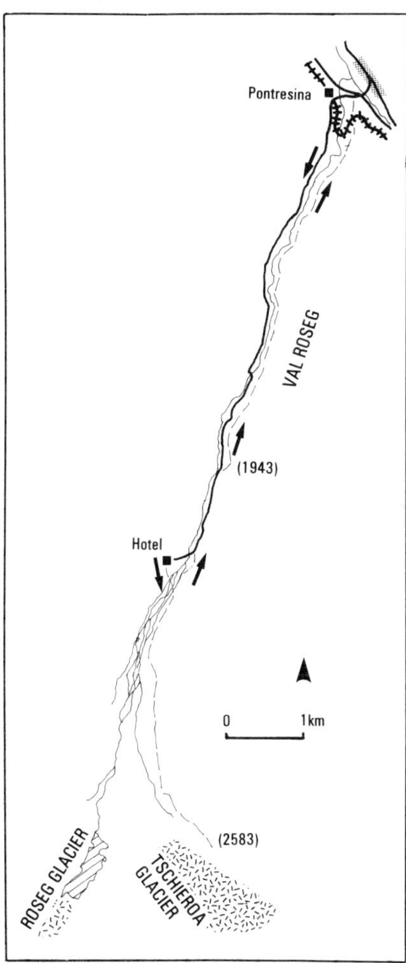

Pontresina, Val Roseg, Roseg Glacier

20km (12½ miles). 6 hours. Easy.
Map: Sheet 268
Straightforward valley walking with close views of glacier scenery.

Take the train to Pontresina and from the station follow the signposted road to Val Roseg, as far as the hotel and continue across the rubble of the terminal moraine to the ends of the Roseg and Tschieroa glaciers. Return the same way, but take the side path which leaves the road about 1½km below the hotel (at point 1943 on the map). This path joins the main road on the Pontresina side of the station, which will be on the left.

There is a beautiful turquoise blue lake at the foot of the Roseg glacier and the dominant peak at the head of the Tschieroa glacier is Piz Bernina.

This is an easy walk to a dramatic viewpoint, but take care not to get too close to the ends of the glaciers as they are dangerous places with a constant fall of rocks.

ROUTE 3

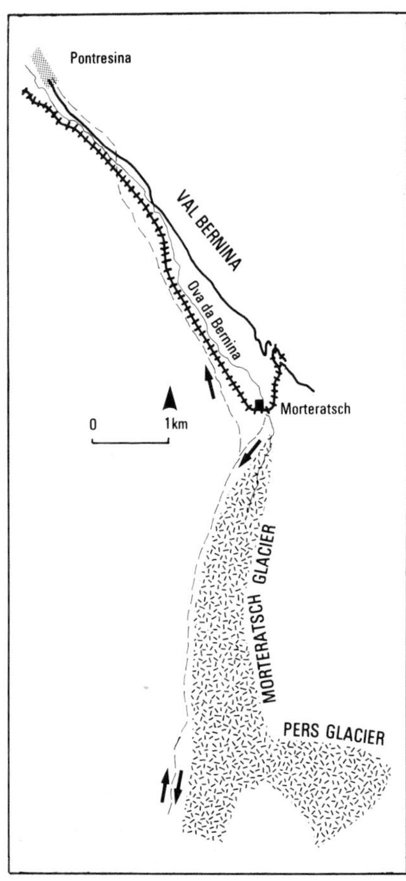

Morteratsch Valley and its glacier system

14km ($8\frac{1}{2}$ miles). 4/5 hours. Easy.
Map: Sheet 268
Another close look at a glacier followed by forest glades. Comparing two different glacial valleys.

Take the train via Pontresina to the Morteratsch valley station and follow the signposted footpath along the valley bottom as far as the dramatic icefalls of the Morteratsch and Pers glaciers. On the return leg turn left before the path descends steeply about 1km short of Morteratsch station, and follow a path above the railway line all the way back to Pontresina.

The sharp peak at the head of the Pers glacier is the famous Piz Palu also known as the Glass Mountain. The Swizz-Italian border follows the skyline above the glaciers of walks 2 and 3. Again do not get too close to the icefalls in case there is a fall of loose rock.

Zuoz village square

ROUTE 4

St Moritz, Lakes Murezzan, Champfer, Silvaplana and Segl, Maloja

18km (11 miles). 5 hours. Moderate.
Map: Sheet 268

A lakeside and woodland walk starting at the fashionable resort of St Moritz.

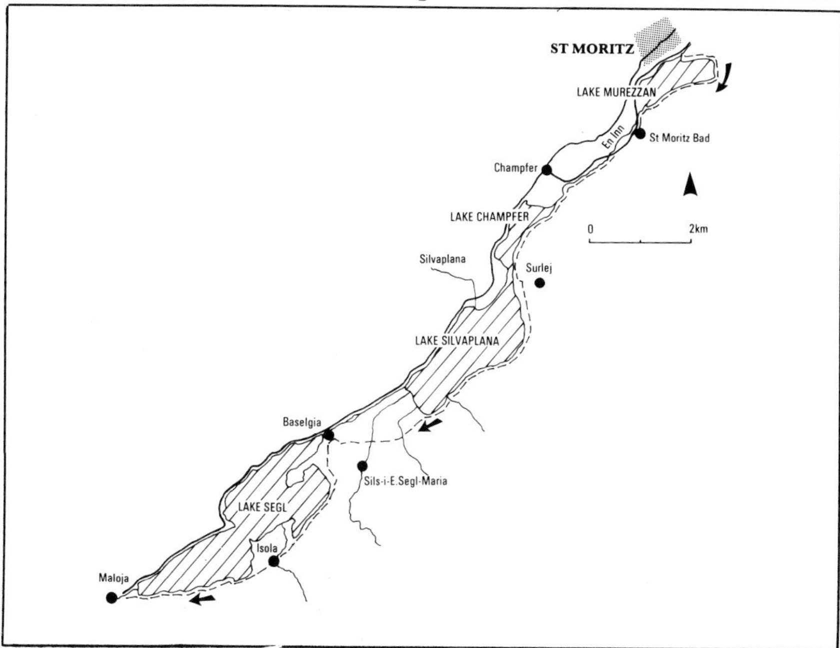

From the railway station in St Moritz cross the main road behind the station complex and walk down to Lake Murezzan. Follow the track round its southern shore as far as St Moritz Bad. Take the Champfer road for about 150m until just before (about 150m) it crosses the river, then turn left on to a riverside path across meadowland. Walk beside the stream and through the forest to Lake Champfer and almost as far as the village of Surlej. Do not go into the village, but turn right off the village road on to a track which crosses a field system before entering the forest ahead. Follow an easy path around the south shore of Lake Silvanplana to the village of Sils-i-E Segl-Maria. Continue slightly uphill through the village and aim for Lake Segl. Follow the path around its southern shore through the hamlet of Isola as far as Maloja where there is a regular bus service back to St Moritz.

This is an ideal walk for a hot day when the trees will offer shade and the water may tempt you to bathe. The only tricky part in this walk is the section through Sils-i-E Segl-Maria; take care to turn left on entering the village when coming from Lake Silvaplana. Walk uphill and at the village square turn right and downhill to where beyond the last house a track turns away to the left to cross meadowland and then down to Lake Segl.

ROUTE 5

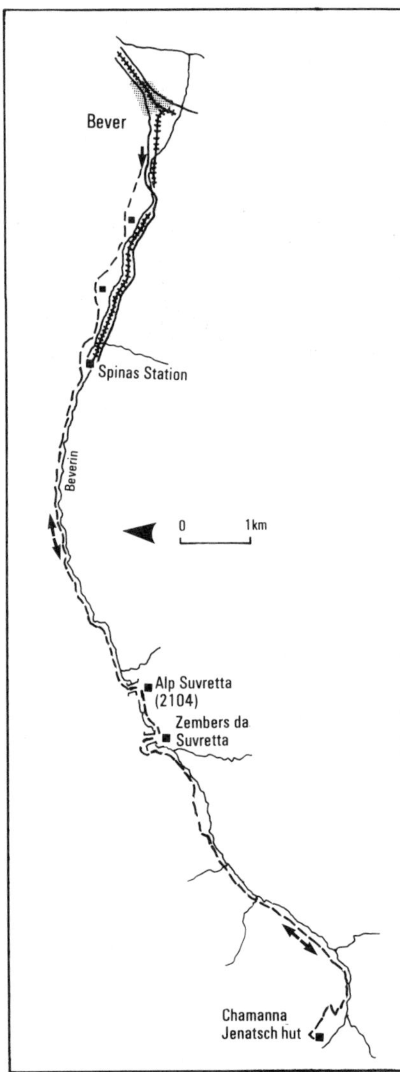

Bever and Val Bever

About 20km (12½ miles). 6/7 hours.
Moderate.
Maps: Sheets 258 and 268
A valley walk beneath high rocky peaks and one which can be extended according to the ability of the party.

From Bever follow the road up the Bever valley as far as the bridge over the Beverin river. Do not cross the bridge but turn right on to a track which climbs gradually up the valley, passing hill farms on the north side of the river. At point 2104 the path crosses over the stream by a plank bridge to follow the south bank for about ¾km and then crosses back opposite the farm of Zembers da Suvretta. Beyond the farm the angle of the climb starts to increase, but the track is still suitable as far as the Swiss Alpine Club Hut at Chamanna Jenatsch.

The return journey for this walk is by the same route and gives different views to those enjoyed when walking uphill. It is recommended that the distance walked be guided by **a** the time, **b** weather and **c** condition of the party. Remember every stride up the valley means an equal number on the return, although of course this is the easiest part of the route.

ROUTE 6

Piz Nair (3,057m), Lake Suvretta, Suvretta Valley, Champfer

10km (6 miles). 5/6 hours. Moderate.
Map: Sheet 268
A downhill walk from an easily climbed mountain, followed by a beautiful alpine lake and a deep valley.

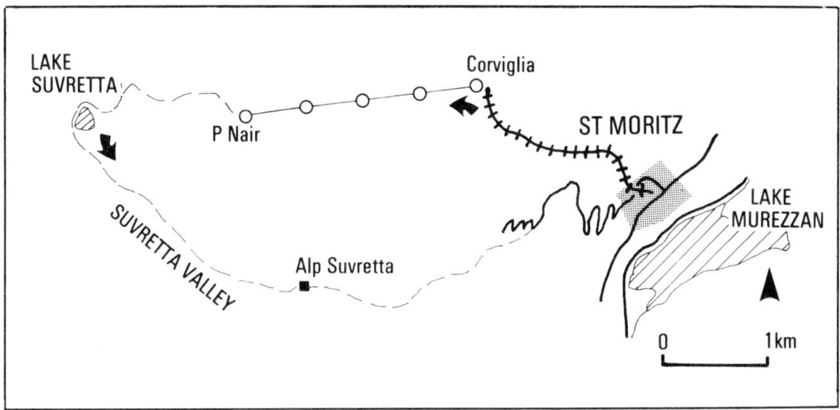

From St Moritz take the mountain train to Corviglia and cable car to Piz Nair. At the upper station follow the signposted path down the side of the mountain away from the cable to Lake Suvretta. Turn left at the lake and again by a steep signposted path down into the Suvretta valley. Where the path forks, just above the farmhouse of Alp Suvretta, turn left on to a gradually improving track to follow the easier gradient in the direction of St Moritz. Ignore a track which climbs uphill to the left about 1½km below the farm, but at the next junction of paths turn right and eventually walk down across the open hillside and wooded slopes above Champfer. Swing round to the left and eventually join a track down to St Moritz.

This route is an easy way to enjoy the high mountain scenery. No problem should be encountered except in bad weather. Corviglia and nearby Sass da Muottas are both excellent viewpoints.

ROUTE 7

Zuoz (1,716m), Val Müra, d'Es-cha Swiss Alpine Club Hut (2,594m), Val d'es-cha, Gualdauna, Val d'Alvra

15km (9¼ miles). 8/10 hours. Difficult
Map: Sheet 258
A tough but rewarding climb to the Alpine Club Hut of d'Es-cha followed by another climb across a slightly lower ridge.

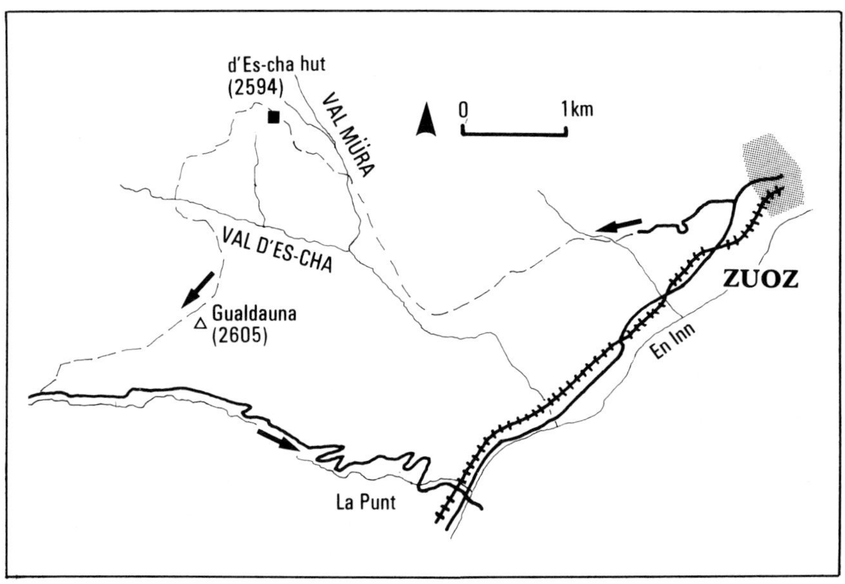

Follow the high level road to the south-west from Zuoz and climb gradually away from the village as far as Val Müra. On entering the valley the angle steepens considerably. At a footpath junction take the one on the right (sign-posted) to climb very steeply to the d'Es-cha hut. Beyond the hut follow the contour round the hillside on an easier path into Val d'Es-cha and cross the ridge ahead by a low col (Gualdauna). Walk downhill on a well defined but steep path to the road and turn left. Follow the road into the valley to La Punt and catch either a bus or a train to ease the strain of the last few kilometres back to Zuoz.

Although this is a strenuous walk with steep gradients and is recommended for fit walkers only, the scenery is marvellous, especially the views southwards towards Piz Palu and its neighbours.

MÜNSTER

Obergoms - (Valais)

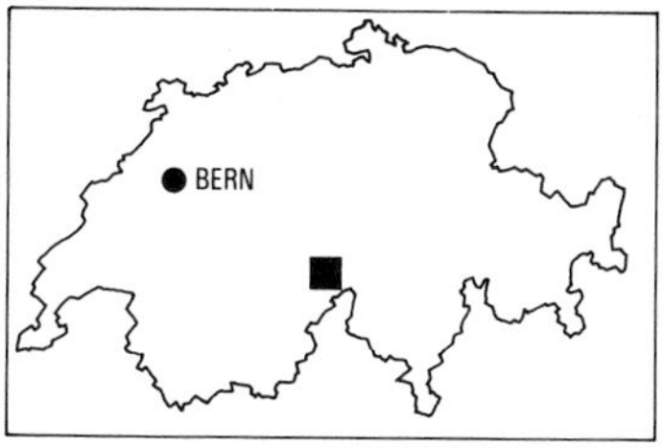

Recommended Map:

Landeskarte der Schweiz (1:50,000 series)
Sheet 265 Nufenenpass and
Sheet 264 Jungfrau

BERN

HOW TO GET THERE

Road: (1) South by European motorway system to Zürich, then via Zug or Lucerne to Altdorf and Andermatt. South-west over the Furkapass and Grimselpass to the Goms valley and Münster. (2) Via Geneva, Lausanne, Martigny to Brig, then north-east along the Goms valley to Münster.

Rail: Main line (trans European/Italian Services) to Brig. Change to rack and pinion line for Münster.

NB Despite the apparent size of Brig main line station, the train to Münster departs outside it from the centre of the main square.

Air: International airports at Bern and Geneva. Connections by rail via Brig.

Main Language: German.

THE AREA

The French claim the Rhône as their own river, but it is born in the Swiss Alps and reaches maturity in Switzerland long before entering France. It starts as the melt waters of the Rhône glacier and soon enters the deep fertile trough of the Goms Valley. This stretch of the river is known as the Rotten Rhône (or Red Rhône). Twelve Alpine villages are spaced almost equidistant along its upper section with Münster being the central and largest.

There are many towns and cities throughout both Germany and Switzerland which bear the name of Münster (the ü is pronounced 'ew' as in dew). The word means minster or cathedral and it is easy to accept the title if it is for a city or large town, but Münster in the Goms valley hardly comes into either of these categories. Certainly its ancient church is a fine example of the baroque style, but then so are the other churches of Obergoms. No doubt it offered sanctuary to early travellers in this high valley, but it can never be classed as anything other than a village church and so the mystery of the name must remain.

Architecture in the Obergoms is mostly based on traditional timber construction. The houses stand on mushroom-like stone pedestals, which lift the whole building a few feet above ground level and keep vermin from entering food stores and similar places. Roofs are solid and overhung to hold the tremendous weight of snow which falls in winter. All the ancient buildings are carefully preserved and modern developments blend with the old to give a pleasant grouping in every village.

The train which climbs up to Münster is the 'Glacier Express' and is one of the most exciting of all the Swiss Mountain railways. This one starts in Zermatt, runs down to Brig, climbs through the Goms valley, then through the Furka tunnel at over 7,000ft, down to Andermatt, over the Oberalp Pass and down through Disentis and Chur before climbing through the Albula valley on the Rhætian section to St Moritz. To climb the many almost impossibly steep gradients it uses rack and pinion — a cog beneath the locomotive engages teeth in a central track or rack. Beyond Münster, where the train climbs to Gletsch, passengers have unbelievably close views of the Rhône glacier. The conveniently slow moving train allows plenty of time to admire the blues and greens of the glacier and photography is made easy as a result.

Lower down the Goms valley from Münster is Fiesch with a cable car to Eggishorn and one of the widest panoramic views in the whole of the Alps. Beneath the summit is the Aletsch glacier which starts at the Jungfraujoch with the Jungfrau itself to the left and on the right is first the Mönch and then the Eiger. Peak upon peak rear up in majesty and even the Matterhorn can be clearly seen far round to the south-east. This trip must be made on a fine day and those who are unlucky enough to find fog on the Eggishorn are deprived of one of Switzerland's finest views.

Münster welcomes the visitor, but does not offer much in the way of noisy entertainment. Daytime activities are mostly of the energetic variety. Apart from walking and mountaineering there is a keep-fit course and trout fishing in the river. Night time finds most visitors satisfied with an after dinner drink or perhaps joining one of the informal dances at the local hotels. Obviously this is not the place to come if you want the neon-lit high life, but if it is quiet hospitality amidst wonderful mountain scenery then Münster is a must.

Food is mainly based on pork or veal with soups a particular speciality, but perhaps the real culinary highlight of a holiday in Obergoms would be a 'charbonade'. This is a kind of indoor barbecue where a metal dish filled with glowing charcoal is placed on a fireproof stand in the centre of the table. Numerous dishes filled with diced meats and small sausages are arranged around the grill together with various spiced sauces. Diners armed with long wooden handled forks grill the meats of their choice and then dip them in one of the sauces before eating. Being beyond the actual wine growing areas there is no truly local wine, but red Dôle is the favourite as elsewhere in the Valais.

Anyone who is interested in trying cross country skiing would be pleased with the Obergoms in winter. The gently sloping broad valley bottom and heavy snowfall, together with plenty of sunshine make this an ideal centre for cross country skiing, known as *lauglauf* in German, or *Ski du Fond* in French. Prepared tracks cover most of the valley bottom and by using the train between Blitzingen and Oberwald a week's good skiing can be enjoyed up and down the valley.

THINGS TO DO AROUND MÜNSTER

Canoeing
Slalom course near Ulrichen and Oberwald (not for beginners). Vantage points along the river bank.

Keep-fit course
Near Ulrichen.

Fishing
River fishing (trout) near Ulrichen. Permits from local hotels or tourist office.

Horse Riding
Stables at Fiesch.

Swimming Pool
Heated indoor pool at Fiesch.

Glacier Viewing

Rhône Glacier   Close views of the glacier from the Belvédère Restaurant on the Furkapass road.

Gries Glacier   From Ulrichen follow the access road to the Griesee lake. The Gries glacier rises directly above the lake.

Alpine Zoo
Collection of alpine fauna at Fiesch (Tierpark).

Road Passes
Grimselpass (2,165m).
Furkapass (2,431m).
Nufenenpass (2,478m) on the Swiss/Italian frontier.

Cable Ascents
Fiesch - Eggishorn   Highly recommended for the panoramic view from the summit of the Eggishorn.
Tel: 028 8 1345

Mountaineering Instruction
Courses organised by the Fiesch Mountaineering School.
Details from:
Verkehrsbüro (Tourist Office),
CH-3984 Fiesch.
Tel: 028 81466

Rail Excursions
By using the 'Alpine Express' places as far apart as St Moritz and Zermatt may be reached by rail. Check train timetables before departure — early workmens' trains are often buses to fit into schedules and do not depart from the station!

Summer walking is very much on the high level, but all the paths are well maintained and follow easy gradients. Unless the visitor is exceptionally early in the season, snow is not usually found on any of the paths. As the tracks are mostly on a higher level than those described in other sections of this guide, the chance of patches of late snow cannot be discounted, consequently extra care must be taken on the walks. The maxim 'if in doubt turn back' is the wisest recommendation which can be offered.

FURTHER INFORMATION

Interesting towns nearby

Zermatt
70km south-west. Famous alpine village at the foot of the Matterhorn.

Montreux
150km west. Lakeside town (Lake Geneva). Famous for its mild climate. Fashionable resort built in the French style which was much favoured by the Edwardians. Famous castle of Chillon nearby, the dungeons of which were used by Byron as the setting for his poem 'The Prisoner of Chillon'. Conference centre and annual film festival. Mountain railway leaves main line station for the Rochers de Naye (6,700ft). Elegant shops and restaurants.

Vevey
155km west. Lakeside town (Lake Geneva). Resort popular with the British since the early nineteenth century. Home of Charlie Chaplin until his death. Centre of an important wine producing region. Interesting market in the main square every Saturday morning. Nearby valley famous for spring flowers. Shops, restaurants.

Fiesch
14km south-west. Small market town. Cable car to Eggishorn. Alpine Zoo. Swimming Pool. Baroque church.

Brig
28km south-west. Busy junction for road and rail networks. Shops and restaurants.

Martigny
105km south-west. At the junction of three important routes through the Rhône Valley. Remains of Roman camp of *Octodorum*. Shops, restaurants. Railway station.

Camp Sites

Oberwald ($7\frac{1}{2}$km north-east).
Ulrichen (4km north-east).

Accommodation

Mostly family run hotels and some rented accommodation. Details from the local tourist office.

Tourist Office

Verkehrsverein Münster,
CH 3985 Münster/Valais.
Tel: 028 73 1745

THE WALKS

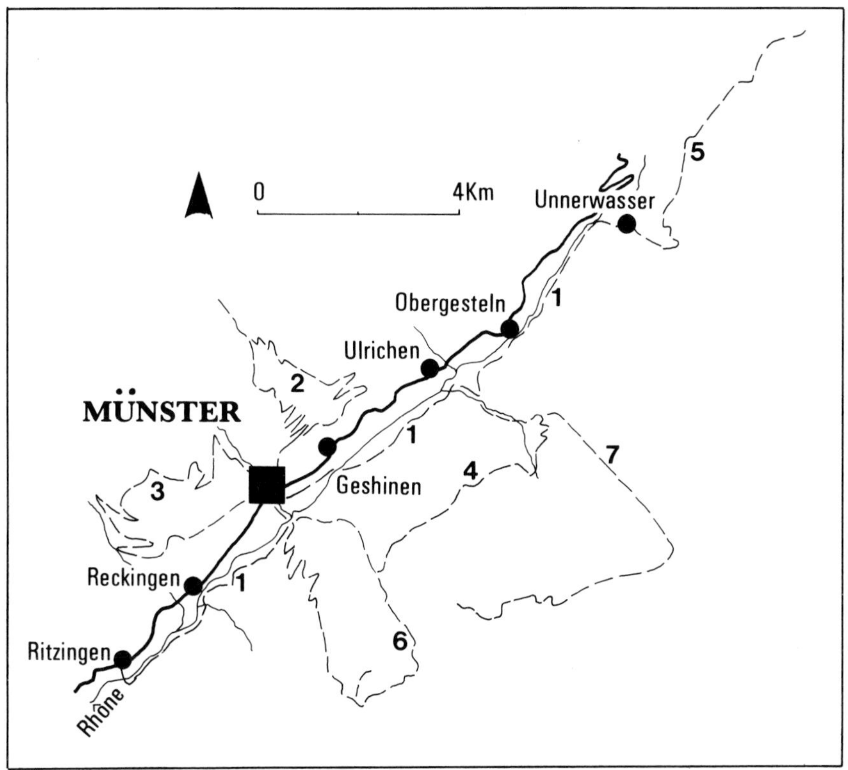

The Gommer Höhenweg

(The Goms Valley Highway)

This is a continuous medium level path which starts at Bellwald and follows a steadily climbing route along the north-west side of the valley all the way to Oberwald. Side paths link with most of the villages and the route is intended to be followed over the course of two or three days easy walking. The Höhenweg route is marked with a white-red-white block symbol. The height at Bellwald is 1,540m and the maximum altitude reached is 1,800m at Bächital in 11½km. Final height at Oberwald is 1,380m and the total distance is 29½km.

ROUTE 1

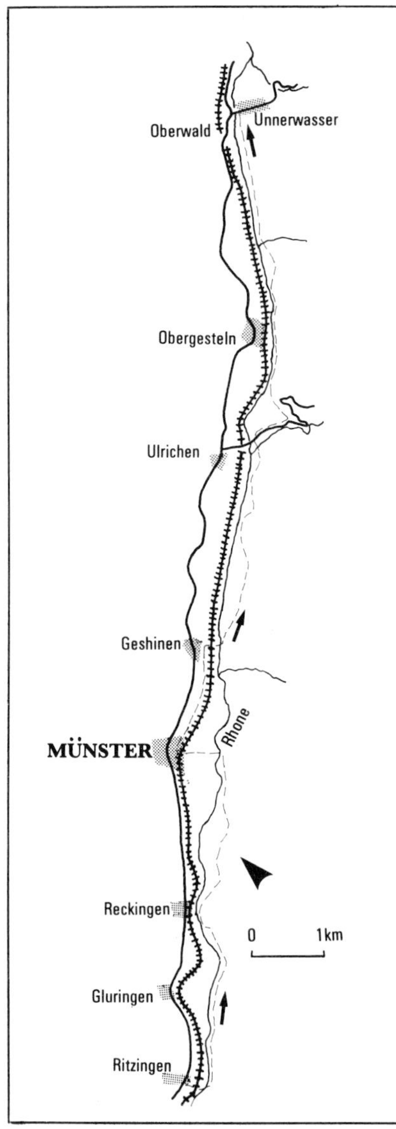

Blitzingen, Münster, Unterwassern, Oberwald

16km (10 miles). 4 hours. Easy. Riverside strolling through alpine meadows.

From Münster, take the train to Blitzingen and from the station cross the river to the café opposite. Turn left along the meadow path keeping on the same bank, ie with the river on your left, until opposite Münster where a short track leads back to the village. This is a possible lunch stop.

Walk down to Münster station and turn left following the track above the railway line until opposite Geschinen where the track crosses the railway and then the river. Turn left and climb a little way above the river on a well defined path which continues up the valley to Unterwassern and its pine fringed lake. Turn left away from the lake and walk the little way by road into Oberwald and catch a train back to Münster.

This is a good way to appreciate the architecture of the timber farm buildings of the Obergoms, as well as the nearby peaks.

The route is known locally as the Rottenweg (Red Way) after the local name for the river.

ROUTE 2

Münster, Münstigergalen, Trützisee, Geschinen

12km ($7\frac{1}{2}$ miles). 6/7 hours. Moderate.
A steep climb rewarded by glorious views culminating in a secluded mountain lake.

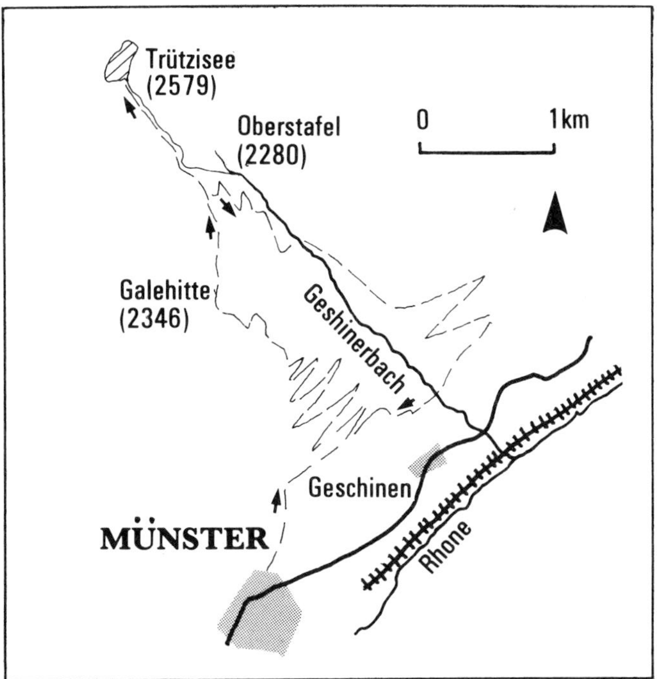

Climb above Münster on path 21 (signposted) which moves away to the right of the side stream, the Münstiger. The angle of the path gradually steepens and climbs the Münstigergalen (2,346m) in a series of zig zags, beyond which the angle eases a little until the junction with a path from the right. Turn left at this point and climb steeply for about 1km to the lake of Trützisee.

Return by the same route as far as the junction of paths, but turn left to take a slightly easier route down to Geschinen. A field path to the right above the village leads back to Münster.

The Trützisee (Trout lake) is sufficient justification for this steep climb with a magnificent panorama of snow covered peaks across the valley.

ROUTE 3

Münster, Münstigertal, Judenstafel, Galmihornhütte, Tränkboden, Alp-Bachi, Millerbine, Reckingen

9km ($5\frac{1}{2}$ miles). 5/6 hours. Moderate.
An alpine stream followed by a climb to a mountain hut, then beneath rocky peaks to descend by an easy track through high alpine pasture.

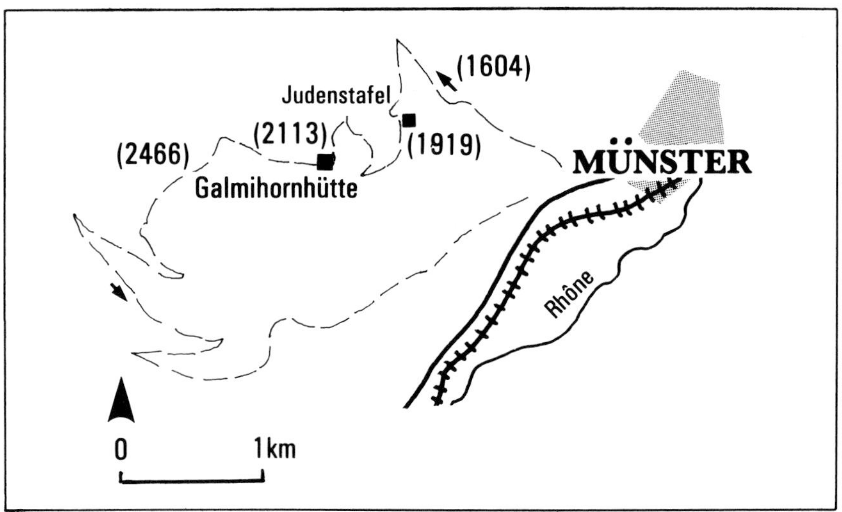

Follow the left bank of the Münstigertal valley behind Münster uphill by path 22 (signposted). At point 1,604* take the left path and climb steeply above the forest to the farmstead of Judenstafel. Turn right at the junction beyond the farm, continuing to climb as far as the Galmihornhütte, which is an obvious place to stop for refreshments.

After lunch the angle of ascent is easier and the path leads to another farm called Tränkboden. Beyond this the climbing finishes on the small unnamed peak at point 2,466*. The path swings downhill in broad zig-zags across the mountain side of Alp-Bachi before entering a pine forest. The farm of Millerbine occupies a clearing, pass this and walk down to Reckingen. Return by road or field path above the village.

This is alpine walking at its best.

* These numbers refer to spot heights on the map and are the most convenient means of identifying features which have no name.

ROUTE 4

Münster, Eiget, Berbel, Chäller, Mossmatte, Agenetal, Ulrichen

17km ($10\frac{1}{2}$ miles). 7/8 hours. Moderate.
Forest and stream followed by a level path across high alpine meadows.

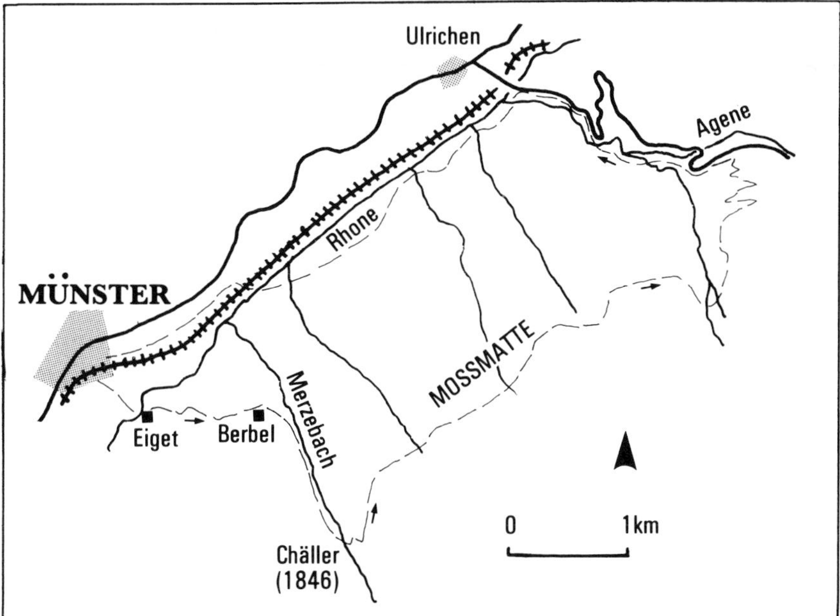

Walk down to the river below Münster, cross over and turn left below Eiget farm. Ignore the farm road but turn sharp right on to a path which climbs along the forest edge to Berbel farmstead. Beyond the farm the track enters a forest and swings round the hillside to follow the Merezenbach stream uphill to a junction of paths at Chäller. Turn left up a steep hill for about $\frac{3}{4}$km to where a level track crosses the alpine pastures of Mossmatte and stretches away into the distance, keeping more-or-less to one contour (path 16). Cross the head of a small valley on your left hand, climb a wooded shoulder then walk downhill and into the Aegina valley. Turn left at the road but leave it at the first bend to follow the stream downhill to the main river. Return to Münster either by train or road from Ulrichen or turn left along the riverside path.

Mosmatten is a riot of colourful alpine flowers in late spring.

ROUTE 5

Muttbach Belvédère, Firbäch, Gand, Gere, Unnerwasser, Oberwald

8km (5 miles). 4/5 hours. Moderate.
A high level walk with views of the nearby Rhône glacier.

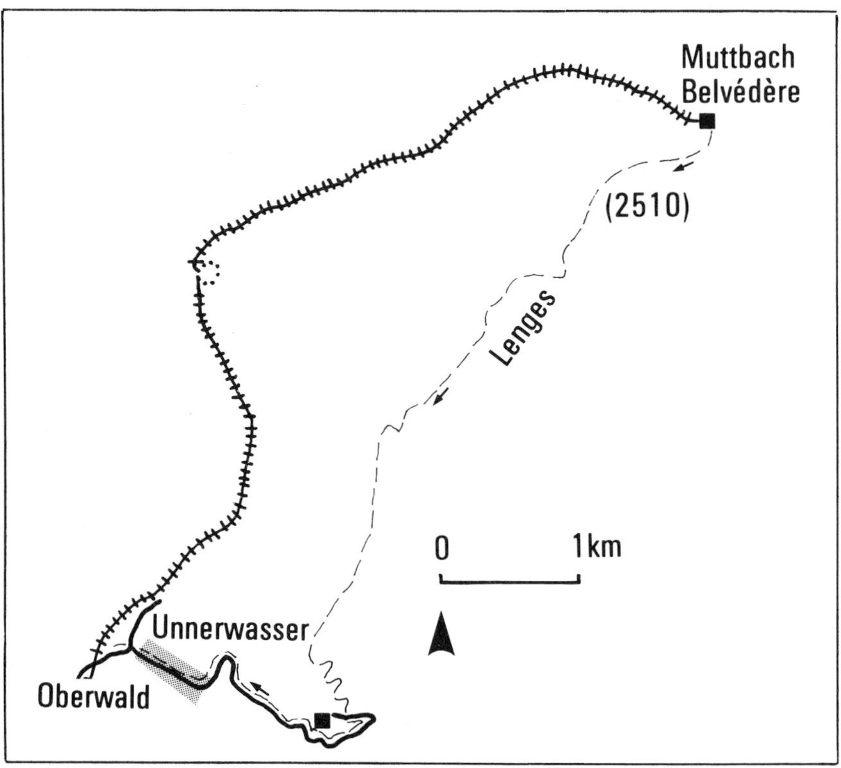

Take the train to Muttbach Belvédère, and then turn right in a south westerly direction away from the railway line, climbing steeply from the station to point 2,510. Walk downhill into the Lenges valley following a path which swings left across the mountain side past Firbach farm and Gand to Gere. Turn right through the village and downhill to Unnerwasser, walk past the lake and join the road to Oberwald and the train back to Münster.

This is an easy walk, mostly downhill, with close views of some of Europe's finest glacier scenery.

ROUTE 6

Münster, Eiget, Abmete, Hochbachchäller (2,027m), Seeve (2,455m), Stock (2,603), Tiefschlücht, Läger, Merezebach, Barbel, Eiget, Münster

15km (9¼ miles). 8/9 hours. Moderate/Difficult.

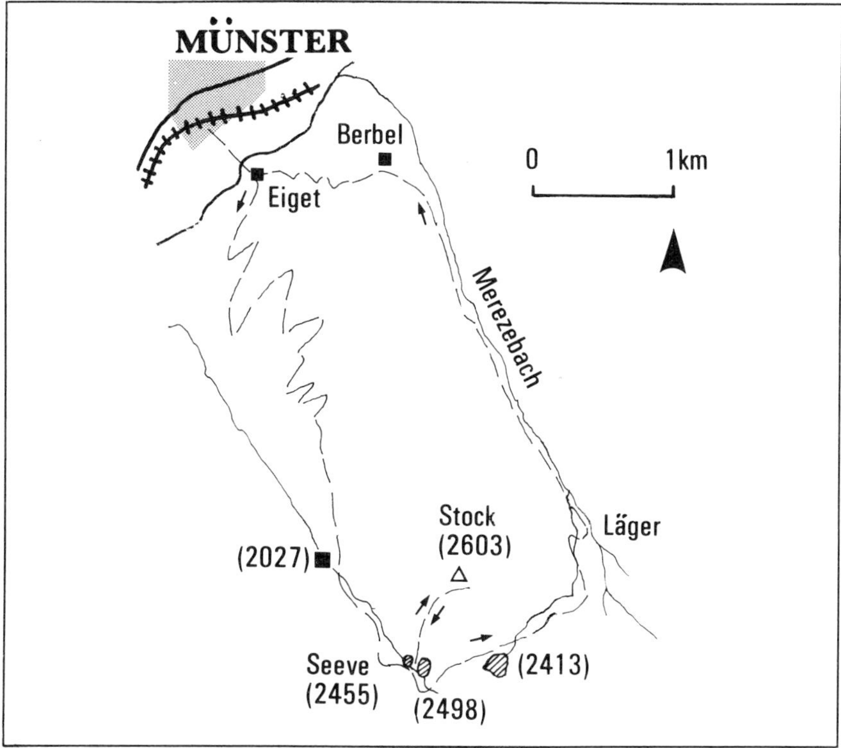

Cross over the river below Münster and turn right at Eiget. Climb through forest and just before Abmete farm turn left through the forest and climb to Hochbachchäller (point 2,027) farm in the Löwwibach valley. Turn left and climb to the head of the valley to the triple lakes of Seeve (2,455m). Those with sufficient energy to spare can now make the short diversion and climb Stock (2,603m). From here the route is mostly downhill. Walk over the col at 2,498m, down to an unnamed lake at 2,413m, then down the Teifschlücht alp. Turn left and go down a steep hill to Läger and follow the Merezebach valley through forest to Berbel, Eiget and eventually Münster.

This is a long walk, without any great difficulties. The short diversion up to the summit of Stock is well worth the climb for the views of the north side of the Blinnenhorn.

ROUTE 7

Ulrichen, Aegenental, Ladstafel (1,925m), Lengtal, Distelsee, Brudelhorn (2,791m)

25km ($15\frac{1}{2}$ miles). 9 hours. Difficult.
A tough high level walk to climb a shapely peak.

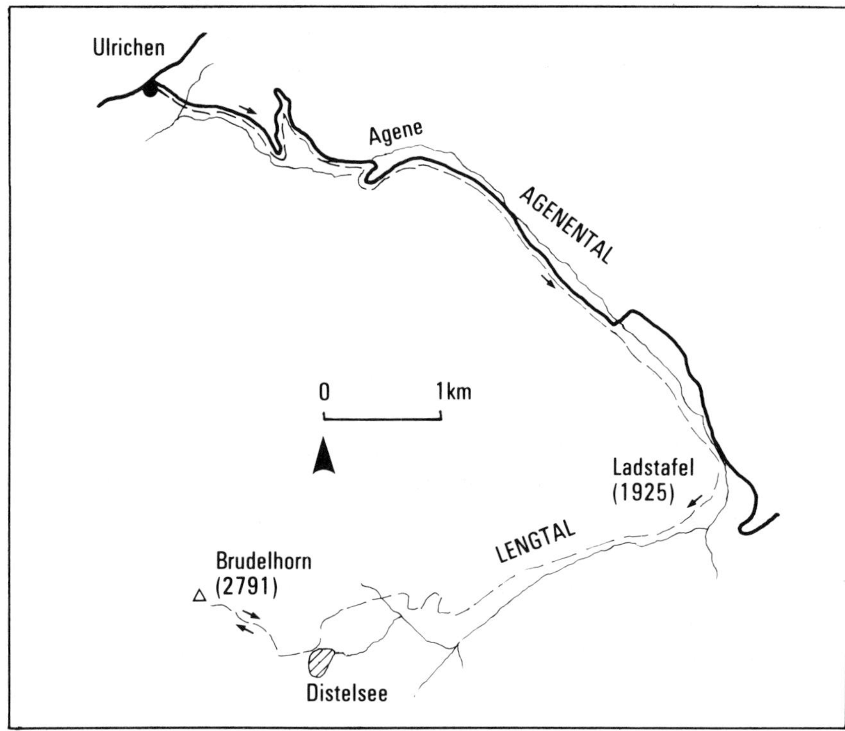

From Ulrichen walk up the Griessee Reservoir access road through the Aegenental valley as far as a junction of four tracks at Ladstafel. Turn right into the valley of Lengtal and follow the path to its head and beyond to the lovely lake of Distelsee. Above the lake the path leads up to the summit of the Brudelhorn which is gained after a short scramble. Return by the same route.

This is a long and hard day and one which should be reserved for the time when you feel at your fittest. The views all around from the summit are just reward for your labours. Countless high peaks and glaciers may be viewed so take your time and enjoy the scenery — you may not be back for sometime!

APPENZELL

Recommended Map:
Landeskarte der Schweiz
Sheet 227 (1:50,000) Appenzell

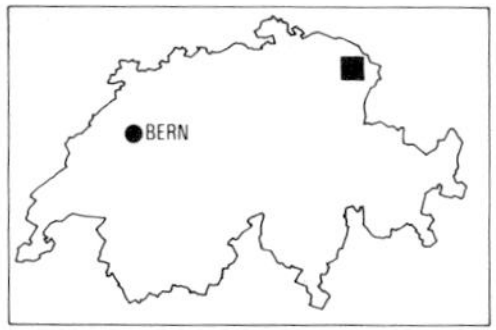

HOW TO GET THERE

Road: (1) South by the European Motorway System to Basel then east to Bodensee (Lake Constance) via Schaffhausen and Rorschach. South via St Gallen to Appenzell. (2) From Basel via Zürich to St Gallen. Gallen.

Rail: Main line network to St Gallen, then local trains to Appenzell.

Air: International airports at Zürich and Basel with rail connections via St Gallen.

Main Language: German.

THE AREA

The north-east corner of Switzerland is where The Alps have their final fling northwards. Parallel limestone ridges march high above the Rhine Valley and to the east, tiny Liechtenstein shelters in the arm of Austria. This is an area where there was much strife in the Middle Ages when feudal barons sought to gain domination over both trade routes and nearby fertile valleys. Appenzell was involved in this activity, but it is many years since Switzerland was directly involved in war and as a result Appenzell remains a tranquil town.

Appenzell gives its name to the canton or self governing region where the 'Landesgemeinde' or open-air parliament is still held. Local men vote by simple 'yes' or 'no' to proposals as far reaching as taxes and changes in the laws of the canton. Each man carries a sword to signify his right to the vote and the assembly is always held annually on the last Sunday in April.

The canton of Appenzell is a charming region of unspoilt villages filled with artistically painted houses which have a backcloth of majestic mountains. It sets out to please and be hospitable to the tourist without being spoilt by commercialism. The countryside of this north-east province is amongst the most fertile in Switzerland and is covered with orchards and meadowland. Dairy farming is the major occupation, with the local Appenzell cheese as the final by-product. These cheeses can be seen maturing or being made at many of the small dairies attached to local villages. The Appenzell cheese is a Gruyère type and is made as large, almost cartwheel-sized, rings. Cheese dishes are naturally high on the menu, especially fondues and

The hiking trail from Hohen Kasten to the Fälensee with the Altmann Range in the background

raclettes (cheese toasted from the whole ring held against a special grill).

Cattle, especially those giving the best milk yield are greatly revered and are dressed up with flowers and massive cowbells for special festivals in spring and early autumn, when the herds are led off to the high pastures and brought back down into the valleys before winter.

Cow bell ringing has become something of a folk art in the Appenzell canton. Some of the bells are so heavy that only the strongest man can lift a single bell, but others are light enough to allow a ringer to use two at a time. Often impromptu concerts are staged in local inns, when a team of three or four men will start to swing the huge bells in unison until gradually an eerie resonance fills the room. Together with accompanying yodelling, the whole effect makes your hair stand-on-end as the sound created by the bells gradually builds up. 'Talerschwingen' is another musical resonance custom. This is the

THINGS TO DO AROUND APPENZELL

Events:

Landsgemeinde. Open-air parliament where all local men may vote on important matters. Held annually the last Sunday in April.

Cow Festivals Heavily decorated animals are led up to the high pastures in late spring and back again in autumn.

Concerts and Dances, etc. Usually impromptu, especially cow bell ringing, yodelling, etc.
Look out for locally advertised special events.

Swimming Pools

Schwimmbad Forren (outdoor).
Town swimming pool near the railway station (outdoor).
Hallenschwimmbad, near by-pass (indoor).

Museums

Music and Flute Museum - Forren.
Folk Museum - Rathaus (Town Hall), Appenzell.

Cruises on the Bodensee (Lake Constance)

Nearest lakeside pick-up points at Rorschach and Romanshorn.

Fishing

Sämtisersee, Fählensee and Seealpsee. Enquire at local hotels for permits and conditions.

Steam Railways, Cable Ascents

Ebenalp (Chairlift).
Hoher Kasten (Cable car).
Kronberg (Cable car).
Säntis (Cable car - from Schwägalp).
Bodensee-Toggenburgbahn — Standard gauge private railway 12 miles between Herisau and Nesslau. Popular with wedding parties.

bell-like sound made by swinging a five franc piece (a taler) inside a large earthenware bowl. The idea is to balance the bowl on one hand and swing the coin higher and higher inside the bowl until it starts to make a musical sound.

Some of Appenzell's buildings date from the sixteenth century. Its town hall, which was built in 1561, has a very fine folklore museum which is well worth a visit. The main street is lined with lovely gabled buildings, mostly used as shops where attractive souvenirs are offered for sale. Hand embroidery is a speciality in this area and many examples of this delicate and intricate craft are available to tempt the tourist.

Hill walking has been made easy with a cable car to the nearby summit of Hoher Kasten above Sämtisersee, as well as a chairlift to Ebenalp from the beautiful Schwende valley. Both these lifts give access to exciting and yet easy ridges where the walker can spend all day exploring the nooks and crannies of these wild heights. Mount Säntis and its glaciers dominate the skyline to the immediate west of the region and although it is essentially the preserve of the skilled

FURTHER INFORMATION

Interesting towns nearby

St Gallen
12km north. Founded by an Irish missionary in AD612. Abbey destroyed during the Reformation, but its library (rebuilt in the eighteenth century), remains and contains over 100,000 volumes and manuscripts, some over a thousand years old. Cathedral built 1756. Theatre. Embroidery Museum. Peter and Paul deer park. Shops, restaurants.

Herisau
15 km north-west. Old town. Privately run steam railway. Shops and restaurants.

Rorschach
25km north. Lakeside town. Largest 'port' on the Swiss side of Lake Constance. Old town is backed by pine forested hills and alpine meadows. Folklore museum. Baroque Churches. Dornier aeroplane factory nearby. Start of rack and pinion railway to Heiden. Shops and restaurants.

Arbon
30km north. Lakeside village. Roman fort built on Celtic foundations. Medieval chateau.Orchards. Museum. Shops and restaurants.

Camp Sites

Appenzell - Kau. Tel: 071 87 1497
Gonten - Jakobsbad.
Tel: 071 89 1131

Cable Ascents

Wasserauen-Ebenalp (Chairlift).
Brülisau-Hoher Kasten (Cable car).
Schägalp-Säntis (Cable car).
Jakobsbad-Kronberg (Cable car).

Bodensee (Lake Constance)
Regular lake cruises to Swiss, German and Austrian resorts.

Accommodation
A wide range of hotels, guest houses and rented accommodation is available in the Appenzell area. Contact the tourist office for up-to-date information.

Tourist Information
Verkersbüro Appenzell,
Hauptgasse 19,
CH-9050 Appenzell.
Tel: 071 87 1693

climber, its summit can be reached by a cable car from Schägalp. To reach Schägalp from Appenzell it is necessary to either go by road or by train through Jakobsbad to Urnäsch and then by post bus to the start of the cable.

Hoher Kasten's limestone ridge is a unique record of many million years of underwater growth during the Carboniferous period. Layer upon layer of plant and animal life were laid one upon the other several thousands of feet thick. Subsequent earth movements have warped these layers or strata into fantastic shapes, all of which can easily be seen from a carefully graded footpath which follows the ridge. Plaques at intervals describe the geology, but even if you can speak good German, they are rather technical and it would be better if more easily understood information was available. However, the ridge and its rock formations represent a slice of the earth's history and it only needs a little observation to appreciate what is around, and of course, the scenery is magnificent.

Railway travel in this region is an entertainment in itself as most of the lines are narrow gauge and steam is a common form of locomotion. The 'main' line meanders from St Gallen to Appenzell with several branches into side valleys, such as the one to Urnäsch or up to Wasserauen and the start of the Schwende valley.

THE WALKS

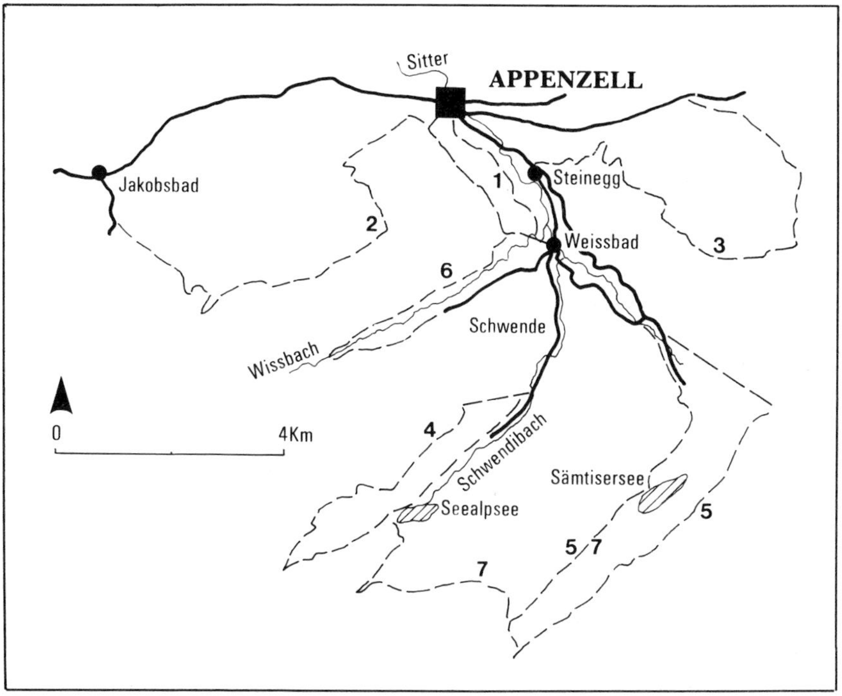

Appenzel

ROUTE 1

Appenzell town, Unterrain, Weissbad

7km ($4\frac{1}{2}$ miles). 2 hours. Easy.

Explore the old town of Appenzell and its nearby meadowland.

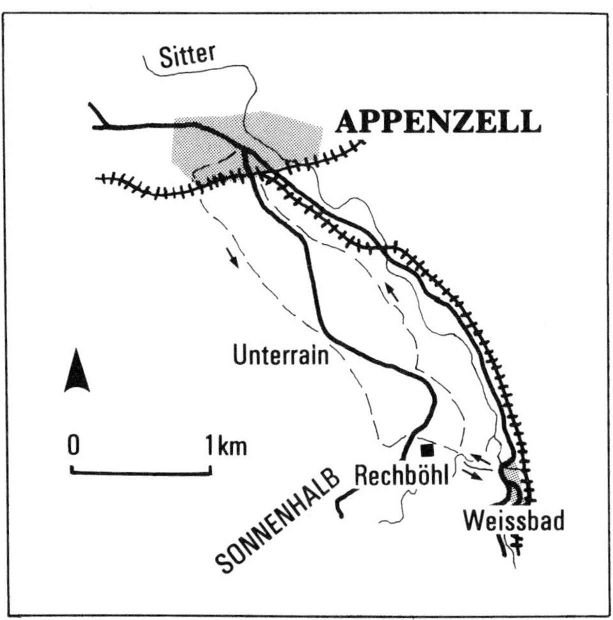

Start in the town centre of Appenzell and wander round its streets admiring the old buildings, then walk uphill beyond the railway station into an area of modern houses. Turn left at a fork in the road at the upper limit of the housing development and almost immediately the town is left behind. The road gradually becomes a well defined track leading past farm houses and through meadowland to join the road to Sonnenhalb at Unterrain. Walk along this road for about 50m and turn right on to a path which climbs towards the forest edge before dropping down again to join the Sonnenhalb road. Cross the road and join a good track downhill past the farm of Rechböhl. A path leads from the farm and across the river to Weissbad where you will probably find refreshments.

Return to the river and across the bridge, but do not go uphill to Rechböhl; turn half right along a well marked track which will be signposted to Appenzell. This track wanders through meadows and through farmyards along the valley bottom to the outskirts of Appenzell.

A pleasant and relaxing first walk of the holiday, but take care not to go beyond the turning to Rechböhl — if in doubt stick to the road at Unterrain as there is usually not much traffic about.

ROUTE 2

Appenzell, Vorder Kau, Sollegg, Wasserschaffen, Dornesslen, Gschwend, Jakobsbad

$10\frac{1}{2}$km ($6\frac{1}{2}$ miles). 3/4 hours. Easy/Moderate.
Mountain pasture followed by forest and ridgewalking.

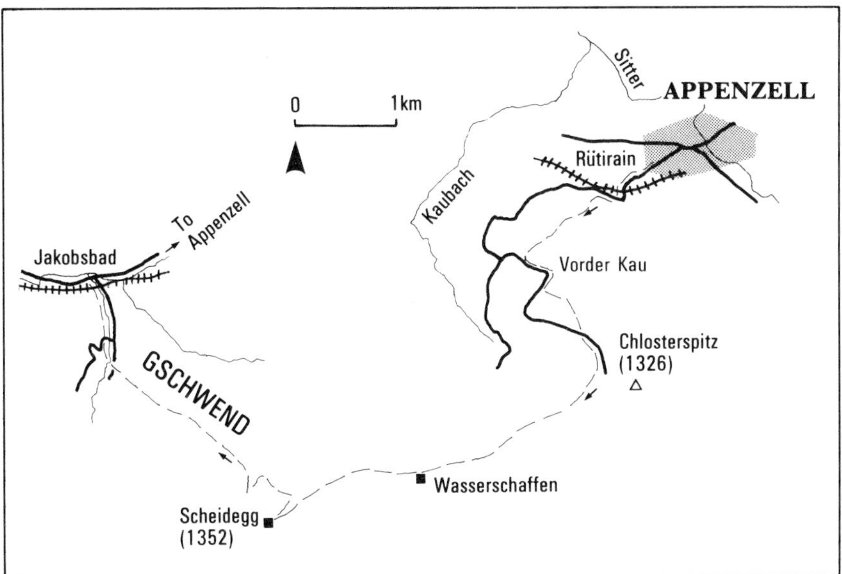

Follow the minor road out of Appenzell in a south westerly direction through Rutirain, over the railway and through a forest as far as a road junction at Vorder Kau. Take the left-hand fork and continue uphill, gradually climbing beneath the Chlosterspitz. At the road end take the track on the right and climb the ridge ahead as far as a hill farm (marked Wasserschaffen on the map). Continue along the ridge for about $1\frac{1}{4}$km and look out for a path to the right which begins at another farm (Scheidegg), and leads down into the Gschwend valley on an improving track to Jakobsbad. Return by bus or rail.

There should be a signpost marking the route into the Gschwend valley, but in case it is missing, do not go beyond Scheidegg farm (ie the second farm along the ridge).

ROUTE 3

Moser valley, Bild, Forstseeli, Forstegg, Hämmeren, Obersteinegg, Steinegg

19½km (12 miles). 7 hours. Moderate.
A high level tour around the Fänerenspitz.

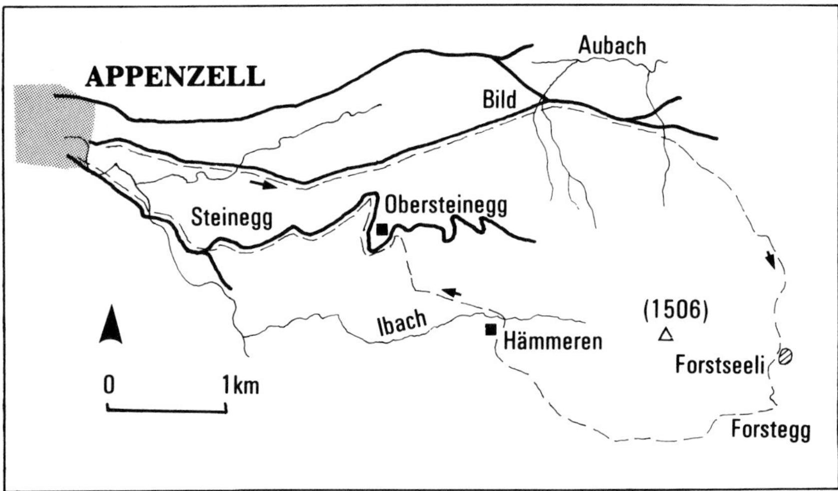

From the town centre of Appenzell cross the bridge beyond the church and immediately turn right along a quiet lane which climbs easily through the Möser valley to the hamlet of Bild.

Join the main road, which comes in from your left, and walk on for 1½km to a fork in the road. Take the right-hand minor road and after about ½km turn right onto a footpath which climbs uphill through patches of forest and across alpine meadows. The path then enters another forest, in the centre of which is the tiny lake of Forstseeli. The path forks just prior to the lake; take the right-hand branch uphill to a junction of paths. Turn right and over the low col of Forstegg. Walk downhill on an improving track and across meadowland to a group of farm buildings at Hämmeren. Turn right away from the farm and cross two side valleys to Obersteinegg and the road down to Steinegg and Appenzell.

This is a long walk with some route finding necessary in the middle section. Do not miss the gem of lake Forstseeli.

ROUTE 4

Wasserauen, Eben Alp, Wildkirchli, Altenalp, Unter-Mesmer, Seealpsee

11km (5½ miles). 6 hours. Moderate/Difficult.
An exciting high-level track to a church carved into the mountainside, followed by mountain farms and a beautiful lake.

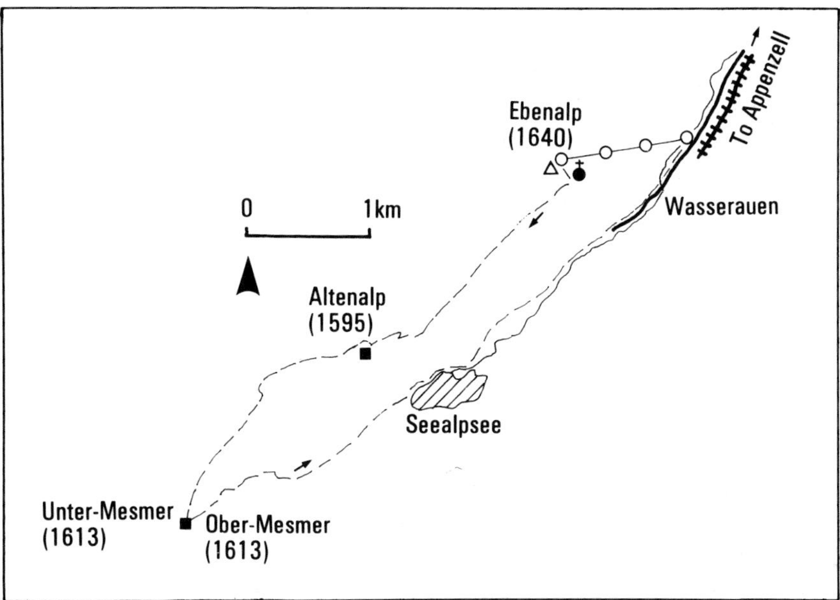

Take the cable lift from Wasserauen to Eben Alp and walk down the steep rocky path (signposted) to the rock church of Wildkirchli. Continue along a rocky ledge on a safe but exposed path and where it divides follow the right-hand upper track across the mountainside to the high summer farmsteads of Altenalp. Walk ahead and downhill to Unter-Mesmer farms and turn sharp left on a rocky path which leads down into beautiful meadows and to a lake (Seealpsee). Beyond the lake an easy track leads to Wasserauen.

This is an exciting walk and much easier than it would appear from the first glance at the map, but do not attempt it in smooth shoes.

ROUTE 5

Brülisau, Hoher Kasten, 'The Geological Way', Staubern Hut, Staubernenchanzlen, Saxerlücke, Furgglen, Sämtisersee, Brüeltobel

14km (9 miles). 7/8 hours. Moderate/Difficult.
A high level route along a limestone ridge.

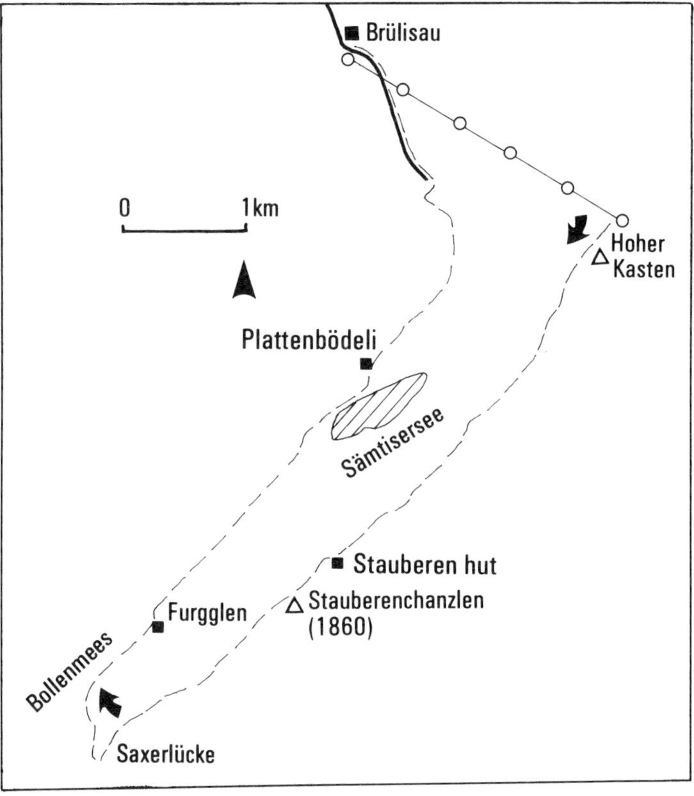

Use the cable car from Brülisau to reach the summit of Hoher Kasten. Turn right and follow the well marked path to the south-west. There are plaques at intervals along here explaining (in German) the various geological features. Continue to the Staubern Hut. An easy climb over the summit of Staubernenchanzlen follows a well marked path down to the narrow col at Saxerlücke. Turn right down the steep hill to Bollenmees, where a path to the right leads to the farmstead of Furgglen. Continue downhill through forest to the lake of Sämtisersee and up to Plattenbödeli where there are refreshments. Follow a woodland track through Brüeltobel back to Brülisau.

The views throughout this walk are magnificent. Look out for interesting rock formations, alpine flowers and marmots.

ROUTE 6

Appenzell, Unterrain, Sonnenhalb, Tüllen, Lehmen, Triberen, Weissbad

13km (8 miles). 3/4 hours. Easy.

A gentle valley stroll after two strenuous high level walks.

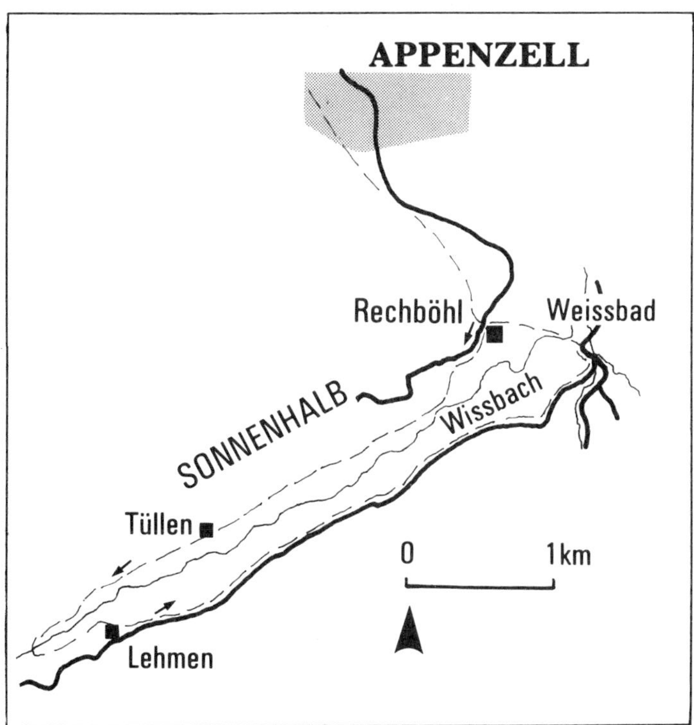

Follow route 1 as far as the turning to Rechböhl. Do not go down to the farm but continue ahead along the Sonnenhalb road. Turn left on a path which follows an easy course along the valley bottom to the farmstead of Tüllen. Continue up the valley and through forest for about 1½km, then cross over the river (the Wissbach) by a forest bridge. Climb up to the road at Lehmen. Turn left and walk down to Weissbad. Return as route 1.

A suitable walk for a rainy day, or as a rest from more strenuous activities.

ROUTE 7

Brülisau, Plattenbödeli, Sämtisersee, Fälensee, Widderalp, Meglisalp, Seealpsee, Wasserauen

16km (10 miles). 8/9 hours. Difficult.
A strenuous walk rewarded by three alpine lakes.

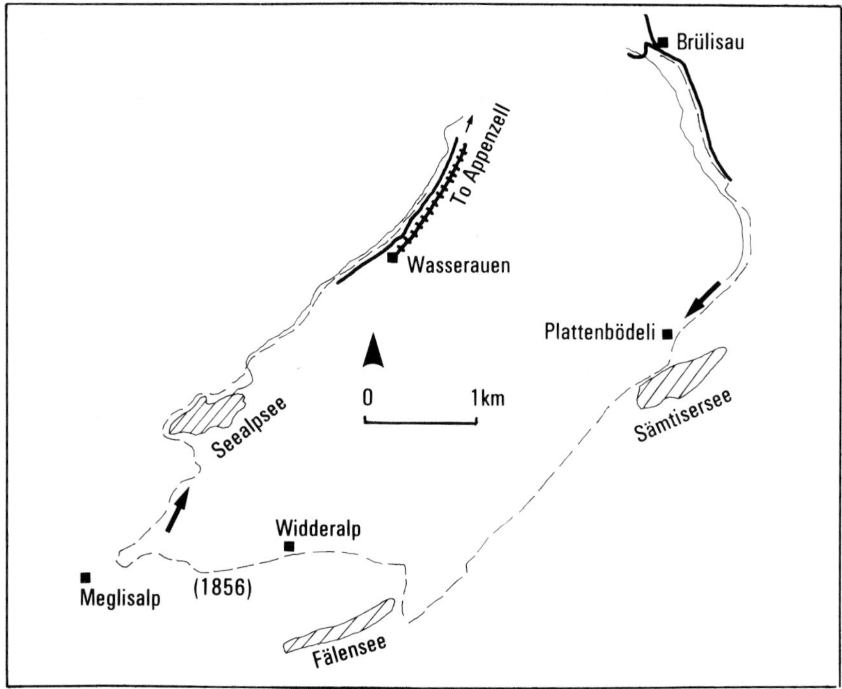

From Brülisau follow the road and track to the Plattenbödeli hut and Sämtisersee. Take the central path through the valley bottom before climbing steeply to Fälensee. Follow the contours around the hillside away from the lake and climb to the alpine farms at Widderalp. Walk over the col (1,856m) and down to Meglisalp. Turn right over the flat alpine meadows for about ¾km then left and down a steep hill to Lake Seealpsee. Follow the valley tracks to the right and into Wasserauen and the road or rail back to Appenzell.

The climb from Fälensee to the col beyond Widderalp is very steep and should only be attempted in boots.

Take care to follow the map on this route and do not attempt it in bad weather. Otherwise it is an excellent and highly recommended walk.

CHAMPEX
(Valais)

Recommended Map:
Landeskarte der Schweiz
Sheet 282 (1:50,000) Martigny

HOW TO GET THERE

Road: (1) South by European motorway system to Lausanne. South-east on routes 12 and 9 via Montreux to Martigny. E21A (St Bernard Pass road) to Orsières then by the steep side road which climbs 572m (1,877ft) in 7½km (4½ miles) in a series of sharp zig-zags to Champex.
Rail: (1) Main line services via Geneva and Martigny. Branch line to Orsières and then post bus. (2) Alternatively by post bus from Martigny itself.
Air: International airport at Geneva. Connections by rail via Martigny.
Main Language: French.

THE AREA

The tourist brochure which describes Champex emphasises the fact that the main attraction to this small secluded holiday village is its situation. Set in a natural bowl high above the Rhône valley and facing south-west, Champex can claim to be one of the sunniest resorts in the whole of Switzerland. High mountain peaks and forested slopes are its backcloth, but without any doubt it is its lake which really sets the scene on an idyllic mountain retreat. The sun shines on Champex all the year round and so justifys its claim to be a 'mile high four-seasons' resort.

Despite being so fortunate in its situation and weather, Champex has never been 'developed' and has not been discovered by too many visitors. Even though it is only a short distance above the busy road to the St Bernard Pass, few tourists take the trouble to climb the steep zig-zags of the road from Orsières, but those who do so find a village of considerable charm and also one of the most beautiful lakes in the Alps.

The Great Saint Bernard Pass, one of the oldest and most famous of the Swiss passes has been used for centuries — first by the Celts in their spread northwards, then later Roman legions crossed its heights during their conquest and administration of Europe. Napoleon led 40,000 troops across it to defeat the Austrians at Marengo in 1800 (where incidentally his cook, in making the most of a scrawny fowl, is

Champex and its lake

supposed to have invented 'chicken marengo'). The hospice on the summit of the pass was opened to help travellers, but now only camera-wielding tourists are interested in the massive St Bernard dogs which were bred to find people lost in the snow. The modern motor road is through an all-weather tunnel, but the old road to the top of the pass is still maintained and is a popular attraction in summer. The Saint Bernard Pass was named after Bishop Bernard of Menthon and the story is that originally the pass, then known as Mons Jovis, was inhabited by highway robbers. Bishop Bernard set out to rid the pass of the robbers and on reaching its summit found a pagan shrine over which he threw his cloak. The shrine immediately turned to dust and equally miraculously the brigands fled away. To cement his hold over the pass Bernard and his followers, built the first hospice which grew in fame and stature throughout the years. The history of the dogs is equally interesting. These originated in Tibet and came to Europe by way of the silk caravans during the time of the Romans, who used them as war dogs. Never happy in the warmer climate of the plains, the dogs work at their best in mountainous terrain and quickly established themselves in snow conditions as ideal search and rescue animals.

THINGS TO DO AROUND CHAMPEX

Boating
Rowing boats and pedaloes for hire on Lake Champex.

Tennis
Two courts: lakeside and village centre.

Swimming
Open-air pool (heated), near riverside east of village.

Climbing Instruction and School of Alpinism
Based nearby at le Fouly (val Ferret).

Alpine Garden
Above village to the north of the camp site. Over 4,000 species of plants on display in natural surroundings.

Fishing
Permits required, enquire locally at the tourist office for current fees. Mostly lake trout.

Cable Ascents
Champex-La Breya.
Sion-Pas de Maimbré.
Verbier-Mont Gelé.

Tour of Mont Blanc
The celebrated long distance walk around Mont Blanc passes through Champex and can be followed by clearly defined route marking. Parts of this route may be followed using Champex as a base and motoring to and from the start of the section being walked.

Grand St Bernard Pass
35km south-east. Hospice, museum, dogs.

Lake Geneva
75km north. Lake cruises, boating and swimming.

Golf
Nearest golf courses at Lausanne and Montreux (both 18 holes and par 72).

Val Ferret
15km south - to upper valley. Access to easy high level walks into Italy (Grand St Bernard, and Italian Val Ferret). Good motor road to Ferret village; regular post bus service.

Martigny is the main town in this area. The Romans used the commanding position of the right-angle bend of the Rhône, where it joins the Drance beneath the St Bernard Pass, to build their fort of *Octodorum.* Even today it marks an important crossroads. Sembrancher is the next town along the Drance valley where the St Bernard road starts its climb through (or at least bypassing today) Orsières, then Liddes and finally Bourg St Pierre where there is an inn which was used by Napoleon. All are attractive sleepy villages, but Champex is best of all.

The countryside around Champex is steeped in tradition as well as history. On festival days the women of this region wear a beautiful and distinctive dress with a hat made from 50yd of ruched silk. Early August is the time of the main festival, when villagers in costume perform a lively dance to the music of country fiddles.

FURTHER INFORMATION

Interesting towns nearby

Lausanne
95km north-west. On Lake Geneva (Lac Leman). Prosperous market town built on Roman foundations. Situated on three hills. Old city clustered around the Medieval Cathedral of Notre Dame founded in twelfth century. Shops, restaurants.

Montreux
75km north. Lakeside town (Lake Geneva). Famous for its mild climate. Fashionable resort built in the French style and much favoured by the Edwardians. Castle of Chillon nearby, the dungeons of which were used by Byron as the setting for this poem 'The Prisoner of Chillon'. Conference centre and annual film festival. Mountain railway leaves main line station for the Rochers de Naye (6,700ft). Elegant shops and restaurants.

Sion
50km north-east. Ancient 'capital' of the Valais region. Commanded by two rocky hills, one topped by a ruined castle and a church on the other. Gothic cathedral with nineth-century Romanesque tower. Seventeenth-century town hall and ancient clock. Market centre for this agricultural region, where fruit is a speciality. Shops, restaurants, etc.

Martigny
25km north. At the junction of three important routes through the Rhône Valley. Remains of Roman camp of *Octodorum*. Shops, restaurants. Railway station.

Vevey
85km north. Lakeside town (Lake Geneva). Resort popular with the British since the early nineteenth century. Home of Charlie Chaplin until his death. Centre of an important wine producing region. Interesting market in the square every Saturday morning. Nearby valleys famous for spring flowers.
Shops, restaurants.

Cable Ascents
Télésiege Champex-La Breya.
Tel: 026/4 1344/42357

Camp Sites
West end of Champex village. First class facilities.

Accommodation
Nine hotels. 200 chalets and other rented accommodation. Contact the Tourist Office for up-to-date details of available accommodation.

Tourist Information
Office du Tourism,
CH-1938 Champex-Lac.
Tel: 026/412 27

Food has a French flavour with cheese fondues topping the list of favourites. These are made from local cheese which is melted and blended with a liqueur, usually Kirsch. The dish is served over a small spirit stove and eaten by any number of participants who dip pieces of bread into a communal bowl. The meal usually develops into hilarious chaos as tradition decrees that anyone losing their piece of bread from his or her fork must pay a forfeit.

With the abundant streams around Champex and also its lake, fish (especially trout) are a speciality and are served in delicious sauces which vary from hotel to hotel, each to a carefully guarded recipe. Dried meats, sausages and fruits are also recommended.

The wines of the Swiss section of the Rhône valley are not so well known as those from France, as production is barely enough to satisfy local demand, but the finest wine from this area is the Dôle, a delicate red, with others from around Lake Geneva in close competition. Of whites, the best is Johannisberg, sometimes known as Sylvaner, a pleasant soft dry wine.

Champex is a holiday resort for the seeker of mountain solitude; the only manmade sporting facilities offered are a small but good tennis court, an outdoor heated swimming pool and boating on the lake. Most visitors come for the walking and are well catered for by an excellent system of well designed paths and a cable lift to the Breya mountain. Lovers of alpine flowers will delight in the area, which is noted for its wide range of species. There is an alpine garden nearby, 'l'Alpine Jardin Florealpe', which has over 4,000 different specimens in a natural setting. The garden is reached by the footpath which starts from the camp site to the west of the village.

THE WALKS

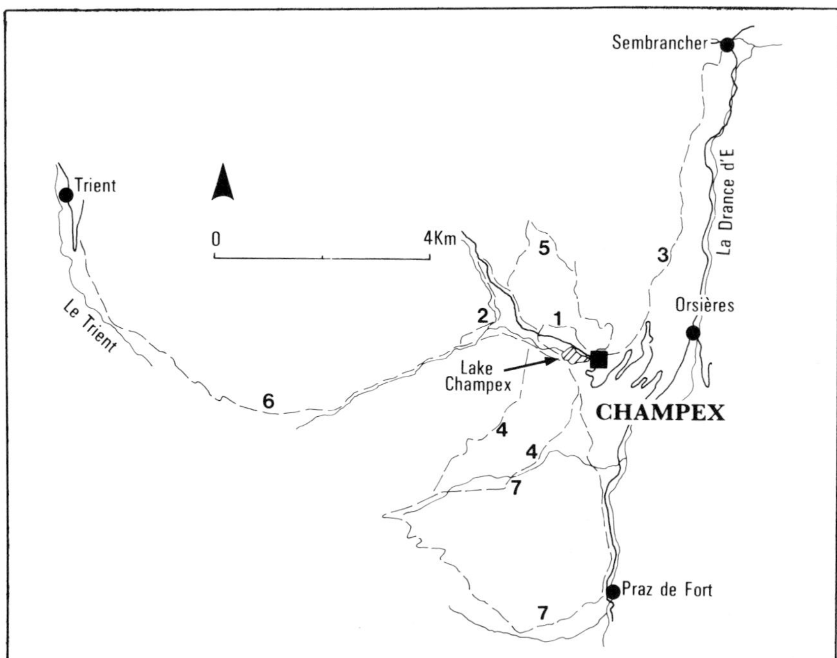

ROUTE 1

Champex village and its lake

5km (3 miles). 1½/2 hours. Easy. A popular local stroll suitable for either relaxation after a long journey or in the evening after dinner.

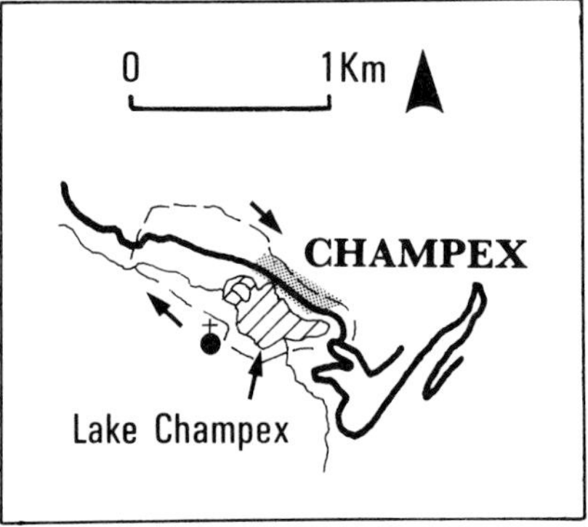

Walk down the Martigny road as far as the camp site and turn right at the sharp bend in the road opposite Les Arollas II. The path known as the Tour de Champex winds gently through meadowland above the village, past the alpine garden and rejoins the road on the far side (east) of lake Champex. Cross the road and walk down to the lake, following its shore by the Tour du Lac path. Opposite the Protestant church the path divides, one arm continuing to the right, round the lakeside and back to the village, the other to the left is the Chemin du Revers. Take this one which meanders through pine forest and across a stream back to the road near the camp site.

ROUTE 2

Lac de Champex, Val d'Arpette, Champex d'en Haut, Champex d'en Bas

8km (5 miles). 2/3 hours. Easy. An excursion into a remote alpine valley followed by forest tracks to unspoilt farming communities.

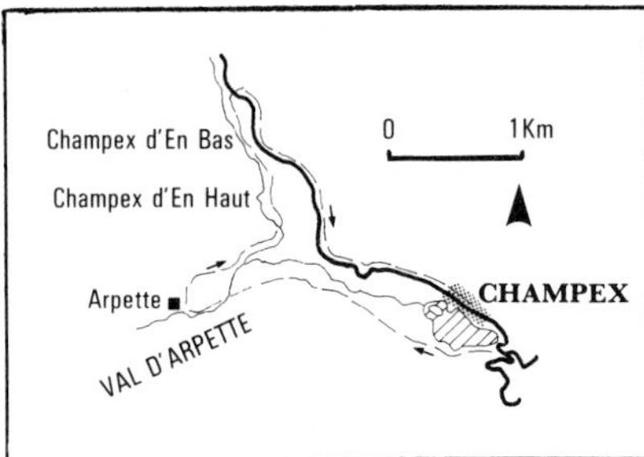

Walk round the south side of Lac Champex and follow the Chemin du Revers as far as the river. Turn left at the river and cross the field ahead to join the Val d'Arpette track. Turn left along this track through pine forest as far as the farms of Arpette. Turn right at the second farmhouse and cross fields to enter more forest. A steep walk down through the forest, leads to the village of Champex d'en Haut; turn left and continue through fields and alongside the river to Champex d'en Bas. Turn right and join the road. Right again and follow the road (which usually has little or no traffic of note) back beneath pine trees to Champex.

Do not cross fields that have crops growing in them.

ROUTE 3

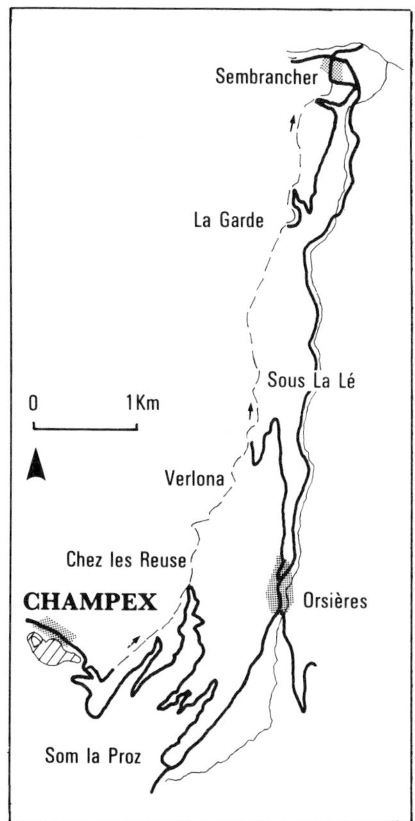

Champex, Verlona, Sous la Lé, la Garde, Sembrancher

8km (5 miles). 4 hours.
Easy/Moderate.
A walk mostly through forest, high above the Val d'Entremont and the St Bernard Pass road.

From the eastern (Orsières) end of Lake Champex take the side road past the Café de la Promenade and walk away from the village. The path enters the forest ahead and continues round the mountain side and downhill above the zig-zags of the Orsières road as far as Verlona, then on to Sous la Lé and la Garde. Do not follow the road down into Sembrancher from la Garde but follow either of the two signposted paths which lead through pinewoods and meadows to Sembrancher and as a result are much more interesting.

Return by bus or train to Orsières and unless you wish to climb the steep road back to Champex, wait for the connecting post bus or take a taxi.

This is a more straightforward walk than a first glance at the map might suggest. The secret is to resist any temptation to use any of the side paths into the valley. Time will be well spent investigating farmhouse architecture along the way.

Champex mountain lake at 3,630ft above sea level

ROUTE 4

La Breya (2,188m), Combe d'Orny, Forêt Voutax, Champex

8km (5 miles). 4/5 hours. Moderate.
An interesting introduction to high level walking, made easy by the use of a chairlift to save 689m (2,260ft) of climbing.

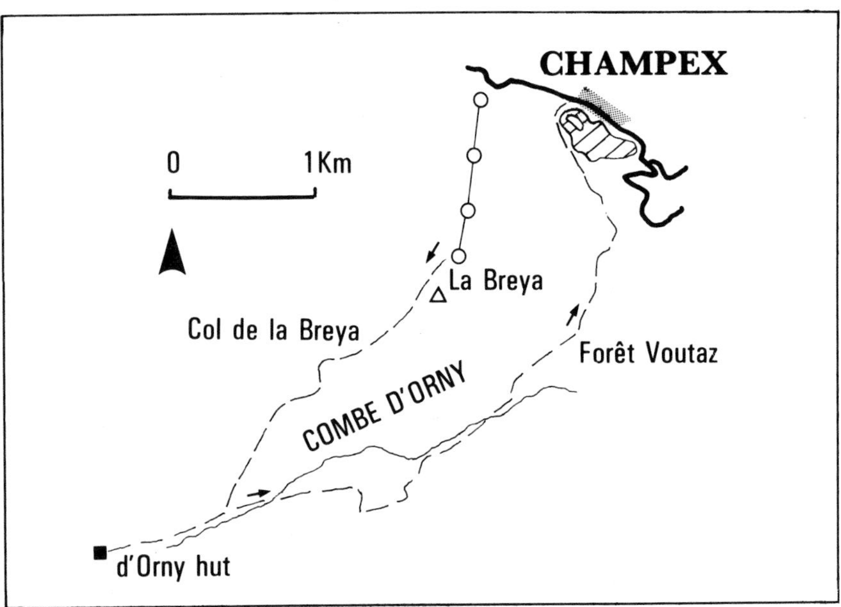

Ascend la Breya by chairlift and from the top station walk forwards along the ridge and down to the Col de la Breya. Turn left and a steep walk down into Combe d'Orny leads to the path from the d'Orny hut. Turn left at the junction and follow a steep path downhill. Follow the river bank for about ½km and look out for a fork in the path. Take the left-hand path which follows the contours across the low col ahead and through the Forêt Voutaz. Continue downhill through forest and back to Champex along a signposted path.

The glaciers at the head of Combe d'Orny lead up to the Aiguille du Tour.

ROUTE 5

Champex (1,466m), le Bonhomme (2,435m)

8km (5 miles). 5/6 hours. Moderate/Difficult.
A stiff climb rewarded by views of the Mont Blanc range.

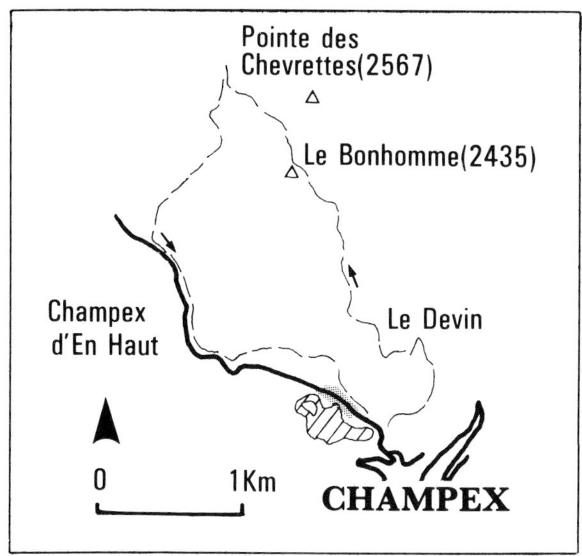

Follow the Chemin du Belvédère path (signposted) beyond the Café de la Promenade and walk up a steep hill through the forest of le Devin. This path leads to the summit of le Bonhomme. Walk ahead on the well graded path beneath the Pointe des Chevrettes ridge until another path from the left is joined. Turn left onto this path and a steep walk downhill leads to the road at Champex d'en Haut. Turn left for Champex.

Boots are essential for this walk. A map covering the Mont Blanc range would help to name the jumble of summits and glaciers seen in the middle distance.

The look out-terrace and the hiking area of La Breya

ROUTE 6

Val d'Arpette, Fenêtre d'Arpette, Trient Glacier, Trient

14km ($8\frac{1}{2}$ miles). 7/8 hours. Moderate/Difficult.
A high valley route to spectacular glacier scenery.

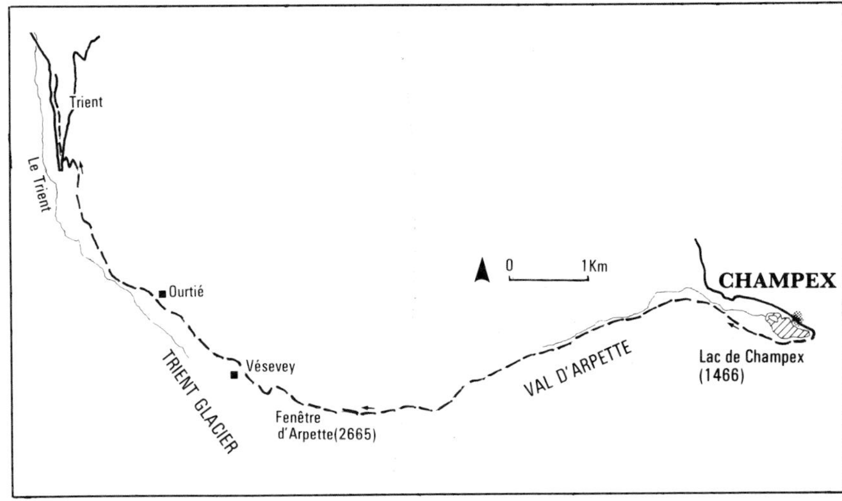

Follow route 2 into the Val d'Arpette and continue up the valley along the signposted path to cross the high pass of the Fenêtre d'Arpette. Walk down a steep hill alongside the Trient Glacier passing the high alpine farms of Vésevey and Ourtié to join the track down to Trient. Return by bus to Martigny and train to Orsières, then by post bus from the latter or direct from Martigny to Champex.

The Trient Glacier is a terrifying jumble of jagged ice formations and makes an exciting climax to this walk. Do not attempt the walk if any great volume of snow is reported on the Fenêtre d'Arpette.

ROUTE 7

Combe d'Orny, d'Orny Swiss Alpine Club Hut, col de Chevrettes, Saleina valley, Praz de Fort, Issert, Prassurny, Champex.

18km (11 miles). 9 hours. Difficult.
A tough and long walk with close views of glaciers and rocky ridges.

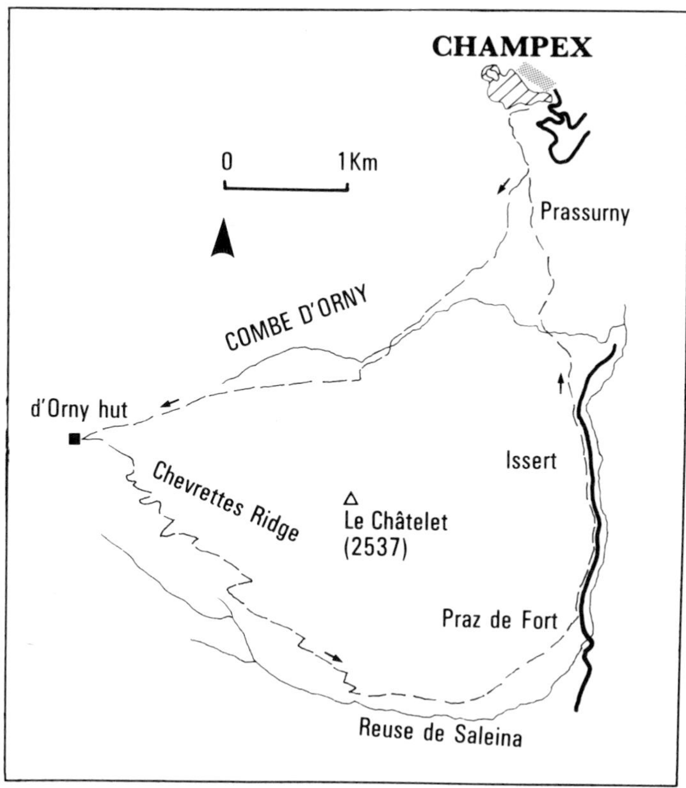

Reverse walk 4 through the Combe d'Orny and continue ahead at the junction with the path from la Breya. After some steep climbing the d'Orny hut is reached. Turn left and climb by zig-zag path across the col below the Chevrettes ridge then downhill into the valley of the Seleina river and into Praz de Fort. Left along the road through Issert. Look out for the signposted path on the left which climbs through the forest of Prassurny and back to Champex.

A really tough walk and only recommended for fit walkers. It can be shortened by using the late post bus from Praz de Fort to Orsières and then Champex (check times locally beforehand), or by taxi.

Austria

DAMÜLS

Bregenzer Wald (Vorarlberg)

Recommended Map:
Freytag and Bernt
Sheet 36 (1:100,000)
Bregenzer Wald

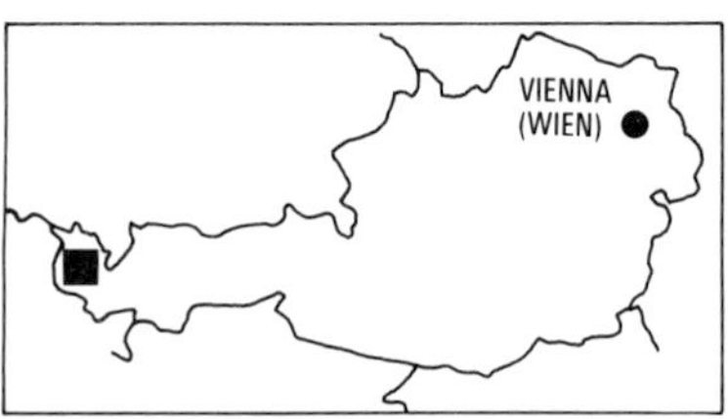

HOW TO GET THERE

Road: (1) Trans-European motorway system to Lake Constance (Bodensee), and Bregenz. Road 1 south to Dornbirn, then road 200 to Au and west by valley road (10km) to Damüls.
NB There is a variable direction flow system in operation on this narrow road. Look out for time schedules at start of the restricted section.
(2) Motorway system south and east via Feldkirch and Bludenz to Arlberg. Road 198 to Warth and 200 to Au (Hochtannenbergstrasse), then as above. (3) Motorway system south from Lake Constance to Rankweil and then 28km east across the Furka Pass to Damüls.
Rail: Via Arlberg on Trans European services to Bregenz. Local service on branch line to Bezau and post bus via Au to Damüls.
Air: Nearest airports with regular direct services from major European cities are Munich and Zürich. Transfer to Damüls by train and post bus as above.

THE AREA

The mountains in the far western corner of Austria are, for an alpine region, comparitively low and are mainly grass covered shales; few are much above 2,000m. Natural forest covers most of the lower slopes and steep sided narrow valleys have carved their way in a complex pattern. This district is known as the Bregenzer Wald, after Bregenz its regional capital. Deep in the centre of the Bregenzer Wald, near the head of the Argen valley and reached by a single track road with a 'tidal flow' traffic system, is the tiny village of Damüls which has been chosen as the base for this section of the guide.

Vorarlberg

Bregenzer Wald ends abruptly where it joins the deep trough of the Rhine valley, which is the border with Switzerland. Germany almost surrounds the rest of the Bregenzer Wald and the tiny principality of Liechtenstein is tucked away to the far south-west of the region. Liechtenstein, despite its close political links with Switzerland, is surprisingly on the east side of the Rhine and therefore, at least geographically, part of Austria.

Walkers who prefer to restrict their mountaineering activities to gentler alpine hills will enjoy the delights of Damüls and its surroundings, for the walking is easier than in the higher regions. Nowhere will the walker be faced with steep rocky gradients, mostly the tracks are on delightfully springy turf and even those on harder ground do not present many problems.

Damüls is built more or less along one street and has become a small holiday resort catering for walkers in summer and skiers in winter and is popular with families. Originally it was simply a staging post between the Lechtal and Feldkirch on a road which crosses the Furka Pass at 1,760m (5,774ft). The Furka is one of Austria's lower and easier passes, but with the demands of modern traffic the road has not developed into a major throughfare and consequently usage is light. Few links with the past remain, apart from a strategically sited

THINGS TO DO AROUND DAMÜLS

Dances, folklore, events, film shows of the surroundings area:
Programmes of film shows and other events organised by the Damüls village tourist association are staged in the tourist hall. Dances organised by individual hotels.

Swimming Pools
Indoor: Hotel Damülserhof.
Outdoor: Bergasthof Walisgaden.
Public pool at Au (9km north-east).

Chair Lift
Uga double chair lift from village to high alpine meadows beneath the Mittagspitze.

Cruises on Lake Bodensee (Lake Constance)
Regular day long cruises from Bregenz (45km north-west), to German and Swiss lakeside resorts.

Castles and Ruins
Roman remains of a fortified trading post of *Brigantium* at Bregenz.
Castle of Schattenberg-Feldkirch. Open to the public. Seat of powerful barons who controlled the Upper Rhine in the Middle Ages.

Fishing
Rivers and Lake Bodensee (check locally about current regulations, fishing permits are required).

medieval church with its 'onion' domed tower, which sits on a commanding height above Damüls. Even today it is a welcoming sight to travellers along the Furka road. Attractive murals with a religious theme decorate its interior walls.

Small rural villages and alpine pastures on natural terraces catch the maximum sunshine of south facing slopes in the surrounding valleys. None have become centres of tourism and yet all, Damüls included, have small friendly hotels. Nothing is wildly expensive and yet all vie with each other to give excellent service and accommodation.

Regional gastronomic specialities are similar to neighbouring Tyrol and pork, beef and dumplings feature on most menus. Fish from Bodensee (Lake Constance) and local cheeses are offered at the more expensive hotels and restaurants. A typical Bregenzer Wald menu might feature: Brot suppe, a vegetable soup with fried bread; Kasspatze, small cheese dumplings eaten either as the main course or as a side dish; Bodensee-felchen (Bodensee salmon trout); Grauer Käse in Essig und Öl, (sheep's cheese in oil and vinegar, served as a salad). No wine grapes are grown locally but one of the best known beers, Mohrenbräu, is brewed in Dornbirn not far to the north-west of Damüls.

A traditional feature in western Austria seems to be the blessing of mountain summits at special times of the year. Damüls honours such a custom when the local bishop climbs to the top of the Damülser

Mittagspitze to conduct a service. The climb is not without danger to the bishop, for he is clothed in his full vestments and in a strong wind on more than one occasion he has had to be held down by his acolytes to prevent him becoming airborne!

Other customs link the region with its ancient past. In February the pre-Lenten festival of 'fasching' is observed where everyone dresses in a disguise and more or less anything goes. Bonfires are lit on the evening of the first Sunday in Lent together with disc fires which are rolled down certain hills, and are said to be a form of purification after the 'sinful' life during fasching. Torchlight processions take place in several places on the first day of May, but high summer is the time when the more modern events take place. There are regattas on Bodensee (Lake Constance) in June. Also in June, and especially July, there are parades and carnivals which feature local costume and

FURTHER INFORMATION

Interesting towns nearby

Bludenz
40km south south-west via the Furka Pass. Old town, shops, restaurants, cable car.

Feldkirch
22km south-west via the Furka Pass. Part of the old town dates from the Middle Ages. Picturesque arcades. Schattenberg castle. Shops, restaurants.

Dornbirn
37km north-west via the Furka Pass. Textile centre, trade fair, music festival, cable car.

Bregenz
45km north north-west. Lakeside resort. Old towns, Roman remains. Music festival on the lake. Cable car, shops, restaurants, casino, deerpark.

Lindau (Germany)
53km north north-west. Lakeside resort. Shops, restaurants.

Camp Sites
Nearest official campsite at Raggall (11km south-west of Damüls).

Cable Car/Chairlift Ascents
Damüls - Uga.
Dornbirn - Karren.
Bludenz - Muttersberg.
Bregenz - Pfänder.
Schoppernau-Au - Diedamskopf.

Bodensee (Lake Constance)
Regular cruises to Swiss and German resorts.

Accommodation
Number of hotels: 11
Most expensive hotel: Hotel Damülserhof
Least expensive: Jagerstuble
Guest houses: 18
Bed & Breakfast accommodation: 2
Rented accommodation: 23

Tourist Information
(Local)
Verkehrsamt Damüls,
A-6884 Damüls.
Tel: 05510/253

(Regional)
Landesverkehrsamt Vorarlberg,
Römerstrasse 7,
A-6901 Bregenz.

music. The regional capital, Bregenz, stages its own cultural festival from mid-July to mid-August with performances of light opera and ballet. Dornbirn hosts a major textile fair in early August, when the fashion shows rival those of Paris. Throughout the year, if you are lucky, you may see colourful local costumes on display at weddings.

Visitors to the area will almost certainly want to visit Bodensee (Lake Constance) where regular lake cruises leave Bregenz to sail to lakeside resorts in Switzerland and Germany. If you go for a cruise and wish to visit one of the numerous and attractive towns around the Bodensee, remember you will be landing in another country. Carry your passport and also sufficient currency or travellers' cheques. Austrian currency may be accepted in shops and restaurants around the lakeside, but you will probably not get a good rate of exchange.

Damüls has eleven hotels, all reasonably priced, most offer some form of entertainment such as dances or film shows and two have swimming pools which are open to non-residents. Transport in and out of Damüls relies on the post bus which travels up and down the valley several times each day.

THE WALKS

Warning: In wet weather the steep grassy slopes of the mountains around Damüls can be very slippery.

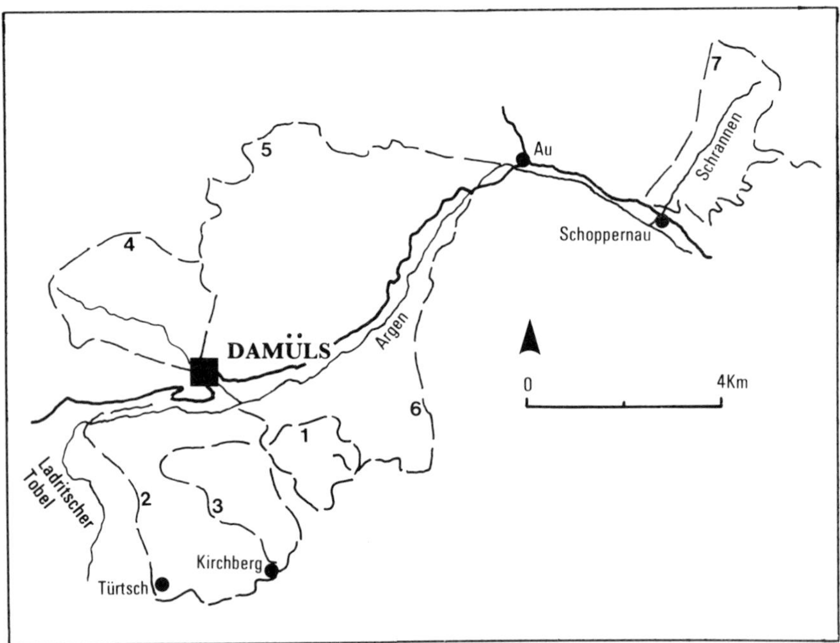

ROUTE 1

Faschina Joch (1,468m), Zafern Horn (2,107m), Zafern-Mais, Faschina

12km (7½ miles). 5/6 hours. Moderate.
A climb across grassy slopes to a viewpoint followed by alpine meadows and forest.

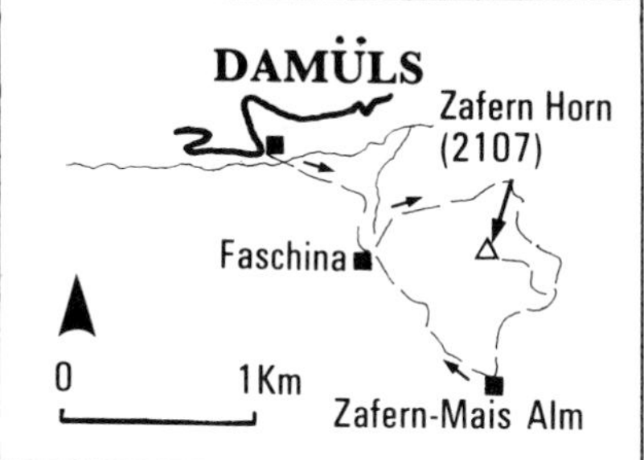

Follow the wide track across the valley which starts behind the general store in Damüls and climb up to Faschina. Turn left for the path indicated with blue and yellow markers and numbered 601. This climbs gradually around the mountain on the right (the Zafern Horn). At a junction of four paths turn right and climb steeply to the top of the Zafern Horn. Retrace your steps back to the junction and turn right down hill as far as a group of mountain farms called Zafern-Mais Alm. At another junction of four paths turn right and walk through forest back to Faschina and the valley track down to Damüls.

This makes an ideal introductory walk and with superb views of the summits surrounding the upper Argen Valley above Damüls.

ROUTE 2

Unterdamülser Alm, Türtisch Alm, Kirchberg, Faschina

15km (9¼ miles). 6/7 hours. Easy. Paths with easy gradients to alpine farms and through forest to a quiet village.

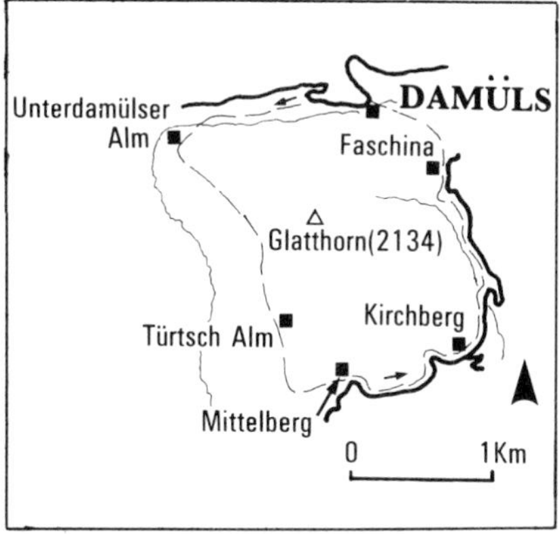

At the first bend in the Furka road above Damüls an excellent path on the left climbs to the top of the valley. Follow this as far as the mountain farmsteads of Unterdamülser Alm. Turn left at the junction with two other paths and cross into the next valley (the Ladnischer Tobel) by an easy track which climbs slightly before holding its height across the slopes of the Türtischorn on the left. Pass the scattered farmsteads of Türtisch Alm and enter a section of forest before reaching the mountain road at Mittelberg. Turn left along the road and go through Kirchberg and Faschina before crossing over the valley to Damüls.

ROUTE 3

Faschina Joch (1,486m), Glatthorn (Damülser Horn) (2,134m), Kirchberg, Faschina

14km (8½ miles). 7/8 hours.
Moderate.
Visit a secluded alpine farming village after climbing Damüls' own mountain.

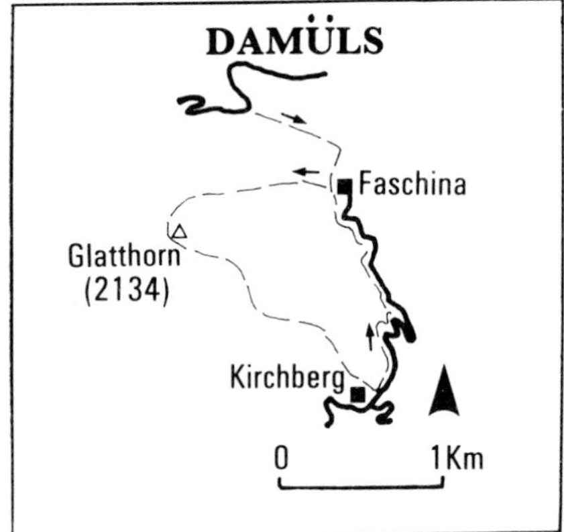

Cross the valley and climb to Faschina Joch as in walk 1. Turn right and climb the grassy ridge ahead to the top of the Glatthorn. Walk downhill in a south-easterly direction to the village of Kirchberg (signposted). Turn left in the village and follow the mountain road to Faschina and the track to Damüls. This walk can be shortened by turning left at the top of the Glatthorn to follow the alternative path back to Faschina.

The mountains to the south seen from the Glatthorn are the Raitikon range.

ROUTE 4

Uga (1,783m), Damülser Mittagspitze (2,095m), Ragazerblanken, Sunser Joch, Portler Horn

10km (6¼ miles). 5/6 hours.
Moderate.
A walk which keeps its easily gained height and has distant views of the Bregenz forest.

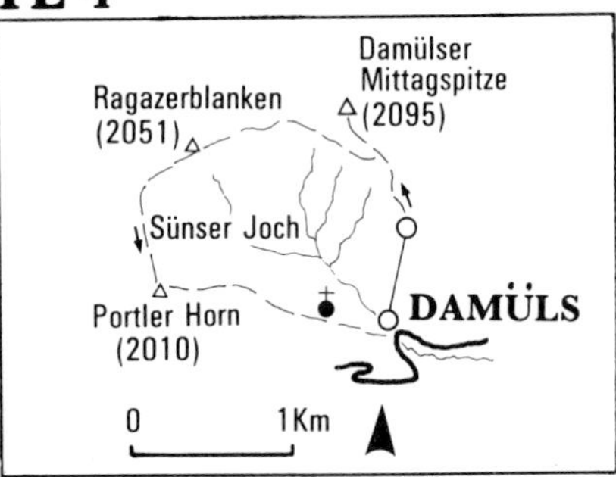

Take the chairlift from Damüls to Uga and follow the signs from the upper station to the steep and narrow grass covered ridge of the Damülser Mittagspitze. Return from the summit by the same path. (*NB Take great care on the ridge especially in wet weather.*)

Turn right (if descending from the mountain) and follow the track around the rim of the combe (ie across the heads of the streams flowing towards Damüls). This track crosses a series of lesser summits to Ragazerblanken before descending to the Sunser Joch col. The path forks in three directions at this point, take the middle path and climb the Portler Horn. From the summit aim towards the Uga chairlift on the opposite side of the valley and walk downhill until you meet another footpath. Turn right along it and almost immediately you will come to a fork. Take the left path and continue downhill to Damüls church.

ROUTE 5

Uga, Kanis Alm, Gasthof Edelweiss, Au

12km (7½ miles). 7 hours. Moderate.
High level walking to a mountain hut.

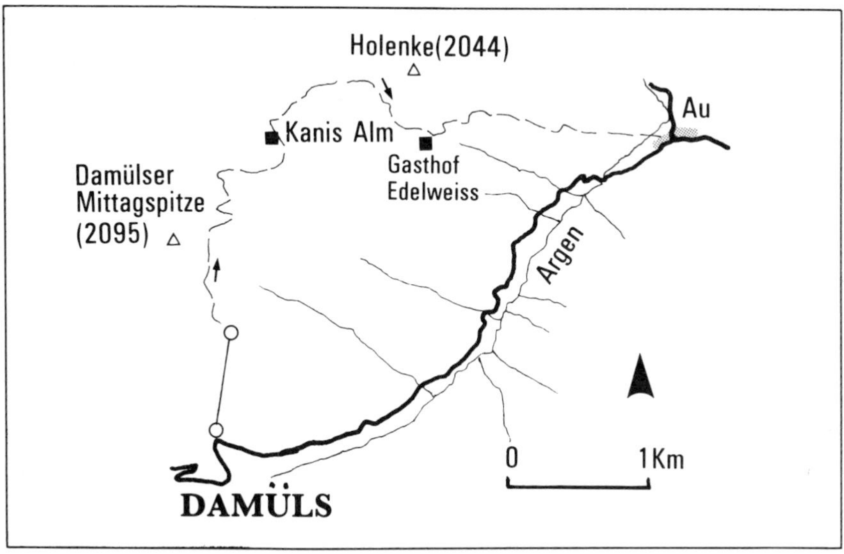

Take the Uga chairlift and walk forwards keeping the Damülser Mittagspitze on your left and continue over the col. Walk ahead and downhill through high pasture to some old farm buildings at Kanis Alm. Beyond the buildings the path divides. Turn right and climb across a wide col beneath Holenke. Downhill to the Edelweiss Restaurant and afterwards continue downhill through pine forest to the village of Au. Return by post bus.

Care must be taken in finding the turning beyond Kanis Alm which can be tricky in mist.

On the Damülser Horn

ROUTE 6

Faschina, Zafern Horn path, Eventobel and Argen Valleys, Argenzipfell

14km (8½ miles). 7/8 hours.
Moderate.
A stiff climb to reach a long downhill forest path.

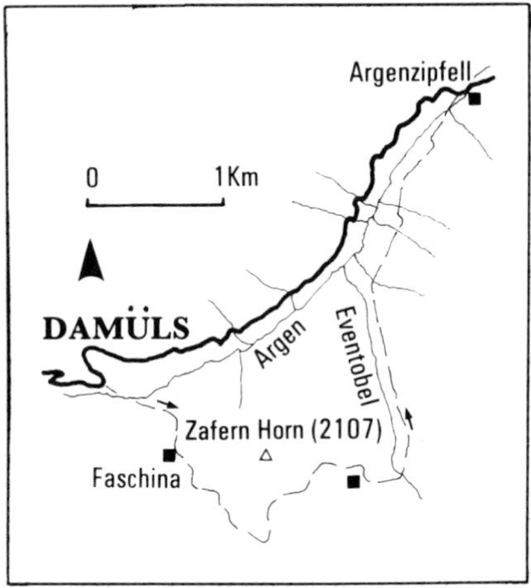

Follow walk 1 through Faschina and beneath the Zafern Horn but leave the summit path before it reaches a low col on the right. Continue ahead on path 601, passing groups of farm buildings. Gradually start to walk downhill and turn left at a fork in the path. This leads into the Eventobel valley where there is an easy route through pine forest downhill to Argenzipfell and the post bus back to Damüls.

The downhill section makes the stiff pull up from Faschina well worth the effort involved.

ROUTE 7

Schoppernau-Diedamskopf chairlift (2,090m), Diedamssattel, Breiten Alm, Falz Alm, Neuhornbach Hut, Am Berg

9km (5½ miles). 5/6 hours.
Moderate.
High mountain walking with the minimum of effort.

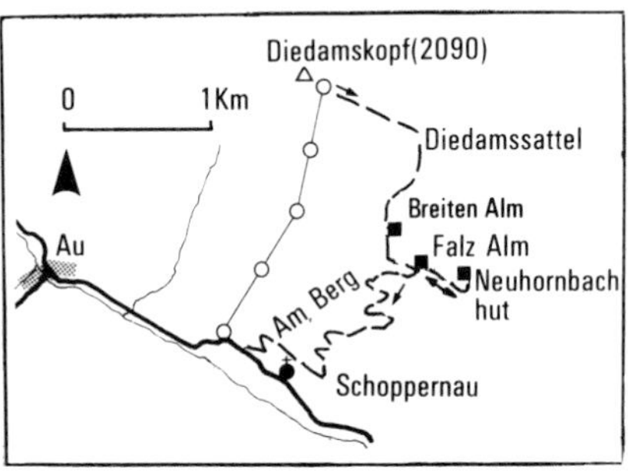

Travel to Au and Schoppermau by post bus, leaving the bus at the chairlift's lower station. Take the lift to the top of Diedamskopf. Turn right away from the upper station and walk downhill to the col at Diedamssattel. Turn right and again downhill to the farmstead of Breiten Alm. Left here and around the shoulder of Falzer Kopf (which is to your left). Enter a stretch of forest and at the farm of Falz Alm continue to the Neuhornbach Hut. Return to Falz Alm and at a fork take the left-hand path downhill through the forest area marked Am Berg on the Freytag-Berndt map. Enter Schoppernau by a track above its church.

It is not essential to visit the Neuhornbach Hut, but if so doing then enquire in Schoppernau or at the chairlift upper station to see if the hut is open.

HALDENSEE

Tannheimertal (Tyrol)

Recommended Map:
Kompass Wanderkarte
Sheet 4 (1:50,000)
Füssen-Ausserfern

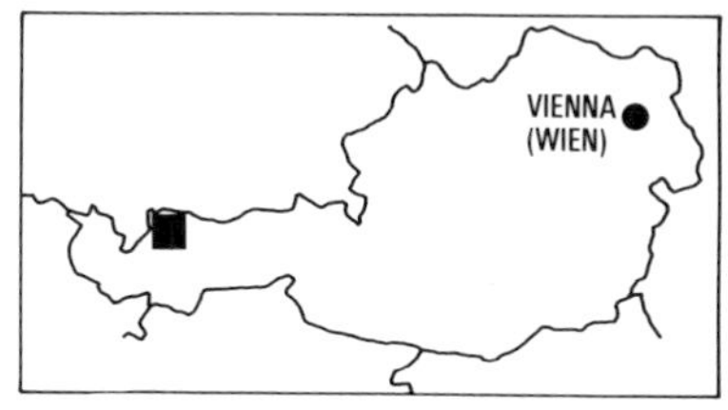

HOW TO GET THERE

Road: (1) South-west from Munich by autobahn, then via Füssen to Reutte. Road 198 to Weissenbach, then 199 north-west into Haldensee.
(2) Via Garmisch-Partenkirchen, then road 24 west to the Austro-German border. Road 187 to Lermoos. 314 to Reutte and 198 and 199 to Haldensee.
Rail: A branch line between Garmisch-Partenkirchen and Kempten passes through Reutte. There is a regular bus service from Reutte through the Tannheimertal to Haldensee. Main lines south from Munich or north from Innsbruck connect with the Garmisch line.
Air: Munich then rail and bus via Reutte.

THE AREA

Tannheimertal means the 'home of the pine trees valley' and was one of the last valleys in Austria to be settled by man. Only a century ago wolves and bears had free run of the valley and land which is now shining with meadow flowers, was all dense forest. Enough trees have been left on the valley sides to make a romantic division between farmland and the mountain ridges, which in turn form the natural barrier between southern Germany and the Tyrol.

The valley is a natural suntrap and access to it is easy, both in winter as well as summer. Southern Germany almost surrounds it and all roads seem to lead back to Germany. It is not surprising then that the valley has been 'discovered' by the inhabitants of industrial Bavaria, who use the area for short holidays or even day visits. Small friendly hotels have sprung up, usually developments from family farms, but none are part of any multiple group and all have family connections going back several generations.

Six tiny villages line the road through the valley and all have their quota of hotels. It is therefore almost arbitrary that Haldensee has been chosen as the centre for the valley, but of all the villages perhaps Haldensee with its lake as an added attraction, has just a slight edge on its neighbours. Also it is the most centrally placed village and therefore has easy access to all the walking areas around the valley.

Throughout both summer and winter holiday seasons there is a full programme of entertainment, usually with a Tyrolean flavour, and hosted in turn by individual hotels. During the summer band concerts are staged in the open air and with the setting sun gilding the rocky summits they can make a true finish to a day spent amongst high places.

Downhill skiing in winter is on the slopes of the Neunerkopf above the village of Tannheim and also above Hindelang over the border in Germany, where most of the downhill facilities are found. The ever growing popular sport of 'langlauf' or cross-country skiing uses the broad flat valley bottom of the Tannheimertal to its fullest extent and long runs are possible. In this way one can enjoy the delights of the countryside around Haldensee in winter as well as summer.

Lake Haldensee is used for sailing and wind surfing and regattas are held there during August. The sport of hang-gliding is also popular in the area.

Small beautifully sited lakes are something of a feature in this valley. Lake Haldènsee is soon obvious to the traveller along the main road, but above the central village of Tannheim and almost on steps in the upper valley of the Vilstal are a series of three jewel-like lakes. As the 'steps' climb higher so the lakes diminish in size, but not in attractiveness. The lowest and largest, the Vilsalpsee, can be reached by car or

Neuschwanstein castle above Hohenschwangau

THINGS TO DO AND PLACES TO VISIT AROUND HALDENSEE

Heute and Zimmer Abends
Folk concerts usually given by local performers in hotels around the area. Check locally advertised times. Also film shows, dances, etc.

Bathing
Lakes: Haldensee, Vilsalpsee.
Indoors:
Sport Hotel Rote-Flüh, Haldensee.
Hotel Sagerhof, Tannheim.
Hotel Jungbrunn, Tannheim.
(All have sauna and keep-fit facilities.)

Squash
Sport hotel Rote-Flüh (Haldensee), 2 courts.

Tennis
Sporthotel Rote-Flüh (Haldensee), 2 covered and 4 hard courts.

Sportcentre (Tannheim), 2 covered and 2 open-air courts.

Sailing
Lake Haldensee.

Fishing
Lake and river.

Hang Gliding
Information:
C/o Kurt Schmid,
A6673 Neu Grän.
Tel: 56 75/6901

on foot. Above it and only reached by an ever steepening path, is first the Traualpsee which is partly man-made, then finally, and without doubt the prettiest, is the Lache which fills the northern combe beneath the Lachenspitze.

Alternatives to hill walking are many; all around and easy to reach are small and often ancient towns on both sides of the Austro/German border. All are worth a visit for either sightseeing or shopping expeditions.

South of Reutte a massively walled fortress commands the route south into the heart of the Tyrol, but the best known of all castles is over the border in Germany. This is Neuschwanstein above Hohenschwangau, a fairytale castle built for Ludwig II of Bavaria between 1869 and 1886. Ludwig II was obsessed with the old germanic legends portrayed in the Wagner cycle of operas and their recurring theme is seen in room after room. Below Neuschwanstein is the older castle of Hohenschwangau, haunt of the Schwangau (or Swan) Knights until the sixteenth century.

Regional gastronomic specialities are based on mountain farmers' or hunters' fare and are as a result high in calories. Dumplings, pork, a large variety of soups, souffles, pancakes and omlettes are a principal feature of the local cuisine. Among the soups are Tiroler Schinkenknödel Suppe (chicken soup with noodles), Schölberlsuppe (beef soup with dumplings) and Lederknödel Suppe (liver soup with dumplings). Typical main courses are Tiroler Gröstli (pork shoulder

FURTHER INFORMATION

Interesting towns nearby

Reutte
20km east. Old town, fortress, shops, restaurants.

Füssen (Germany)
24km north-east. Lakeside promenade, shops, restaurants.

Hohenschwangau (Germany)
28km north-east. Neuschwanstein castle and other relics of King Ludwig II of Bavaria.

Oberammergau (Germany)
45km east. Passion Play staged every ten years. (That held in 1984 to commemorate the 350th anniversary is out of sequence, others will follow in 1990, 2000 etc).

Hindelang (Germany)
16km west. Holiday town, shops, restaurants.

Camp Sites

Grän.
Haldensee.
Nesselwängle.
Reutte.

Accommodation

Mostly small hotels and some houses have rooms to let (Zimmer Frei).

Cable Car Ascents

Grän-Fussener Joch (chair).
Tannheim-Neunerkopf (chair).
Nesselwängle-Krinnespitze (chair).
Höfen-Reutener (cabin).

The Zügspitze

The highest mountain in Germany (2,961m), can be ascended by cable car from either Ehrwald (Austria) or Eibsee (Germany).

Museums and Art Galleries

Reutte
Folklore and art of the region.

Hohenschwangau
Neuschwanstein Castle. Murals of Wagnerian influence.

Tourist Information

Up-to-date details of available accommodation and events are available from the local tourist office: 6673 Grän-Haldensee.
Tel: 5675/6285

Guest Cards

Obtainable from the tourist office and most hotels. Available for visitors staying minimum one week in the area and give special rates for various facilities and events.

cut into small thin pieces and roasted with finely sliced onions and potatoes), and Tiroler Leber (fried calf's liver with capers and sour cream sauce). Some of the desserts are: Tirolerkoch (pudding with nuts, raisins, bread crumbs and wine), Schneenockerl and Hupfauf (both souffles). Wines are usually Kalterer and Magdalener, both reds and made from grapes grown in the South Tyrol.

An inexpensive but very filling dessert is the Kaiserschmarren, a dish which is linked with of all things the colour of Austrian public buildings. Apparently, so the story goes, the Emperor wanted all public buildings to be painted the same colour. The shade he had in mind was egg yellow so he summoned his advisors and told them about his plan, instructing them to break an egg in order that they could see its colour. Unfortunately the yolk was not exactly the right shade and another had to be broken, this was also wrong so more were brought. The Emperor decided that probably the correct colour would appear if they were all mixed, but this was not so. After great deliberation milk and flour were gradually added until the colour met with imperial approval. From that day the colour, the shade of eggs mixed with milk and flour, has been used on all public buildings in Austria. How the mix then became a dessert is due to Austrian frugality. On being told to throw the rubbish away, a courtier decided rather than waste such a quantity of food, he would have it cooked in a thick pancake which unfortunately broke in the pan, so it was chopped up further and served with jam. Kaiserschmarren means imperial fluff, or rubbish, and is a popular dish in mountain huts.

Public transport throughout the Tannheimertal is based on the reasonably frequent bus route linking Reutte in the Lechtal valley with Hindelang in Germany. Across the frontier by the Oberjoch pass a whole area is made accessible by this convenient bus route. It is possible to walk from the Tannheimertal valley into Germany and return by bus from the village of Oberjoch.

THE WALKS

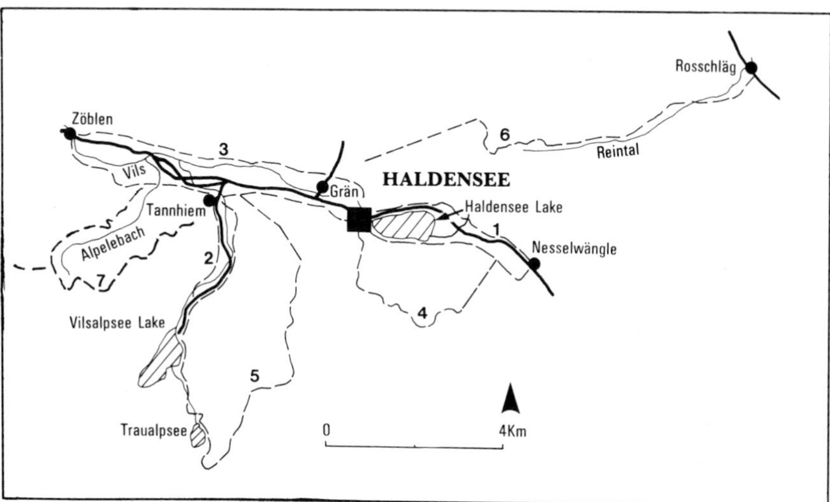

ROUTE 1

Haldensee, Nesselwängle (campsite), Haller

10km (6 miles). 3 hours. Easy.
Lakeside and valley.

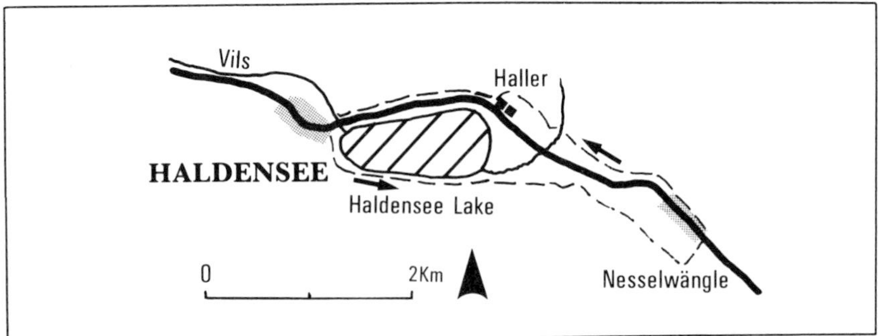

Follow the path on the south side of Lake Haldensee and then the river bank to the campsite opposite Nesselwängle. Cross over the main road and go through the village to a farm lane leading towards meadow land. Turn left in Nesselwängle along this lane which is followed to Haller and Haldensee.

This walk can be extended at several points and is an ideal one for the first day of a holiday.

Tannheimertal in wintry garb

ROUTE 2

Tannheim, Bogen, Schmieden, Vilsalpsee

16km (10 miles). 5 hours. Easy.
Through forest to a hidden lake.

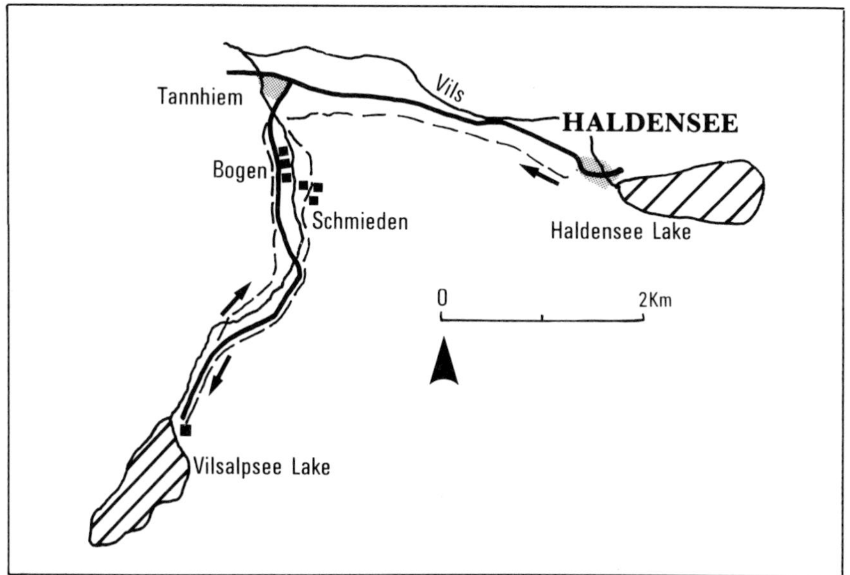

From Haldensee follow a farm track parallel to the main road westwards as far as Tannheim. Turn left in the village by a signposted path (421) through Bogen and Schmieden and along the back road to Lake Vilsalpsee. Walk round the lake (refreshments at the road end). Return by same route for about 1¼km and turn left and across the river to follow a field path back to Schmieden and Tannheim.

Try to pick a hot sunny day for this walk — the lake is ideal for open air bathing.

ROUTE 3

Tannheim, Höfer See, Zöblen, Berg, Grän

12km ($7\frac{1}{2}$ miles). 3/4 hours. Easy/Moderate.
Unspoilt forest and interesting villages.

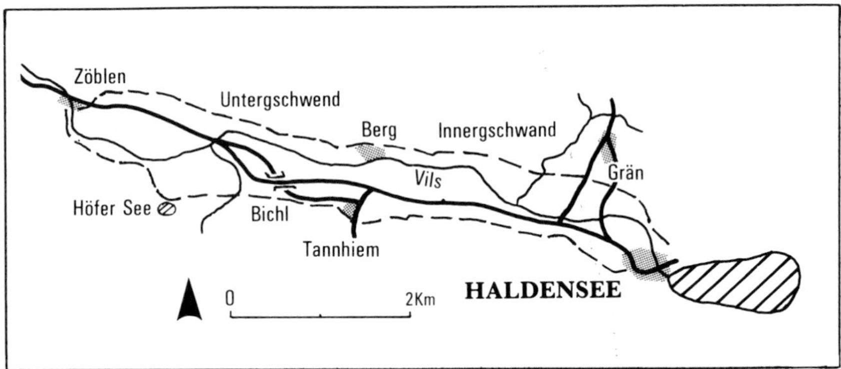

Either take the bus or walk, as route 2, to Tannheim. Walk out of the village by road in a westerly direction to Bichl. Where the road swings right to cross beneath the bypass, take the first farm track on the left before the bypass. Follow this track into the forest as far as the tiny lake of Höfer See. Turn right at the lake and leave the forest to cross open meadows and skirt round another section of forest. The path descends to the river which is followed to Zöblen. Cross the main road and climb slightly above the village to follow a field path which passes through the villages of Untergschwend, Berg and Innergschwend to reach the main road at Grän. Walk through the village in an easterly direction and turn right on to a side road which leads back to Haldensee.

A nice feature of this walk is the way in which refreshment stops are spaced at regular intervals. Spend a little time exploring the farm house architecture along the way.

ROUTE 4

Nesselwängle, Krinnespitze, Jaunstation Nesselwängle, Haldensee

8km (5 miles). 4 hours. Moderate.
Forest and mountain walking.

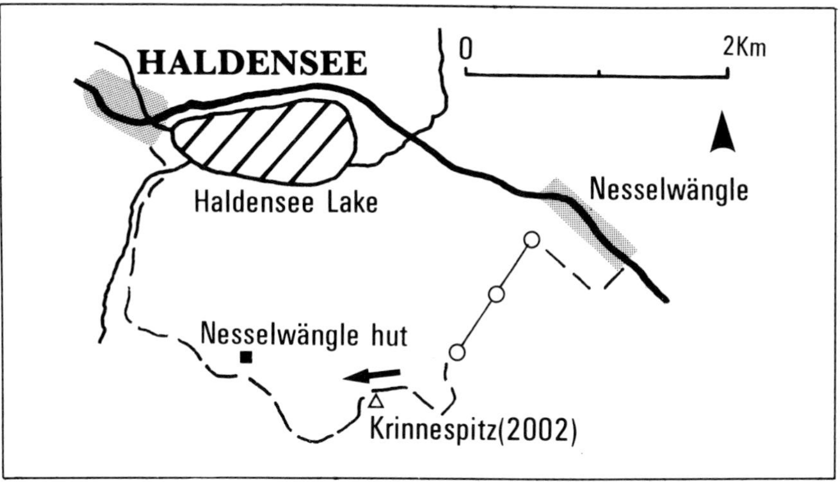

Take the chairlift from Neselwängle and from the top station follow footpath 19 (signposted), this is the Gamsbocksteig which goes over the Krinnespitze (2,002m). On now to footpath 14 which goes down to a slight col and on to the Nesselwängler hut. Continue downhill on path 15 to Haldensee.

The Gamsbocksteig may be slippery in wet weather; also take care to find the correct path at the many junctions, otherwise this is an easy to follow walk in the mountains.

ROUTE 5

Tannheim, Vilsalpsee, Traualpsee, Lachesee, Schochenspitze, Sulspitze, Neunerkopf

13km (8 miles). 7/8 hours. Moderate.
Three lakes and three mountain summits.

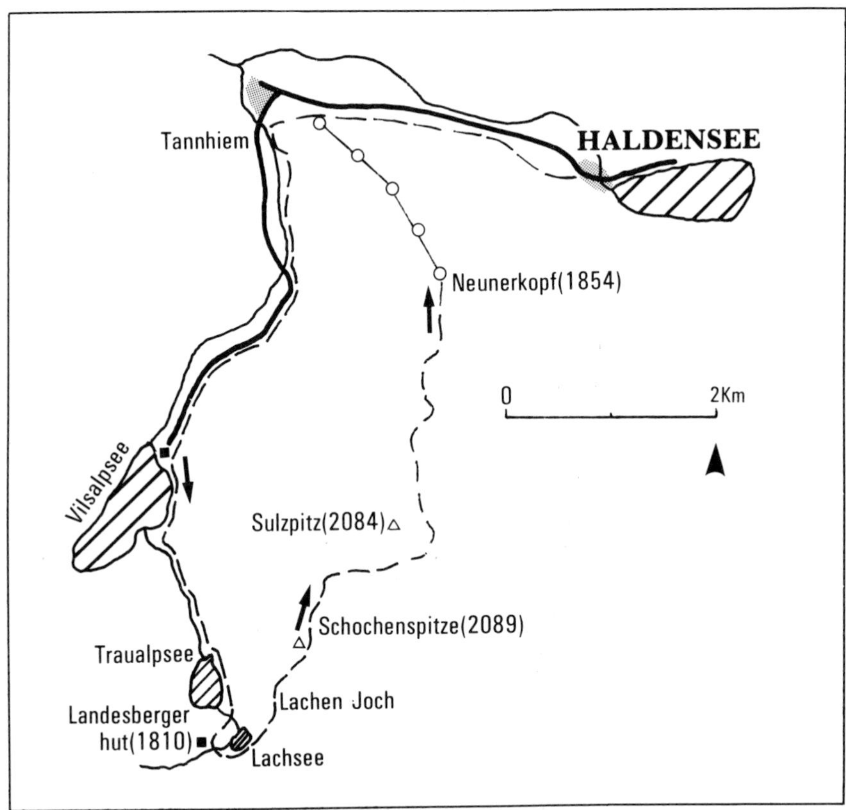

As route 2 to the Vilsalpsee then follow path 425 up a steep hill to Traualpsee and on to the Landesberger hut. Left at the hut on path 421 past Lachesee and over Lachen Joch pass to Schochenspitze and Sulspitze. Turn left below the summit of Sulspitze on an un-numbered path as far as the top of the Neunerkopf. Return to Tannheim by chairlift from the Neunerkopf.

This is true mountain walking at its best. The Sulspitze (1,097m) is slightly off route, but is worth the diversion.

Reversing the direction of this walk ie by using the Neunerkopf chairlift to gain height will reduce the amount of climbing, but the views of each lake when reached by the uphill route are well worth the extra effort.

ROUTE 6

Grän, Füssener Joch, Hallergernjoch, Reintal, Rosschläg

8km (5 miles). 4/5 hours. Moderate.
Two alpine passes and a forest valley.

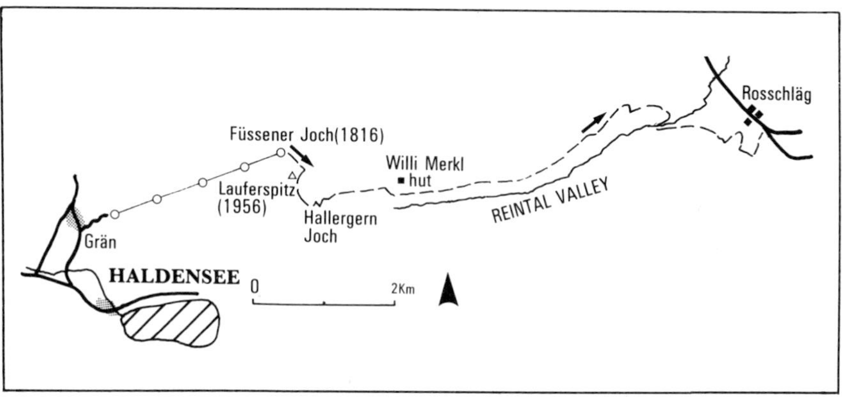

Take the chairlift from Grän to the Füssener Joch pass. Turn right on path 413 and climb round beneath Läuferspitze to the col at Hallergern Joch. Go over the col and downhill past the Willi Merkl hut into the Reintal valley. Walk down the valley road to Rosschlag to catch a bus to Reutte and then to Haldensee.

Although this involves complicated route finding, it is an enjoyable walk through high alpine scenery followed by a pleasant easy track down the Reintal valley.

ROUTE 7

Tannheim (1,097m), Rossalpbach, Rossalpe, Zirleseck (2,872m), Alpelebach

14km ($8\frac{1}{2}$ miles). 8/9 hours. Moderate/Difficult.
A climb on a little-used path and rewarded with views into Southern Bavaria.

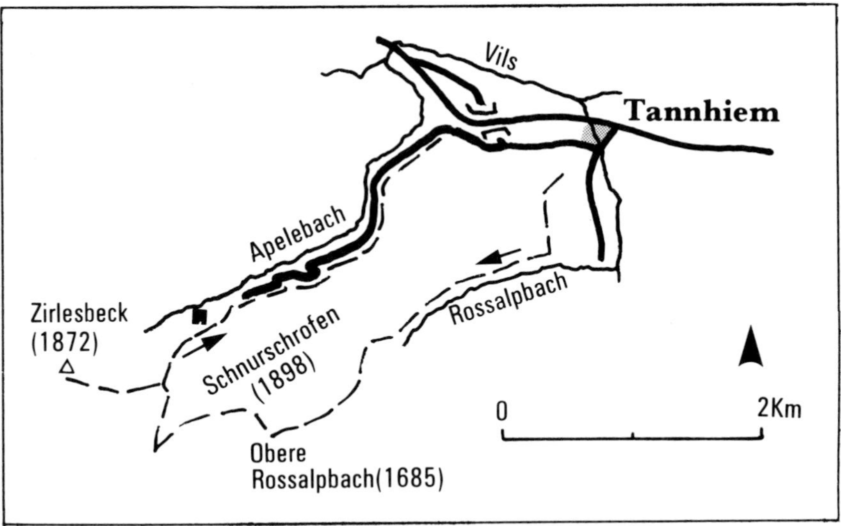

South-west from Tannheim a path climbs steeply up the side of the Rossalpbach valley to a junction just before Obere Rossalpe. Turn right and climb the ridge of the Schnurschrofen to another footpath junction marked by a Calvary shrine. Left on path 423 to the summit of Zirleseck. Retrace the route back to the shrine and turn left. Walk downhill past the Alpele mountain restaurant and follow the track through the Alpebach valley (423) to Tannheim.

This is a steep climb which will take all day, however the views are worth all the effort involved. The Alpele restaurant is a welcome sight later in the day.

SEEFELD

(Tyrol)

Recommended Maps:

Seefeld Umgebungskarte (1:25,000)
Freytag-Berndt : Sheet 34 (1:100,000) Wettersteingebirge

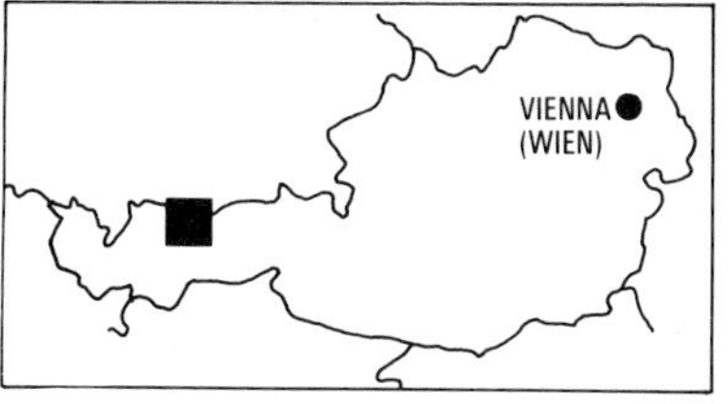

HOW TO GET THERE

Road: South from Munich by autobahn to Garmisch-Partenkirchen to join the Austro-German autobahn (Route 2 in Germany and Route 185 in Austria). Cross the border at Scharnitz and Seefeld is a further 9km along the road. Regular bus services link with Munich and Garmisch-Partenkirchen.

Rail: (1) The Munich to Innsbruck line passes through Seefeld. (Station is in the centre of the town.) (2) Trans-Europe via Arlberg and change at Innsbruck.

Air: Munich then rail or bus.

THE AREA

The gap between the Wetterstein and Karwendel ranges which are a part of the bastion of mountains guarding the long western arm of Austria, has provided one of the few all-weather routes between Southern Germany and Austria. High above the Inn Valley and now by-passed by the Austro-German autobahn (185), Seefeld has become a popular holiday area not only for those from northern Europe, but also as a 'near to home' centre for Bavarians. As a result of this popularity the countryside around the small town Seefeld has developed a series of pleasant paths on easy gradients through predominantly pine forest.

THINGS TO DO AND PLACES TO VISIT AROUND SEEFELD

Heute-abends, roughly meaning 'evenings at home'. Local entertainments, music, dancing in bierkellars of local hotels. Look out for advertised times of dances, film shows, etc.

Casino
Casino-Austria, Seefeld.

Summer Toboggan Run
Leutasch.

Indoor Swimming Pool
Seefeld.

Golf
Lottenseehütte Golfplatz. (18-hole). Near Wildmoos, 4km west of Seefeld.

Bathing
Wildsee Strandbad, 5 minutes from centre of town.
Wildmooser See, 4km west.
NB This lake can dry up in drought conditions.
Waidach See - Between Waidach and Kirchplatzl, 4½km north-west of Seefeld.

The numerous small lakes all have their promenades and bathing beaches and the whole area has that essential feature of all walking tours in Southern Germany or Austria — the forest café or gastof providing excellent coffee and cakes. Most of the mountain peaks and ridges which surround Seefeld are safe territory to the competent walker, but as with any mountain walking due respect must be paid to weather conditions. In summer all the nearby peaks should be snow free from July to late September.

Seefeld is probably better known to most as a winter sports area. Not only is the downhill skier catered for, but the increasingly popular sport of cross-country skiing has developed in the area with an extensive range of tracks throughout the forest. Some of these are up to Olympic standards. A number of lower footpaths are kept open throughout the winter and this makes it possible for walkers to enjoy the delights of alpine snow and sun.

In summer well marked and easy-to-follow footpaths wind their way through the forests where the dappling effect of sunshine between pine boughs gives way to tantalising views of tiny meadows brim full of alpine flowers, or perhaps where the trees frame a vista of the Inn Valley far below. Above all this soar the dramatic peaks of the Seefelder Spitz to the east and the Hohe Munde in the west, while the wall of the Wetterstein range makes a backcloth to the north and is also the border with Germany.

Seefeld has a wide range of accommodation, from high class hotels to more humble but very comfortable guest houses. Night life is found most evenings in one or other of the hotel bierkellers. Shops abound offering a wide range of Austrian artifacts from wood carvings to lace or from wine to sausages. About 6km to the north-west is the quieter Leutasch Valley with a number of small friendly inns, usually run by the same families who have dispensed hospitality for generations.

The mountains in this area are comprised of limestone and a number of interesting fossils can be found to the east of Seefeld on the lower slopes of the Seefelder Spitze.

On the nearby border stands the ruins of the fortress of Portia Claudia and during the Napoleonic wars it was defended by an Austrian garrison, commanded oddly enough by an English Colonel. Little now remains of the fort, which was sited to guard the narrow gap in the border north of Scharnitz.

Across the border the first town in Germany is Mittenwald, which can also be approached by a quiet side road from the Leutasch valley. Mittenwald is one of those gems to be found in southern Bavaria or the

Tuxertal above Lanersbach, Mayrhofen

Zillertal to the Inn Valley, Mayrhofen

Tyrol, where the tradition of decorating the exterior walls of houses with frescos is still carried on. Violin making is an historic trade in Mittenwald with skills handed down throughout the generations. These skills are aptly displayed in the tiny, but attractive museum behind the town square. Oberammergau with its Passion Play is not too far away by road via Mittenwald. Turn off the autobahn at Oberau and follow road 23 for about 9km.

Transport in the area is easy, for the Austrian authorities still recognise the usefulness of the humble bus and a regular service runs

FURTHER INFORMATION

Interesting towns nearby

Innsbruck
19km east. Administrative capital of the Tyrol. Buildings centred around Maria-Theresien Strasse link with the zenith of the Austro-Hungarian empire. Shops, restaurants, cafes.

Mittenwald
14km north-east. Frescos, Violin Museum, shops and cafes.

Scharnitz
8km north-east. Border with Germany. Ruins of Porta Claudia Fortress.

Leutasch Valley
9km north. Quiet unspoilt villages. Interesting chapels and wayside shrines.

Oberammergau
44km north-west. World famous for its Passion Play with cast composed entirely of locals which was first performed in 1634, then in 1680, and every ten years since. Performances start at the end of May and continue until the beginning of September (about 90 performances). Essential to book seats in advance.

Mountain Guides
Sporthaus Kirchmair, Seefeld.

Alpine Zoo
Weiterberg, Innsbruck.

Cable Car Ascents
- Seefelder Joch
- Harmelekopf
- Karwendel Spitze (from Mittenwald)
- Zugspitze (from Garmisch-Partenkirchen)

Accommodation
Seefeld has the better class hotels, also some houses offer rooms to let. Look for the sign 'Zimmer Frei'.
Gasthofs, mostly in Leutasch Valley, plus rooms to let.

Camp Sites
- Seefeld, Wildsee.
- Leutasch, Neuleutasch (2km north of Seefeld).
- Waidach, Leutasch.

Tourist Information
Verkehrsverein A1200 Seefeld.
Verkehrsverein A1130 Leutasch.

Oberammergau Passion Play
Geschaeftsstelle der Passionsspiele,
Schnitzlergasse 6,
8103 Oberammergau,
West Germany.
NB The 350th anniversary production will be held in 1984, otherwise every tenth year from 1990.

between Seefeld and the Leutasch Valley. Cable cars take the effort out of climbing the Seefelder and Karwendel Spitzes and fast local train services run between Garmisch-Partenkirchen, Mittenwald and Innsbruck.

THE WALKS

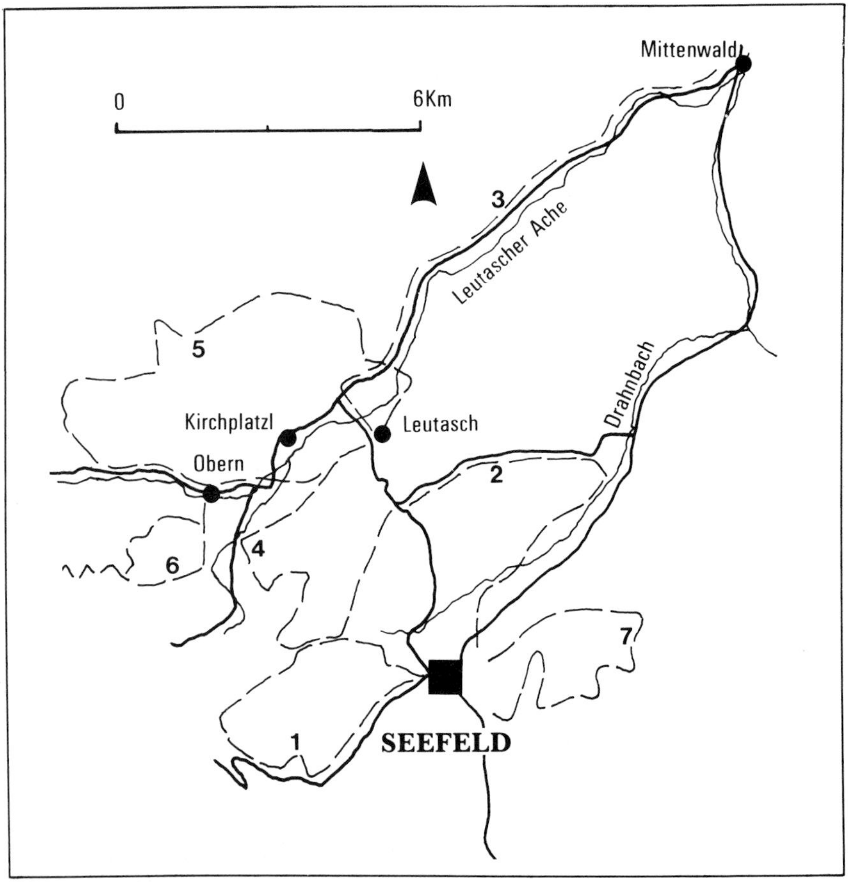

Mittenwald
0
6Km
3
Leutascher Ache
5
Drahnbach
Kirchplatzl
Leutasch
Obern
2
4
6
7
1
SEEFELD

Wildmoos, Seefeld

ROUTE 1

Mösern, Wildmoos and Wildmooser Alm

12km (7½ miles). 4 hours. Easy.
A pleasant stroll through pine forest and alpine meadows.
NB This path is kept open in winter.

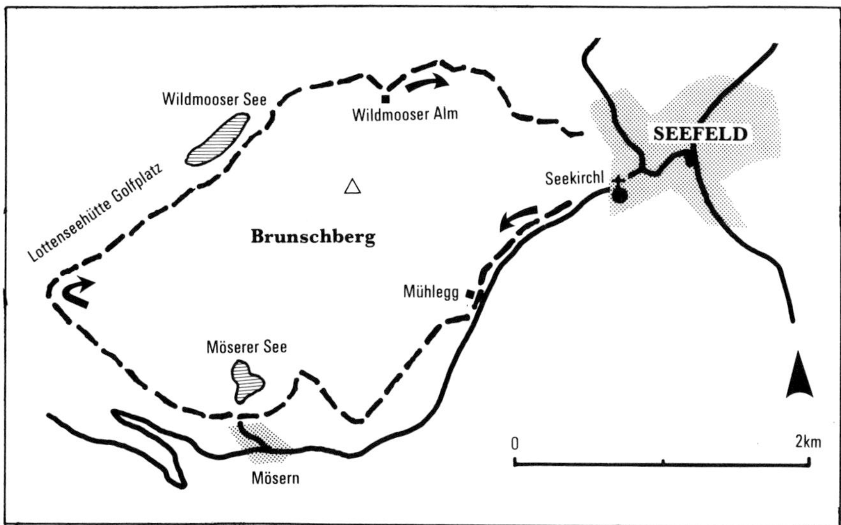

From the centre of Seefeld take the Mösern road (south-west from the town) as far as the chapel at Seekirchl. Turn right into the wood opposite the chapel to follow an easy path climbing gently uphill to the farmstead of Mühlegg. Pass in front of the farm buildings and join the road which is followed for about 200m in the direction of Mösern. Turn right across a stream and aim for the outskirts of woodland ahead, continuing to walk slightly uphill. At a crossing of four paths continue ahead and downhill to the lake of Mösern See. Beyond the lake a level track follows the contours around the hillside to the Lottenseehütte golf course. Keeping this on the left walk as far as Lake Wildmooser, beyond which is a children's holiday camp. Continue forwards to the restaurant at Wildmooser Alm and turn right along a path which leads to the Leutasch road into Seefeld.

The stretch of path between Mösern and the golf course has spectacular views into the Inn Valley far below.

ROUTE 2

Durch den Boden - Drahnbachtal

10km (6 miles). 3/4 hours. Easy.
An easy to follow forest track with distant views of mountain peaks.

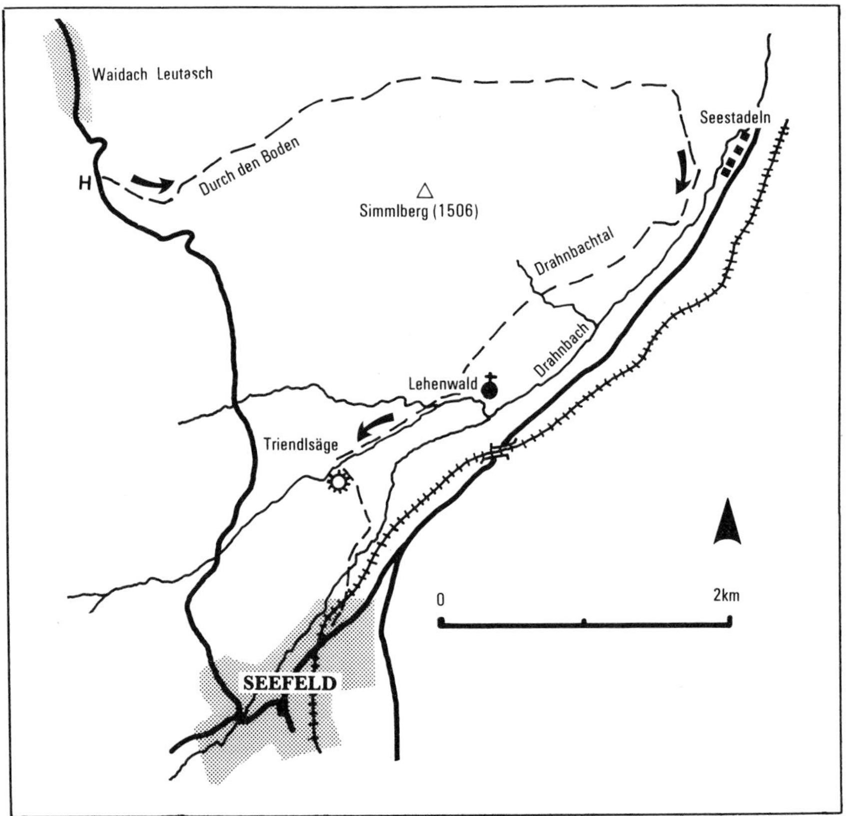

Take the Leutasch bus to Durch den Boden. Follow the track adjacent to the bus stop and climb gently to the north-east into the forest. After about 4km and on the downhill stretch turn right at the junction into the shallow valley of Drahnbachtal with the hamlet of Seestadeln ahead. Before reaching the stream turn right along a track which climbs gently for a while before dropping down to the tiny village of Lehenwald. Turn right here as far as the water mill at Triendlsäge and its café. Go left and then out of the forest to cross a series of meadows alongside the stream into Seefeld.

The best mountain views are from the highest point along the Durch den Boden road and also from Lehenwald.

ROUTE 3

Unterleutasch, Austro-German frontier, Mittenwald

10km (6 miles). 2/3 hours. Easy.
A quiet road walk to a picturesque town famous for violin making. Suitable in wet weather or fine.

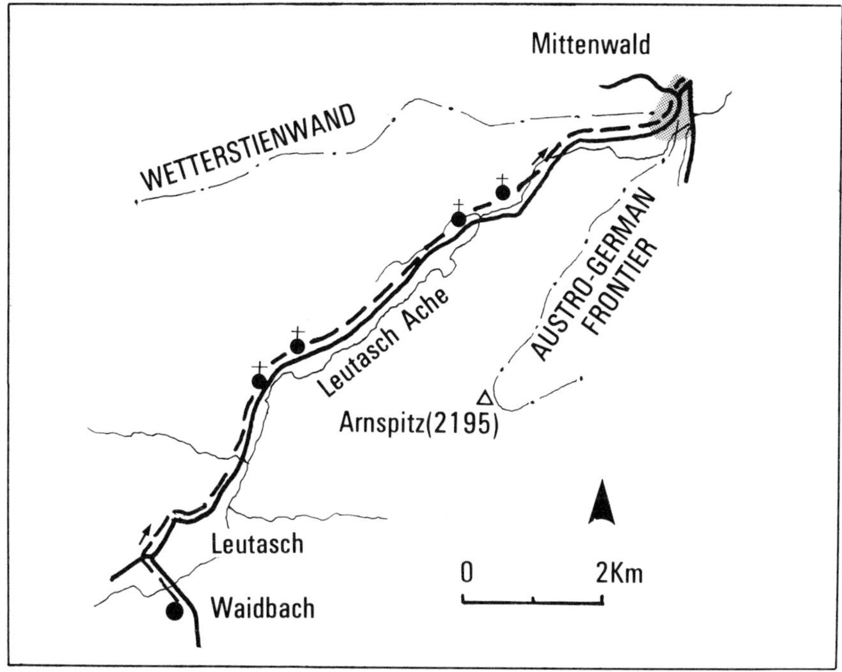

Take the bus to Waidach in the Leutasch Valley. Turn right at Gasse and simply follow the road down stream past several interesting chapels and wayside shrines to the frontier. Go through both Austrian and German posts always keeping to the road. *Passports may be checked at the frontier – so it is essential to carry them just in case.* Climb through the pine forest and down to Mittenwald and its attractively decorated houses. The violin museum is signposted from the town square. This walk may be combined with a cable car ascent of the Karwendel Spitze. Return by bus or train to Seefeld.

NB As this walk is into Germany, arrangements should be made to exchange sufficient currency for the trip either before or in Mittenwald.

The Karwendel Spitze is seen on the way down through the forest and also as a background to Mittenwald.

ROUTE 4

Fludertal, Wildmoos, Oschbach, Waidach

9km ($5\frac{1}{2}$ miles). 2/3 hours. Moderate.
A forest and lake walk.

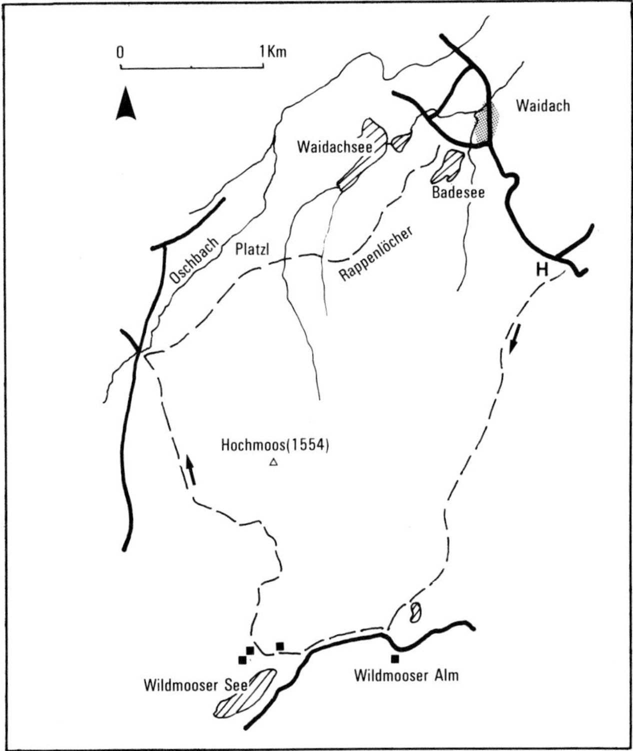

From the Durch den Boden bus stop take the track opposite which climbs steadily through the dry valley of Fludertal (marked Kellental on some maps). Ignore any side tracks until you reach the restaurant at Wildmooser Alm. Turn right along the Wildmoos road, but turn right again before the lake and follow a footpath to the Youth Camp, where another right turn climbs up through the forest for about 500m to a junction of paths. Keep left here and descend slightly towards the Buchen-Leutasch road which is reached where it crosses the Oschbach river. Do not join the road, but turn right to the north-east along a path towards Platzl. Right turn again and downhill across an area known as Rappenlocher and into Waidach.

This is an ideal walk for a hot day.

ROUTE 5

Waidach, Plaik, Hammermoosalm, Wangalm, Puitbach, Leutasch

16km (10 miles). 6 hours. A moderate climb.
Meadows, farms and a glimpse of the higher peaks.

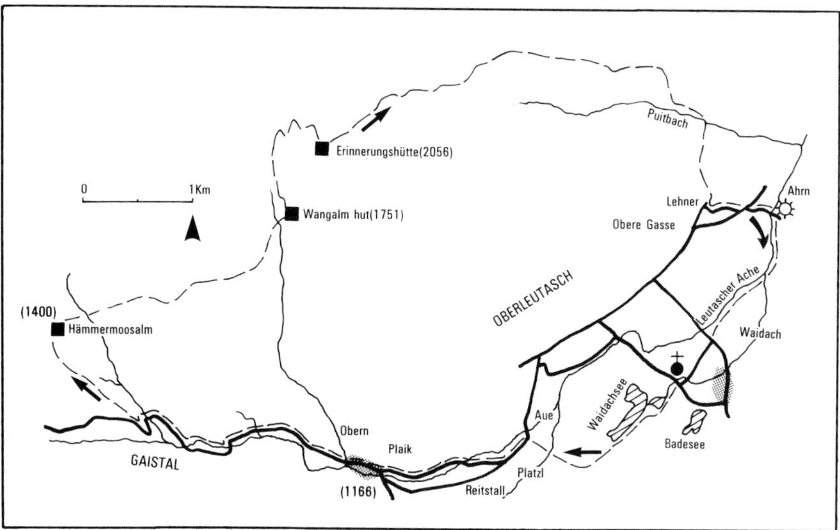

Take the bus to Waidach as far as the church and follow the path on the south side of Lake Waidach to Aue. Turn left at the road and fork right at Reitstall. Follow this quiet road through Plaik and Obern along the Gaistal valley. The track crosses the Leutasch river three times. Turn right at a signpost to Hammermoosalm Restaurant and climb uphill. Continue along a well made footpath to the Wangalm hut. Left along a path climbing steeply up to and across the Scharnitzjoch (col) to the Erinnerungshütte. Left down a path across high meadows to the Puitbach Valley and into Lehner. Cross the valley road and river by a side track and opposite the water mill at Ahrn turn right to follow the river upstream back to Waidach.

This is a delightful introduction to high level walking, but should only be undertaken in fine dry weather.

ROUTE 6

Hohe Munde (2,661m)

8km (5 miles). 6 hours. Moderate to Difficult.
A mountain climb suitable for walkers.

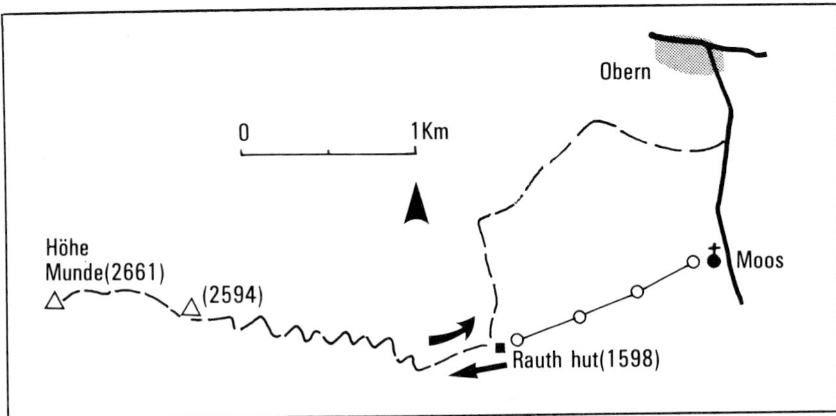

From Obern at the head of the Leutasch Valley follow the Buchen road to the chairlift above Moos. Use this to climb to the Rauth hut (1,598m). The path up Hohe Munde starts immediately behind the hut and climbs the steep east slope of the mountain by a series of zig-zags to the summit. Use the same path for the descent taking great care not to slip on any loose stones. At the Rauth hut either use the chairlift again or if you prefer to walk, turn left across high pasture to Moosalm and walk downhill through forest back to Obern.

The view from the top of the Hohe Munde is considered to be one of the finest in Austria.

As the climb up and down the mountain is on a very steep track great care must be exercised at all times. The walk is only suitable in fine weather, but is well worth the effort involved.

ROUTE 7

Rosshütte (1,748m), Schonangersteig, Nordlinger Hut (2,238m), Reither Alm

8km (5 miles) including cable railway. 6 hours. Moderate to Difficult. High mountain walking.

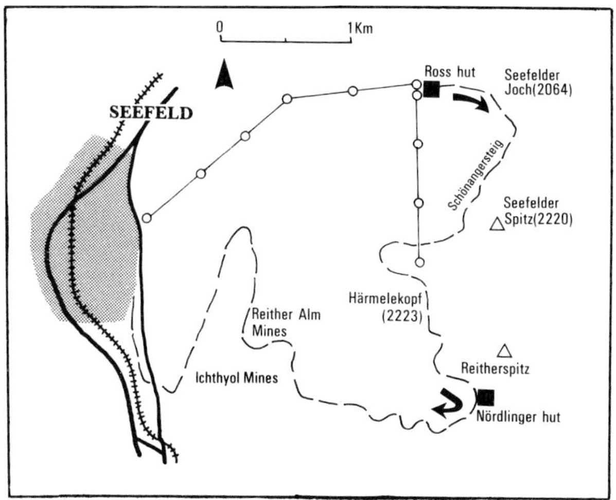

From Seefeld use the cable railway to gain height as far as the Ross Hut. Continue uphill by footpath from the hut in the direction of the Seefelder Joch, but turn right along the Schonangersteig path, which follows a well engineered route beneath the Seefelder Spitze and around a high rocky spur, before climbing to the left past the upper station of the Harmelekopf-Rosshütte cable car. Take the lower right-hand path which contours around the mountain side to the Nordlinger Hut. Go downhill from the hut and right after 350m, to follow a path which gradually swings back around the hillside. At the quarry on Reither Alm follow the track downhill in a sweeping zig-zag back to Seefeld.

This is a safe high level walk in good weather for competent walkers and gives a hint of the ridges found in the Karwendel range which starts here and continues eastwards for about 25km or so. The walk can be shortened by using the cable car from the Ross Hut to Harmelekopf.

Look out for fossils on the way down especially around Reither Alm.

All the preceeding walks are clearly signposted, especially in the vicinity of Seefeld. They and others can be followed from an excellent 1:25,000 map produced by the local tourist association. The map is called an 'Umgebungskarte' or in English a 'Map of the Surrounding District' (of Seefeld). The walks as described in this book often link a series of shorter routes which are marked on the map and have been included to give the visitor a selection of the best walking available in the area.

MAYRHOFEN

Zillertal (Tyrol)

Recommended Map:
Freytag and Berndt Sheet 15 (1:100,000), Zillertaller Alpen

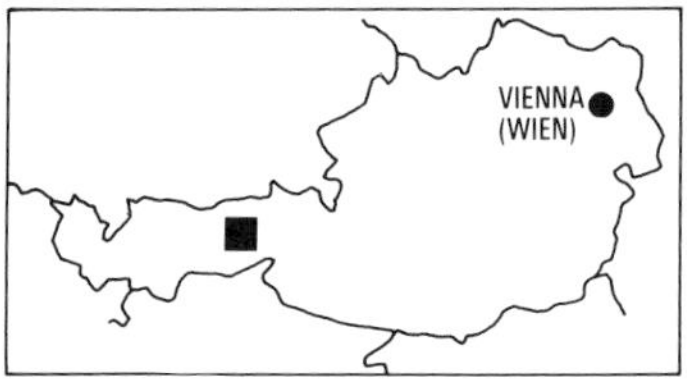

VIENNA (WIEN)

HOW TO GET THERE

Road: South-east by autobahn (E11) from Munich to the Rosenheim interchange. South to Kufstein then south-west by autobahn to the Weising-Achensee interchange which leads immediately to the Zillertal road. Mayrhofen is about 26km from here.
Rail: Main trans-European lines to Innsbruck and Jenbach. Branch line to Mayrhofen.
Air: (1) Munich or Salzburg then rail via Innsbruck. Services from most of the major European cities. (2) As above then connecting local flight to Innsbruck followed by rail.

THE AREA

The deep valley of the Ziller which opens to the south off the main Inn Valley is rather a disappointment at first. All the way up to Zell am Ziller it is broad and flat, but from there onwards it becomes a real mountain valley, narrowing as it climbs beneath the ever steepening snow clad peaks of the Zillertal Alps. At Mayrhofen the Ziller Valley splits into four. Three of these are called Grunds (grounds): the Zillergrund, Stillupgrund and Zemmgrund. Each is narrow, but all are pretty and strike deep into the heart of the Ziller Alps. The fourth is the Tuxor Tal and although the main valley's name is carried by one of the Grunds the Tuxor is the true continuation of the Zillertal. Roads climb all four valleys but none of them have exits, each one ends beneath a high col under the snow and ice of the high mountains. Mayrhofen is a market town of 3,500 inhabitants, the third largest in the Tyrol and has been well known as a walking centre for over a century. It offers a wide range of accommodation with approximately 2,400 beds in hotels and inns, 5,650 in bed-and-breakfast houses and farmhouses as well as an official campsite.

Buses run a regular service from Mayrhofen to the villages of the higher valleys and are a convenient aid to wider exploration. At almost 1,500m (5,000ft) above sea level at the head of the Tuxer Tal, the village of Hintertux is easily accessible and has become something of a spa. It boasts a small thermally heated swimming pool and amongst other attractions the traditional craft of wood carving is

Hochfeiler above Mayrhofen

THINGS TO DO AND PLACES TO VISIT AROUND MAYRHOFEN

- Guided walks
- Riding
- Claypigeon shooting
- Swimming (Indoors and out)
- Sauna
- Fishing
- Mini Golf
- Bowling Alleys
- Discotheques
- Cycle Hire
- Keep Fit Course

All these facilities are available in Mayrhofen, details of addresses, costs, etc are found in a booklet published by the local tourist office called *Kleiner Urlaubsberater.*

Special Courses
(Details from tourist office):

- Hang Gliding
- Skiing
- Canoeing
- Alpine Climbing

Zillertalbahn
Narrow gauge steam railway run and maintained by enthusiasts.

carried on and some fine examples are offered for sale locally.

The beautiful Christmas hymn ' Silent Night, Holy Night' has links with the Ziller region and might have disappeared if it was not for the observance of a local organ repairer. The story is told that the famous hymn was composed and written to be performed once only as an emergency measure by the village choir in Oberndorf near Salzburg, as mice had chewed holes in the organ bellows. After the performance the text and score were stuffed behind the organ pipes and forgotten. Purely by chance they were discovered by an itinerant organ repairer some years later and taken back to the Zillertal. About that time (the early nineteenth century) the people of the area were famous glove makers and as a publicity stunt decided to give a recital of the hymn at the Leipzig Fair. 'Silent Night, Holy Night' was an immediate success amongst the German speaking nations and before long became known all over the world.

Folk music has strong traditions in this area going back over several centuries. Beautifully voiced choirs and soloists perform at local festivals, usually to the accompaniment of the harp or zither; zither playing is especially renowned in the Zillertal.

The Zillertal is a valley of festivals and carnivals from the pre-Lenten frolicks of 'fasching' when anything may happen, to the Gander festival held the first weekend in May. The first part of the Gander festival is a procession and then contests are held between mountain cattle to decide the dominant cow or 'queen' which will lead the herd back up to the high alpine pastures. Young men from the outlying villages take part in the competition with a form of wrestling called Preis-Rangeln in which the opponents lock hands and try to throw each other. The competition goes on until a final champion remains.

Being a town devoted to providing tourist accommodation, Mayrhofen has plenty of entertainment to offer. At night most of the hotels offer some form of folk concert (Tiroler Abends), or maybe informal dances which are usually announced by an advertised programme. In this way you can easily find out what is on, and where. Daytime diversions are many and range from canoeing on the river Ziller for the energetic and skilled, to swimming either indoors or out; also tennis, squash, horse riding, outdoor chess, cycle hire, ten-pin bowling, fishing and that unique but growing facility of a specially laid out keep fit court (Fitness-parcours) where one can jog round a woodland track laid out with various obstacles. A small explanatory plaque usually accompanies each obstacle, which may range from a set number of

FURTHER INFORMATION

Interesting towns nearby

Innsbruck
60km (by rail or road) north-west. Links with the Austro-Hungarian Empire. Museums, art galleries. Interesting buildings: Goldenes Dachl (Golden Roof) in Maria-Theresien Strasse.
Shops, restaurants, public gardens, cable car ascents of Karwendel mountains.

Zell am Ziller
8km north. Shops, restaurants. Trout fishing at Gasthof Bräu.

Hintertux
18km south-west. Thermal swimming pool. All-year-round skiing facilities.

Camp Sites

Mayrhofen.
Zell am Ziller.
Finsing.

Cable Car Ascents

Mayrhofen-Penken Gschösswand.
Mayrhofen-Ahorn.
Finkenberg-Penkenjoch.
Zell am Ziller-Rosenalm.
Hintertux-Olperer glacier.
Hainzenberg-Gerlosstein.

Accommodation

First class hotels to bed and breakfast, rooms available throughout the valley.

Facilities

Swimming Pools (both indoor and outdoor) at Mayrhofen and Hintertux.
Horse Riding
Tennis
Ice Skating and Curling (Winter)
Car Rental on Inter-Rent-Austria

Guest Cards

Obtainable only from hotels, entitles guests to reductions on the following:
Entertainment at the Europahaus.
Tirolean evenings (folk concerts).
Babysitting service.
Cable car journeys on the Ahorn and Penken lifts.

Tourist Information

Up-to-date information of available accommodation, courses and other facilities can be obtained from the local tourist office:
Mayrhofen,
Post Code 6290.
Tel: 5285/2305 and 2635

Zell am Ziller,
Post Code 6280.
Tel: 5282/2281

Hintertux,
Post Code 6294.
Tel: 5282/207 and 374

press-ups to a rope climbing exercise. The idea is to time yourself daily around the course and then try to improve your 'score' on subsequent days.

Summer skiing takes place above Hintertux on the slopes of the Olperer glaciers which are linked to the valley by a series of cable cars and ski tows. In winter the opportunities for all grades of downhill skiing from easy to very difficult are available on the slopes surrounding the Zillertal. Cross country or langlaufloipen trails cover over 22km of the valley bottom and some are illuminated for night skiing.

Transport from Mayrhofen is excellent with buses to most of the higher villages. The railway links the Inn Valley, while cable cars climb easily to the higher ridges and can be used to take the walker into another environment. What better way to enter a holiday area than by a narrow-gauge steam train, which pulls a handful of passenger coaches and the occasional goods wagon from Jenbach to Mayrhofen.

THE WALKS

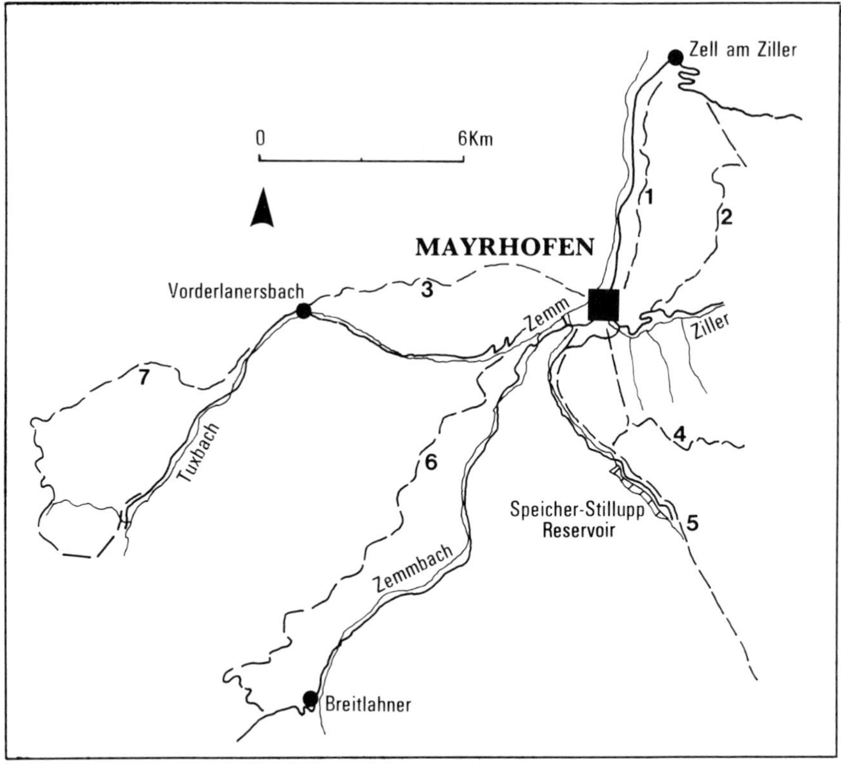

ROUTE 1

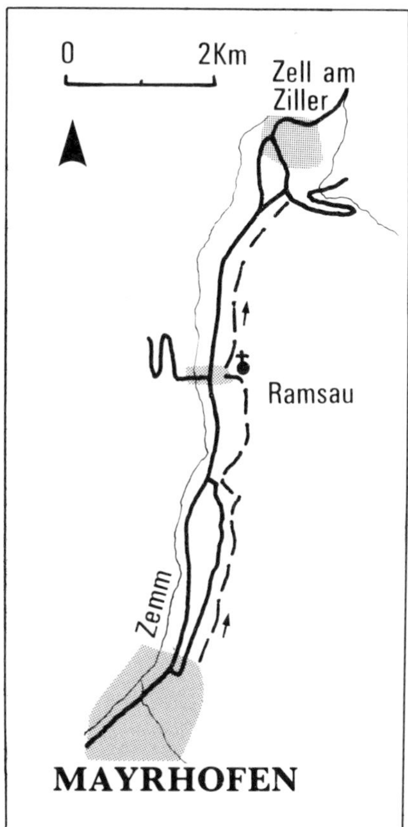

Mayrhofen, Ramsau, Zell am Ziller

9km (5½ miles). 2/3 hours. Easy. A valley walk through meadows along the forest's edge.

Walk uphill past the Europahaus Centre towards the forest. Turn left on the path which starts beyond the last houses of Dursterstrasse. Follow this field path along the forest edge and through meadows to Eckartau village. Walk downhill through the village and turn right along a cart track (signposted) to Ramsau. Turn left into Ramsau and right at the church along a track which leads through the meadows to Zell am Ziller. Return by bus or train.

Some interesting old farm buildings may be seen along the track. Careful timing is needed to link with the train for the return journey.

Train travel through the meadows of Mayrhofen

ROUTE 2

Hainzenberg, Gerlosstein, Karl Alm, Steiner Kogel Hut, Mayrhofen

8km (5 miles). 3 hours. Easy.
A gentle mountain walk, mostly downhill.

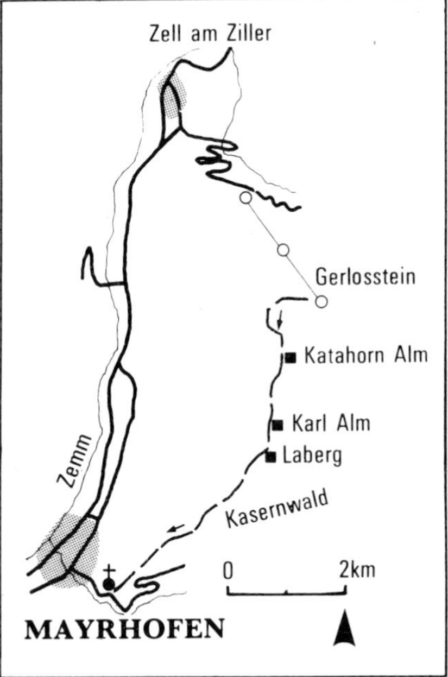

From Zell am Ziller take the Gerlos bus to Hainzenberg and then the cable car to Gerlosstein. From the top station follow footpath number 50 which carefully follows the contours of the hillside all the way past the alpine farms of Katahorn Alm and Karl Alm to Laberg. The path then starts to descend fairly steeply, but in fine weather should present few problems. Enter a stretch of forest (Kasernwald) and eventually the Steinerkopf hut is reached. Beyond the hut the path is steeper and care is needed, especially in wet weather. This path drops down into the Zillergrund valley and joins the Mayrhofen road by the side of a chapel. Turn right at the church to reach the town.

The views to the south from Karl Alm and Laberg are of the Zillertal Alps and careful map reading should help to name the major peaks in view.

The Gerlossteinwand (2,166m) can be climbed as a deviation away from the top station of the cable lift and the main route rejoined by following path 8 from below the summit to Katahorn Alm.

ROUTE 3

Gschössberg, Penken, Schrofen, Vorderlanersbach

9km ($5\frac{1}{2}$ miles). 5/6 hours. Moderate.
By quiet mountain tracks across an easily climbed summit.

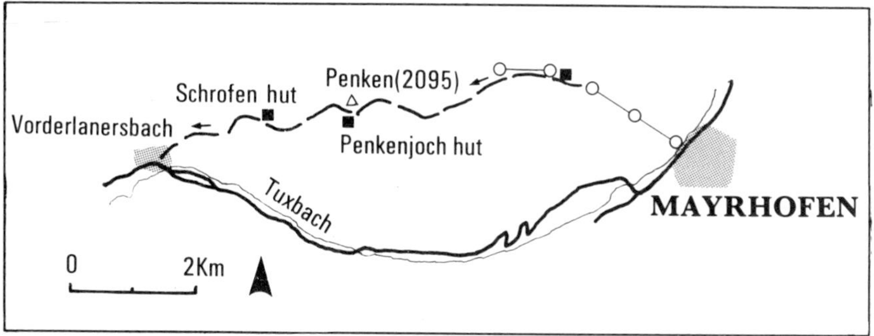

Use the Gschössberg cable to climb from Mayrhofen. Follow path 23 to the upper hut and continue uphill beneath the higher cable. This path follows an easy ridge across the minor summit of Knorren to Penken (2,095m) and the Penkenjoch hut. Turn slightly right behind the hut and walk downhill along the ridge to where the path divides. Follow the left-hand track down a steep hill and then to the right across a broad valley head for the Schrofen hut. Follow the path downhill through the forest and join the valley road at Vorderlanersbach where there is a bus connection back to Mayrhofen.

Careful navigation is necessary to find the path down from the Penken ridge, but if it is missed then another way down is from the mountain farm at Wangl Alm.

Any tired walkers can use the cable car for the last downhill section from Schrofen Alm to Vorderlanersbach.

ROUTE 4

Filzenalm, Edel hut, Ahorn Spitze

8km (5 miles). 5/6 hours.
Moderate/Difficult.
An introduction to mountaineering.

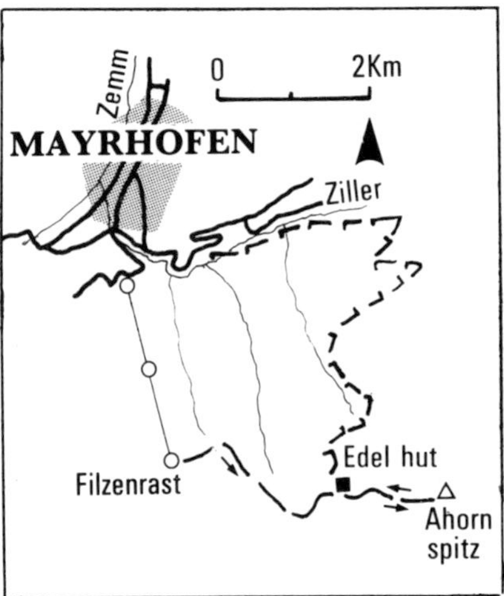

Take the Ahorn cable car from Mayrhofen to Filzenalm. Turn left from the upper station along path 514 which follows a level course to Edel hut. If the weather is suitable climb the Ahorn Spitze by path 42 (waymarked from the hut) to the summit. Return by same route.

On no account should inexperienced and ill-equipped walkers (ie without an ice axe) attempt the climb of the Ahorn Spitze if there is any snow about. The rock is safe when dry, but slippery and dangerous under snow. A suitable way down from the Edel hut, if the summit of Ahorn is under snow and yet the area around the hut is clear, would be to continue along path 514 downhill past Ahornach Alm to the Zillergrund. However this is a long steep descent and requires about 2½ hours.

ROUTE 5

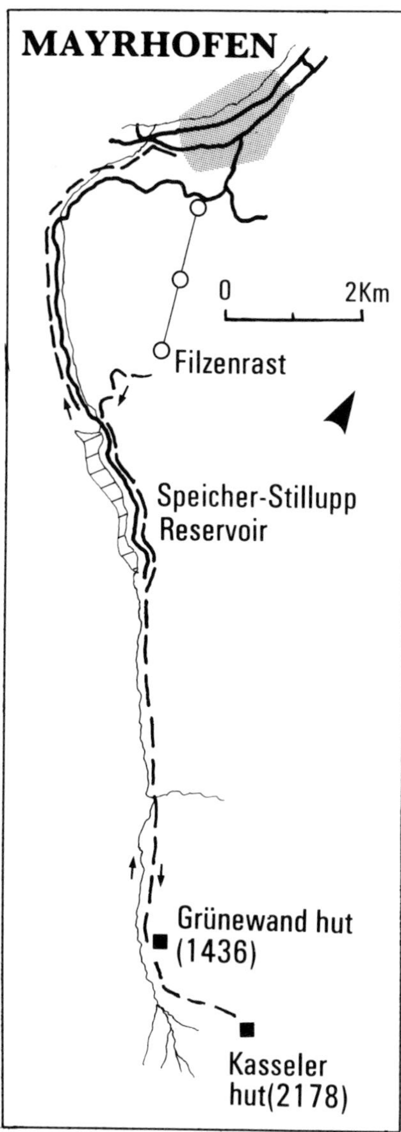

Filzenrast, Speicher-Stillupp Reservoir, Grünewand Hut

20km (12½ miles). 6/7 hours.
Moderate/Difficult.
A dramatic approach route to the high mountains.

Use the Ahorn cable car to reach Filzenrast. Turn right away from the upper station along path 514 (signposted) and walk down a steep gradient to the Speicher-Stillupp dam. Turn left along the side of the reservoir and follow the Stillup Grund all the way to the Grünewand hut. If you feel fit enough, continue on up to the Kasseler hut, but remember it is another 740m (2,427ft) higher, so think carefully as it is a long walk back to Mayrhofen.

Return the same way as far as the dam, but continue downhill on the service road if you do not wish to climb up from the dam.

This walk may be shortened or lengthened according to the ability of the party.

The peaks seen ahead as you walk up the valley are, from right to left: Grosserhöffler, Keilbach Spitz, Grünewand Spitz, Wollbach Spitze and Hinter Stangen Spitze.

ROUTE 6

Breitlahner, Wesendlekar Lake, Kessel Alm, Berliner, Höhenweg, Gams Hut

20km ($12\frac{1}{2}$ miles). 7/8 hours. Moderate/Difficult.
A high terrace walk.

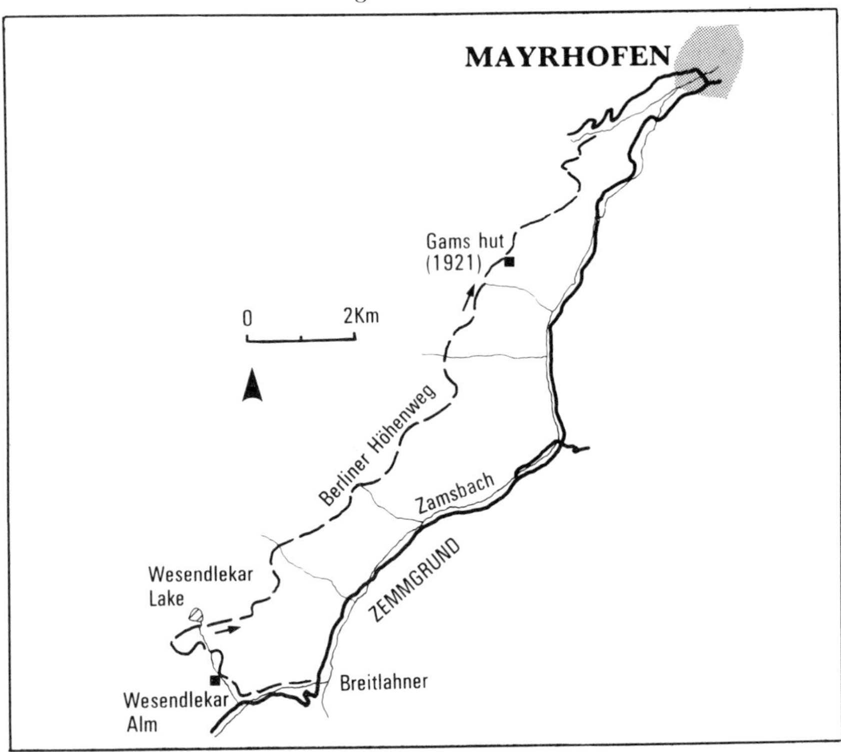

It will be necessary to hire a taxi to reach the start of this walk unless a driver in your party volunteers to take a car up into the Zemmgrund Valley.

Start from Breitlahner in the upper Zemmgrund. Turn right on path 530 across the Zamsbach river and follow its tributary, the Zamser, upstream for about $1\frac{1}{2}$km (1 mile), and turn right to follow a steep side stream uphill to the Wesendlekar Alm Farm.

After more steep climbing a path to the right is eventually joined and more level ground is reached. This path follows the shape of the mountain side high above the Zemmgrund Valley for 10km (6 miles) to the Gams hut. Its number is 533, but is better known as the Berliner Höhenweg. From the Gams hut a steep walk downhill above the cliffs of the Nesselwand leads into the Tuxertal valley and eventually back to Mayrhofen.

The Berliner Höhenweg is a classic footpath with marvellous views of the Zillertal range to the south-east. The view makes the hard climb up from Breitlahner worth while.

ROUTE 7

Tuxer Joch Hut, Weitental, Junsbach, Juns

10km (6 miles). 6 hours. Difficult.
Interesting hill walking with views on to the Olperer Glacier.

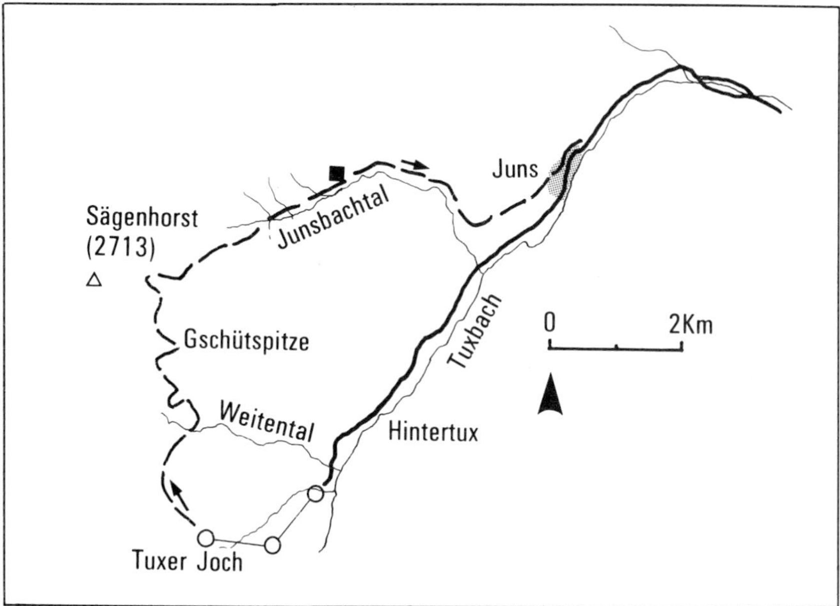

Go to Hintertux by bus and walk uphill along the road to the cable car station. Take the cable car and then the chair lift to Tuxer Joch. Turn right away from the upper station along path 323 (signposted) and down into the upper section of the Weitental valley. Climb steeply out of the valley to the small col beneath the Gschütspitze. Continue around the headwaters of the Madseit valley and over the ridge between the Dunkle Spitze and Sägenhorst. Turn right after 200-300m and walk downhill into the Junsbachtal valley. Cross six side streams before reaching the mountain settlement of Junsalm Hochleger. Beyond the farms the walking is easy all the way to Juns and the road.

There are a number of steep sections both uphill and down on this walk and it is, therefore, not recommended for anyone who is not completely fit. Boots and warm clothing are essential.

NEUKIRCHEN

Grossvenediger (Oberpinzgau)

Recommended Map:

Freytag and Bernt
Sheet 38 (1:100,000)
Kitzbüheler Alpen und Pinzgau

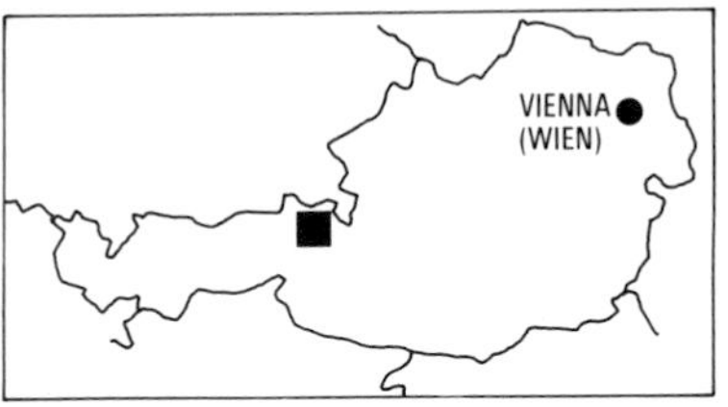

HOW TO GET THERE

Road: (1) South-east by autobahn (E11) from Munich to the Rosenheim interchange. South to Kufstein then south-west by autobahn to the Wörgl-Ost interchange. East on E17 to St Johann in Tyrol. South by road 159 via Kitzbühel to Mittersill and west along 169 to Neukirchen.
(2) From Salzburg south-west on E11 to Lofer. Then south on route 168 to Zell am See. West on 159 and 168 via Mittersill.
Rail: Via Salzburg to Zell am See and local train to Neukirchen.
Air: Munich or Salzburg with connections by rail.

THE AREA

Today a modern motor road over the Gerlos Pass connects the Zillertal to the valley of the Salzbach, but for centuries the only link would be a little used track open only in summer. As a result of this two major and close alpine valleys developed along entirely different lines. Even though the walking centre of Neukirchen is only about 35km away from Mayrhofen in a direct line, the atmosphere and character is entirely different. The only similarity is the overall friendliness of the people and the sunny climate.

The Salzbach valley, or to give it its regional title — Oberpinzgau — runs due east from the Gerlos Pass and is much broader and perhaps less shut in than the Zillertal. Villages are sited to take the maximum advantage of the shape of the valley, which is a natural sun trap. Further down the valley, castles, some still inhabited, evoke the feudal atmosphere of long ago. Schloss Mittersill is typical and is now used as an exclusive rendezvous for hunters.

Even though Neukirchen has been a popular tourist centre for many years, nevertheless it remains completely unspoilt and unassuming even though it was a favourite hide-away of the late Emperor Franz Josef, who occasionally came this way to relax from the problems of being head of the crumbling, but once mighty, Austro-Hungarian empire.

Neukirchen is often used as a base for climbers attempting the peaks and glaciers of the northern side of the Venediger Group. These

Neukirchen

visitors will be in the minority as the more average walker finds tremendous scope for mountain expeditions without the need to enter the realms of eternal snow and ice. There are plenty of safe high-level routes which give spectacular views of the peaks, although some of those described in this section will require the walker to spend a night or so in mountain huts. The bulk of walking however, is without a lot of hard climbing, and also well sited cable lifts will take the walker from the valley to higher levels. Roads over the Gerlos and Thurn Passes can also be used to gain height for some very pleasant walking through sunfilled forest glades.

Another motor road which is usually used purely for the experience of taking a car over 8,000 ft is the Grossglockner road. This road climbs steadily south from Bruck along the Fuscher valley almost to its end and then starts to climb in dramatic loops and bends to its summit at Hochtor where the motorist finds himself in a glittering world of permanent snow and ice. High peaks seem almost a hand's breadth away. A small toll is charged on this road which descends into South Tyrol, but most sightseers usually take a side road to a dead end at the Franz Josef hut beneath the Pasterzen Glacier. The road is usually open between mid-May and mid-November although early and late snows may prevent this. Fog is an ever present hazard and night

THINGS TO DO AND PLACES TO VISIT AROUND NEUKIRCHEN

Folklore Events, Informal Dances, Discotheques, etc
Organised on an individual basis by local hotels. Check locally.

Facilities found in and around the village
- Open-air heated swimming pool
- Mini golf
- Bowling alleys
- Tennis courts
- Horse riding
- Sauna
- Cinema
- Open-air concerts

Boating and Lake Bathing
Zell am See (average summer temperature 73°F/23°C). 40km east of Neukirchen.

Castles in the area (all east of Neukirchen)
- Schloss Farmach.
- Schloss Dorfheim.
- Schloss Lichtenberg.
- Schloss Mittersill (private).

Museums
- Pinzgau; Christmas Crib Museum.
- Pinzgau; Schloss Lichtenburg.

Grossglockner Road
The road (which is subject to toll) is due south from Bruck, near Zell am See. It follows the Fuschertal to Lukashause before starting to climb steeply by dozens of hairpin bends to its highest point at Hochtor (2,575m). Continue by a side road to the Franz Josef Haus for views of the Pasterzen Glacier.
Parking away from official places is prohibited.

crossings are not recommended. Restaurant and tourist accommodation is well catered for. Parking except in the spots provided is dangerous and therefore forbidden. Remember that at this altitude the temperature can be considerably lower than in the valley and so if you intend to spend any time walking around admiring the views, then take warm clothing.

There are many interesting diversions to lure the walker away from the mountain tracks and as we have already seen, the Grossglockner road is an exciting way to climb into the highest mountains of the region by car. Down the valley is the beautiful and popular lake resort of Zell am See where boats can be hired or a day just spent sunbathing. The water in summer reaches temperatures warm enough to satisfy most outdoor swimmers. To the north are the famous ski resorts of St Johann in Tyrol and Kitzbühel.

In Neukirchen itself there is an open-air heated swimming pool, also tennis courts, ten-pin bowling alleys, a cinema and horse riding facilities. Folklore concerts, dances and film shows are offered by individual hotels in this most hospitable resort. In winter the avalanche free slopes of the Wildkogel are a mecca for downhill skiers and the level valley bottom gives an excellent system of linked cross-country ski trails.

Natural features abound, but it is probably the Krimml waterfall 12km south-west of Neukirchen which is the prime attraction of the area. Dropping 1,250ft in three stages, the falls are Europe's highest. The best time to see them is at noon when the overhead sun makes the water sparkle like millions of diamonds. In summer the falls are illuminated at night, but whenever you visit them remember to take a waterproof as the spray travels quite some distance.

Transport up and down the Salzbach valley from Neukirchen is easy and the walker has a choice of either bus or rail. If you intend using an early train, check carefully, because as often happens in alpine areas, some early trains are buses departing from outside the station rather than from within!

The lower mountains of the Pinzgau are an ideal playground for the mountain walker who wants to experience the comradeship of mountain hut life. A number of the walks described in this section will necessitate the use of the hut system for overnight accommodation. It is not usual to book in advance, although a phone call beforehand might let you know if the hut is likely to be crowded. Information regarding their opening times or local weather conditions can be obtained from local tourist information centres.

FURTHER INFORMATION

Interesting towns nearby

Mittersill
15km east. At the foot of the Thurn Pass. Castle now used as an exclusive hunters' club.

Zell am See
40km east. Lakeside holiday resort. Boating, bathing and sailing.

Krimml
12km south-west. Europe's highest waterfall (1,250ft), restaurants, etc.

Kitzbühel
30km north-east. Fashionable ski resort, shops, restaurants.

Camp Sites

Wald.
Krimml.
Mittersill.
Zell am See.

Cable Car Ascents

Neukirchen-Wildkogel.
Zell am See-Schmittenhöhe.

Accommodation

The most expensive hotel in Neukirchen is the Jagdhaus Graf Recke, a hunting lodge/pension owned by Count Recke-Volmerstein. The remainder are inexpensive family run gasthofs and pensions. Self service and bed-and-breakfast accommodation is widely available.

Tourist Information

Up-to-date details of available accommodation and events can be obtained from the local tourist office:
Verkehrsverein Neukirchen,
A-5741 Neukirchen am
Grossvenediger,
Oberpinzgau, Austria.

THE WALKS

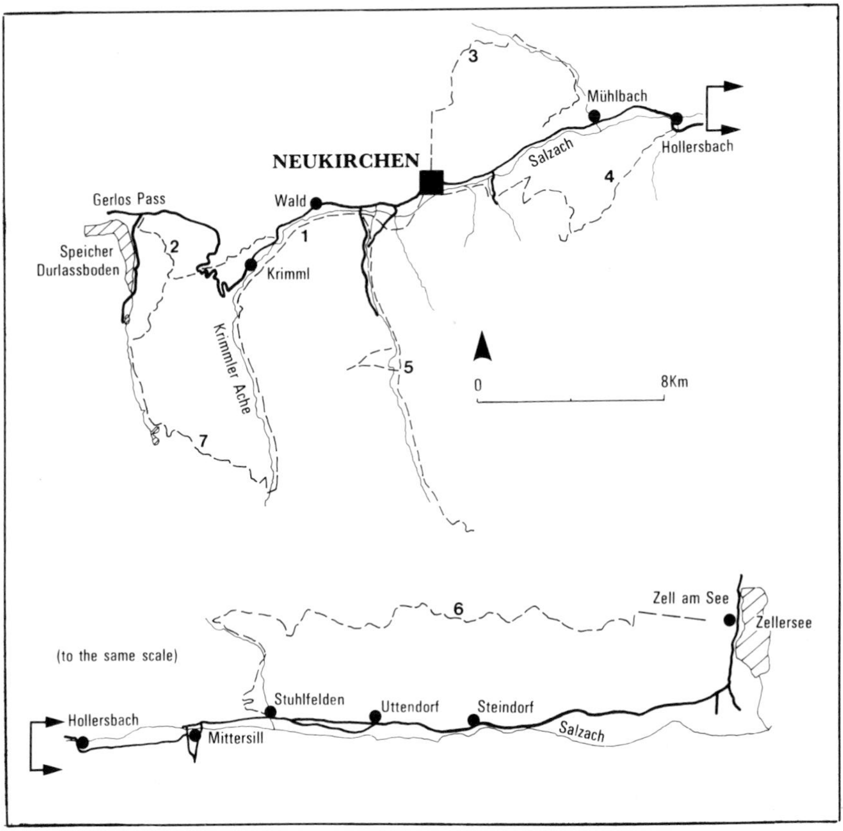

The potential for walks of all standards with or without the use of huts in this area is almost limitless and the visitor can spend many happy hours working out new routes for himself. The routes described above are only a representative selection of what is available.

Horse riding, Neukirchen

ROUTE 1

Salzbach valley, Sulzau, Krimml, Krimml Waterfall

12km ($7\frac{1}{2}$ miles). 4 hours. Easy.
Riverside and forest paths to the highest waterfall in Europe.

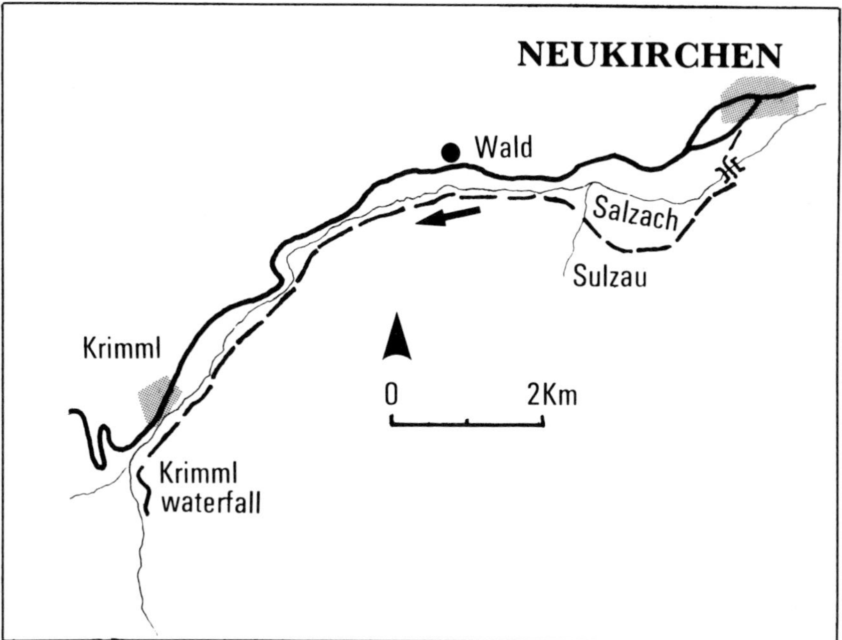

Follow the lane opposite Neukirchen's church down towards the river (go under the bypass road and railway, and follow the line as far as the river). Cross the river by a wooden bridge and turn right, but keeping outside the forest, walk through meadowland to Sulzau. On through fields again to join a riverside path which enters the forest opposite the village of Wald. Follow this path (signposted 37) all the way to the Krimml waterfalls. Return by bus from Krimml.

A most relaxing walk with the highlight of the falls as its climax.

ROUTE 2

Gerlos Pass, Platten Kogel, Krimml

9km ($5\frac{1}{2}$ miles). 3/4 hours. Easy.
An easy high-level walk mostly through forest and along well maintained paths.

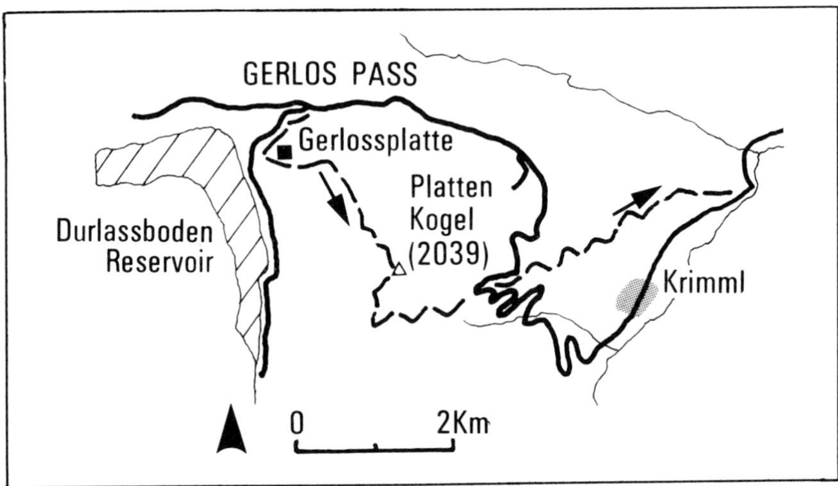

Take the bus to the top of the Gerlos Pass. Turn left away from the road and walk down to the Durlassboden reservoir. Turn left away from the reservoir and walk up a steep hill to the Gerlossplatte restaurant. Continue up to the summit of the Platten Kogel (signposted). Turn right at the summit and go downhill to a junction of four paths on a narrow col. Turn left and go steeply downhill through forest and across the main road following a path into Krimml. Continue as far as the railway station.

Platten Kogel is a good vantage point for views down the whole length of the Salzbach valley.

ROUTE 3

Wildkogel (2,225m), Mühlbachtal, Bramberg

14km (8½ miles). 6 hours. Moderate.
An easy mountain climb followed by forest and valley walking.

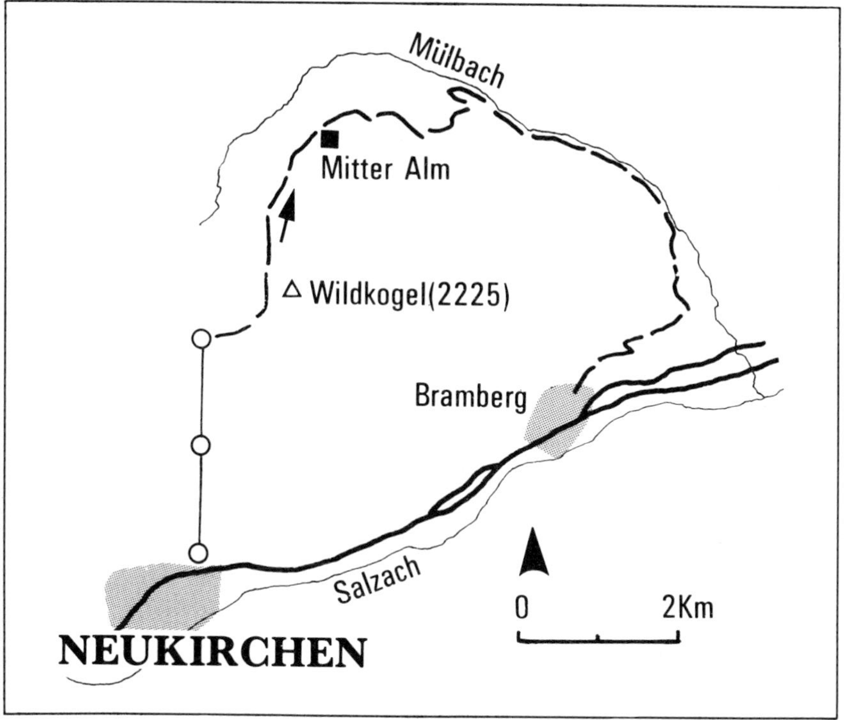

Take the chairlift from Neukirchen on to the flank of the Wildkogel. From the top station turn right along path 740 (signposted), to the summit of the Wildkogel. Retrace your steps for about ⅓km to a junction of four paths and turn right along path 739 (signposted). This path descends easily over rocky ground before crossing some alpine pastures. A mountain farm (Mitter Alm) marks the forest edge. Continue on path 739 and turn right into the forest; gradually descend in and out of clearings and across meadows, as far as the Mühlbach river. Join path 714 at this point and turn right down stream as far as a junction of paths. Turn right across the shoulder of the hill and continue downhill to Bramberg where a short bus ride will take you back to Neukirchen.

The mountain range to the south as seen from the top of the Wildkogel is the Venediger group with the Grossvenediger (3,674m) at its highest point. Alpine flower lovers will want to spend as much time as possible on the section between Wildkogel and Mitter Alm farm.

ROUTE 4

Habachtal (833m), Karsee (2,085m), Zwölfer Kogel (2,282m), Reitlehen

17km (10½ miles). 8/9 hours. Moderate/Difficult.
A stiff climb rewarded by fine views.

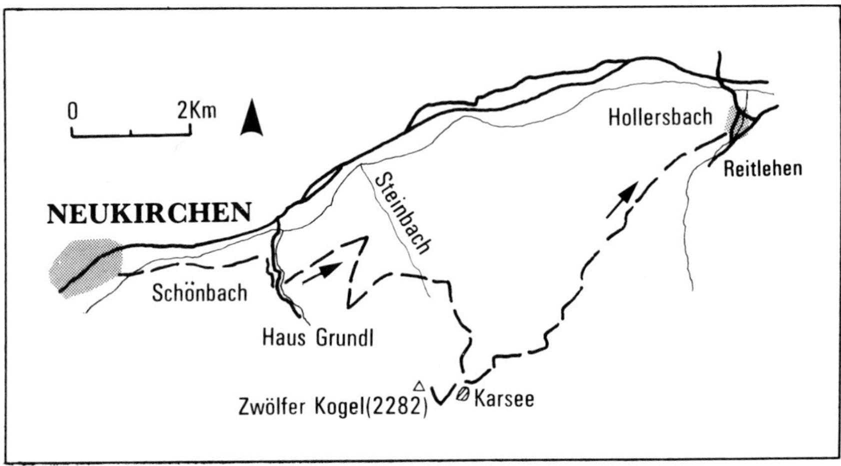

Take the road from Neukirchen station down to and across the river. Turn left downstream through Schonbach and as far as the Habachtal road. Turn right and walk along the road for about ¾km, turning left opposite Haus Brundl. Take the right of two paths ahead and climb into the forest. After about 4km (or 1½ hours of climbing), a small stream the Steinbach, is crossed and soon a path from the left is joined. Turn right uphill along this path (932) to the tiny lake of Karsee. A right turn will find the path to the summit of the Zwölfer Kogel. From the summit return to the lake and walk ahead and downhill over rocky ground on path 933, following a steady course to the north-east across several minor summits. The angle of descent steepens through forest as far as Reitlehen. Return by bus from Reitlehen or train from Hollersbach.

The forest should offer shade on the uphill section on a hot sunny day. Allow plenty of time for admiring the views from the Zwölfer Kogel. The Breitkopf (2,420m) can be climbed as an alternative to the Zwölfer Kogel, but remember it is another 138m (453ft) higher.

Although the following walk 5 could be completed up and down in one day by a strong party, the use of huts for overnight accommodation is recommended on this and all of the following routes.

ROUTE 5

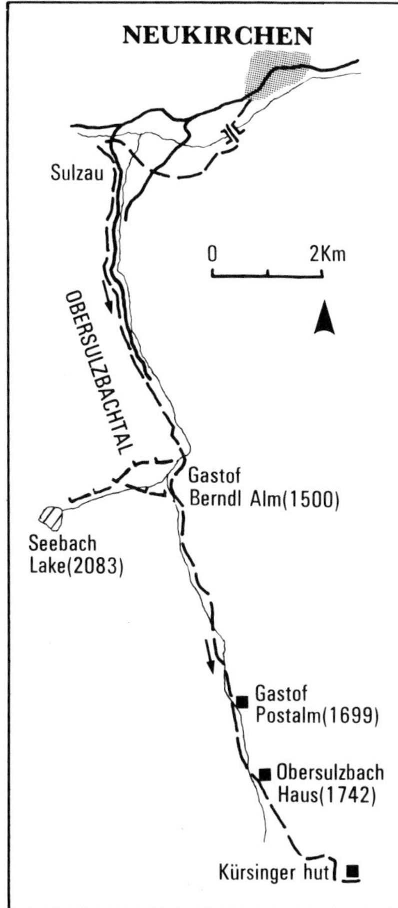

Obersulzbachtal, Gasthof Postalm, Kürsinger Haus (2,403m)

36km (22 miles). 12/14 hours (8/9 hours up and 4/5 hours down). Moderate.
A valley which climbs steadily into the heart of the Venediger range.

Follow walk 1 along the main valley to Sulzau and turn left along the Obersulzbachtal valley road to the Gastof Berndl Alm (1,500m). (A diversion could be made by climbing to the Seebach lake (2,083m) and rejoining the main route above the hut.) Continue up the valley past Gastof Postalm (1,699m) to the Obersulzbach Haus (1,742m) where the track divides. Take the left-hand path and climb steeply up to the Kürsinger hut (2,403m). Return the same route.

Assuming that the party is staying at the Kürsinger Hut, climb the ridge behind the hut for close-hand views of the Obersulzbach glacier and its attendant peaks — the Gross-venediger dominates them all.

This walk could be varied by a party wishing to just explore the Sulzbachtal, by walking for half the day uphill and returning as time or energy dictates.

ROUTE 6

Zell am See, Schmittenhöhe, Pinzgauer-Spaziergang, Bürgl Haus, Stuhlfelden

28km (17 miles). 10/12 hours. (8/10 hours to the Burgl hut from the Schmittenhöhe). Moderate.

A panorama walk along a well engineered 'balcony' path.

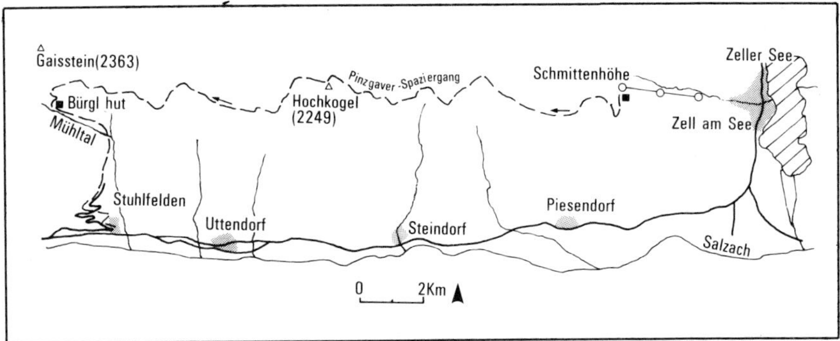

From Zellam See take the cable lift to the Schmittenhöhe and stay the night in either the Schmittenhöhe hotel or the Pinzgauer Haus hut. The walk is then to simply follow path 719, the Pinzgauer-Sapziergang (signposted) along a delightful route which carefully follows more or less the same contour beneath a series of summits all the way to the Bürgl Haus hut. From the Bürgl Haus hut follow the jeep track down the Mühltal valley to Stuhlfelden.

This is mountain walking at its most enjoyable. If time allows, a diversionary climb of the Hochkogel can be made en route. Also it is possible to climb the Gaisstein from the Bürgl hut before descending, but both climbs require a good head for heights and dry weather.

Mayrhofen

Mount Blanc range, Courmayeur

The Dolomites

ROUTE 7

Krimmler Achental, Tauernhaus, Gerlos See, Zittauer Haus, Wildergerlostal, Leitenkammersteig, Gerlosplatte

30km (18 miles). 16/18 hours (total walking). Difficult.
An experience of high mountain, hut-to-hut walking.

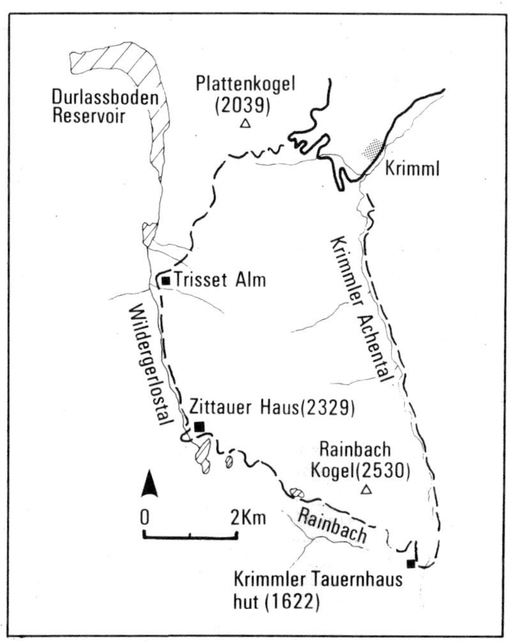

From Krimml follow path 40 (signposted) above the Krimml Falls to Gasthof Schömegerl. Continue by path 519 alongside the Krimmler Achental stream as far as the Krimmler Tauernhaus hut (possible night stop). Turn right up the Rainbachtal valley on path 512; after about 1¼km turn right on path 511 which is a steep climb uphill beneath the Rainbach Kogel peak. Pass three pretty mountain lakes before reaching the Zittauer Haus (possible night stop). Walk downhill on path 540 alongside the Wildergerlostal stream as far as Trisset Alm mountain farm. Turn right (signposted) along the Leitenkammersteig path as far as the junction of four paths beneath the Plattenkogel peak. Turn right downhill through forest and eventually Krimml is reached. If time allows the route can be extended by walking alongside the Salzbach river all the way back to Neukirchen (reversing route 1).

Allow about 4/5 hours between the Krimmler Tauernhaus and Zittauer Haus huts. Consideration should be given to spending nights at both huts and spread the total walking time over three days. This would allow plenty of time for further exploration.

Italy

COURMAYEUR

Aosta Valley (Piedmont Region)

Recommended Maps:

Kompass Wanderkarte (1:50,000) Sheet 85 Massicio del Monte Bianco

Didier & Richard (1:50,000), Sheet 8 Massifs du Mont-Blanc

HOW TO GET THERE

Road: (1) By motorway south via Geneva to Chamonix and the Mont Blanc tunnel, or via Lausanne and the St Bernard tunnel to Aosta. (2) Regular long-distance coach services serve this area from Geneva and Milan.

Rail: (1) Geneva to Chamonix then bus or taxi through the Mont Blanc tunnel (22km). (2) Milan or Turin to Aosta and connections to Pré St Didier then taxi or bus (4km).

Air: Geneva, Milan or Turin then rail as above.

Language: Italian or French.

THE AREA

The south face of Mont Blanc, Europe's highest mountain presents a steep wall beneath which the Aosta valley ends abruptly. This background enhances the beauty of a valley steeped in a history which started in Roman times, and all along its length and that of its tributaries, ancient towns and villages await the visitor's quiet investigation.

Courmayeur, which is a mixture of old and new, has given comfortable hospitality to mountain wanderers and skiers since mountains began to be enjoyed in their own right during the last century. As a resort it has developed considerably since the early mountaineers came this way. Then their journey might have taken days, but now Northern Europe is only a matter of hours away, thanks to the trans-European motorway system and the massive engineering projects of the Mont

Mont Blanc from Courmayeur

Blanc and St Bernard tunnels. The building of the Mont Blanc tunnel is commemorated locally in a tiny chapel above Entrèves close by the southern entrance. In the chapel is a dramatic plaque which shows the moment when French and Italian engineers broke through to meet each other deep beneath the mountain.

The walker can easily enter the world of the mountaineer by exploring the ridges which run parallel to the south face of Mont Blanc and see at close hand across the Veni and Ferret valleys such famous features as Mont Dolent, where three nations meet, or the impressive rock towers of the Grandes Jorasses, the Aiguille du Géant and two awe-inspiring glaciers, the Brenva and Miage. The summit of Mont Blanc itself sits above all this grandure in snowy majesty.

A cable car from Courmayeur to Pian Chécrou below Mont Chétif takes the effort out of walking around the westerly ridges, but as yet, there is no similar service to the east. To the north there is the ambitious system of lifts which start at la Palud above Entrèves, crosses the Mont Blanc glaciers as far as the Aiguille du Midi and then down to Chamonix. As a result of this project all-the-year-round skiing is possible on the Glacier du Géant and above the Vallée Blanche.

The Brenva and Miage glaciers both grind down into Val Veni, carrying rocks which started their slow journeys centuries ago high up in the snow-filled recesses of the ridges and peaks, to be dumped (often

THINGS TO DO AND PLACES TO VISIT AROUND COURMAYEUR

Mont Blanc Tunnel
Toll. Interesting commemorative chapel near southern entrance.

Tennis
Public courts on the outskirts of Courmayeur.

Mini Golf
Near tennis courts.

Swimming Pool
Near tennis courts.

Fishing
Trout in the river below Pré St Didier. Check locally for permits.

Notre Dame de Guerison
Chapel above Val Veni.

Col de la Seigne
Ruins of pre-war fortified customs post.

Alpine Flowers
Especially interesting around the head of Val Sapin.

Gran Paradiso National Park
Sanctuary for mountain flora and fauna. Reached via Val di Cogne to the south of Aosta.

with alarming sounds) on to the terminal moraines in the valleys beneath. Melt water flowing out into the valley is a greenish grey colour from the heavy load of silt it carries and which is eventually deposited lower down on the fertile plains of Northern Italy.

Opposite the terminal moraine of the Brenva Glacier there is a chapel perched high on a rocky outcrop. This is Notre Dame de Guerison where miracles are said to have taken place. That is if the number of crutches and other invalid aides lining the chapel walls are to be believed.

French is the second language spoken in the upper Aosta valley, even the place names have a French ring to them, but it is more courteous to speak Italian. At one time the Veni and Ferret valleys had busy smuggling routes into France and Switzerland. Frontier posts below Col de la Seigne and Col du Grand Ferret are now in ruins, so today's hill walkers can pass freely over frontiers which until fairly recently were heavily guarded.

Downstream from Courmayeur the streets of Aosta are still laid out in the regular pattern of the original roman garrison town which was founded by Augustus Praetoria in 25BC. There is still a well preserved triumphal arch of Augustus, together with the remains of a Roman theatre, forum and the Prætorian gate.

Romantic castles dominate vantage points throughout the Aosta Valley, such as those found at Fennis, Sarre, St Pierre and Aymaville, which all guarded the ancient route into northern Italy. Hannibal took his elephants into Italy by the Little St Bernard pass.

FURTHER INFORMATION

Interesting towns nearby

Aosta
Built on a roman city founded in 25BC. Roman theatre, triumphal arch, forum and Prætorian gate.

Turin
Capital of the Piedmont. Many beautiful squares. Medieval churches. Cathedral on Piazza San Giovanni houses the 'Turin Shroud', which some believe to be the shroud in which Christ was wrapped.

Asti
Centre of a wine growing region. Famous for its sparkling vintages (Asti Spumante), as well as a number of reds: Barbera, Barbereso, Barolo, Gattimara and Grignolio. Vermouths also come from the Piedmont area.

Fennis and Issogre
Ancient villages with fourteenth-century castles.

Cable Cars, etc

La Palud Chamonix complex.
Stations at Rifugio Torino, Aiguille du Midi, Plan d'Aiguille.
Courmayeur-Pian Chécroui.
Morgex-Jacod.
Villair (above Morgex)-Fenêtre.
Aosta-Pila.

Accommodation
Being off the normal tourist route, prices in Val d'Aosta tend to be lower and off season bargains are often available. The choice is varied and most of the better modern and high class hotels are in Courmayeur. Older family-run comfortable establishments are found in the surrounding villages. Rented rooms and villas are also available, but prior booking is essential.

Camp Sites

Planpincieux - Val Ferret.
Sarre - Riverside near Aosta.

Tourist Office
(Local)
Azienda Autonoma di Soggiorno,
Courmayeur,
Val d'Aosta.

(Regional)
Ufficio Informazioni Turistiche Regionalo,
Piazza E Chanoux,
8-I-11100 Aosta.

To the north of the city of Aosta the road climbs the Grand St Bernard Pass into Switzerland, but today with the opening of the tunnel there are none of the dangers which were associated with the pass in earlier times. The monks who gave shelter to travellers and their famous St Bernard dogs are there by the side of the old road, which still remains in use as an alternative to the tunnel. In summer it is a pleasant drive up to the col at 2,469m.

A little to the south of the region is the Gran Paradiso National Park. No further superlatives beyond a translation of the title are needed — The Great Paradise — a paradise of mountains and wildlife. Flowers and animals such as the rare ibex abound in this park, and it should be high on the list of priorities for any visitor.

Most forms of relaxation are catered for in and around Courmayeur, the region has a number of excellent dishes and restaurants vie with each other to reach the highest standards of catering. Nightlife is lively and there is even a casino in St Vincent, lower down the valley. Courmayeur has a miniature golf course and tennis courts.

Local transport is good with a regular bus network up to and including Val Veni and Val Ferret.

THE WALKS

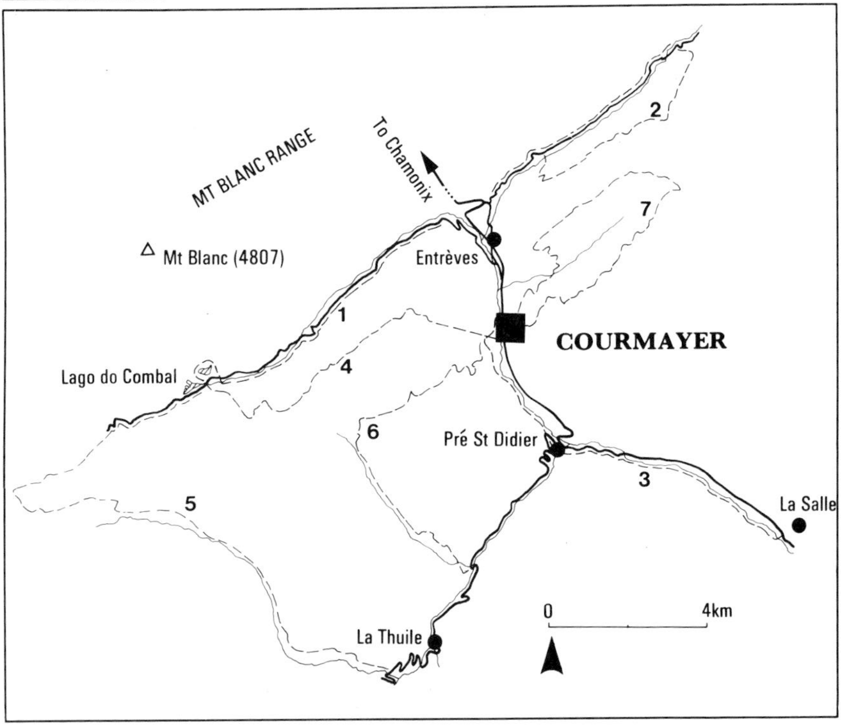

MT BLANC RANGE
To Chamonix
Mt Blanc (4807)
Entrèves
COURMAYER
Lago do Combal
Pré St Didier
La Salle
La Thuile
1
2
3
4
5
6
7
0
4km

Ponte Romano, Aosta

ROUTE 1

Val Veni and Lago del Miage

18km (11 miles). 5 hours. Easy.
An easy road walk beneath the south face of Mont Blanc passing the terminal moraines of the Brenva and Miage glaciers.

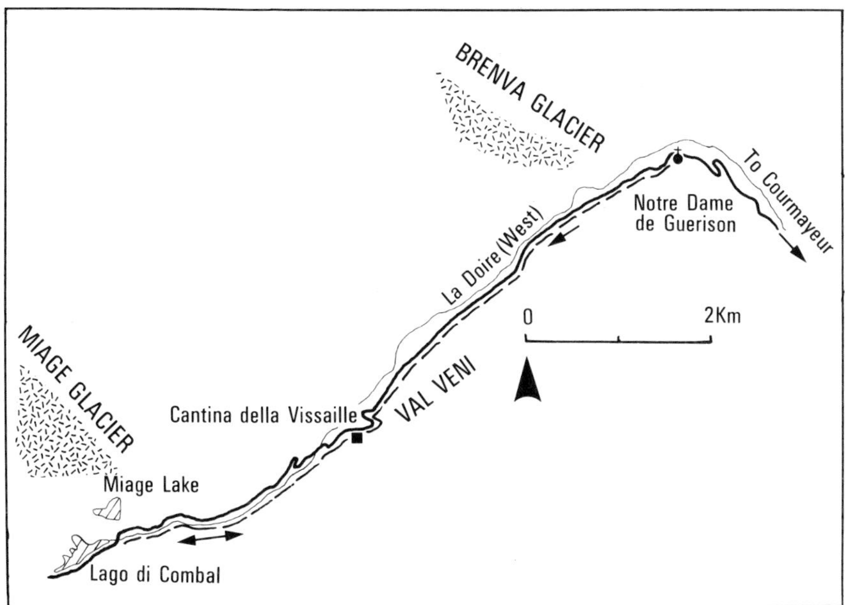

Take the Val Veni bus as far as the church of Notre Dame de Guerison and walk up the road, passing the huge terminal moraine of the Brenva galcier on the right. Continue uphill beyond the restaurant of Cantina della Vissaille until you are opposite the Miage glacier. Descend, but do not go beyond the Miage lake. From here it is possible to get really close views of the glacier. Return as far as the Vissaille restaurant, which is also the bus terminus and if necessary the walk can be shortened by using the bus back from here.

This is a safe way to get close to the spectacular sight of the final stages in the life of a glacier, but do not stray from the path, especially when near the moraine.

ROUTE 2

Val Ferret

15km (10 miles). 6/7 hours. Moderate.
Dramatic views of some famous peaks.

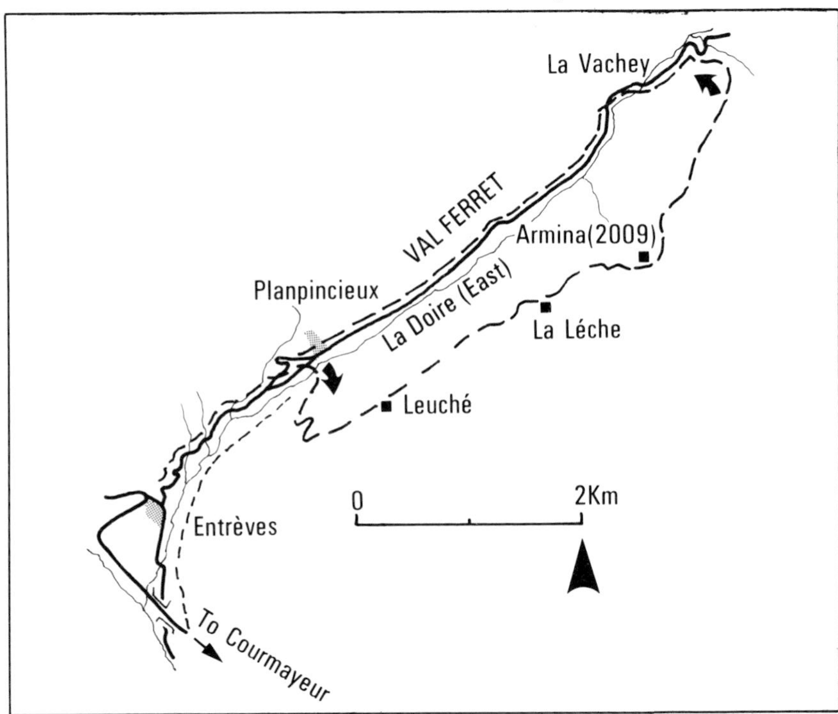

From Entrèves follow the Val Ferret road as far as Planpincieux and turn right to cross the River Doire. Climb an easy path which zig-zags up the hill-side to the farmsteads of Leuché. Turn left along a track which follows a more-or-less level route across the hillside and above a small forest to another farm at la Lèche. Climb slightly uphill and aim for another section of forest above which is yet another group of farms called Armina. Ignore tracks right and left from Armina, but continue ahead and downhill through forest to join the val Ferret road beyond la Vachey. Turn left along the road and back to Entrèves.

The walk can be extended on the return leg by crossing the river again at Planpincieux to follow an easy path by way of la Saxe into Courmayeur, but this will add another 5km (3 miles) to the journey.

Not only is a map essential for normal navigation on this walk, but it will help in an interesting diversion, that of naming all the giant peaks on the opposite side of the valley.

ROUTE 3

Courmayeur, Dolonne, Pré St Didier, Morgex, la Salle

12km ($7\frac{1}{2}$ miles). 3/4 hours. Easy.
An easy valley and forest walk to interesting old villages.

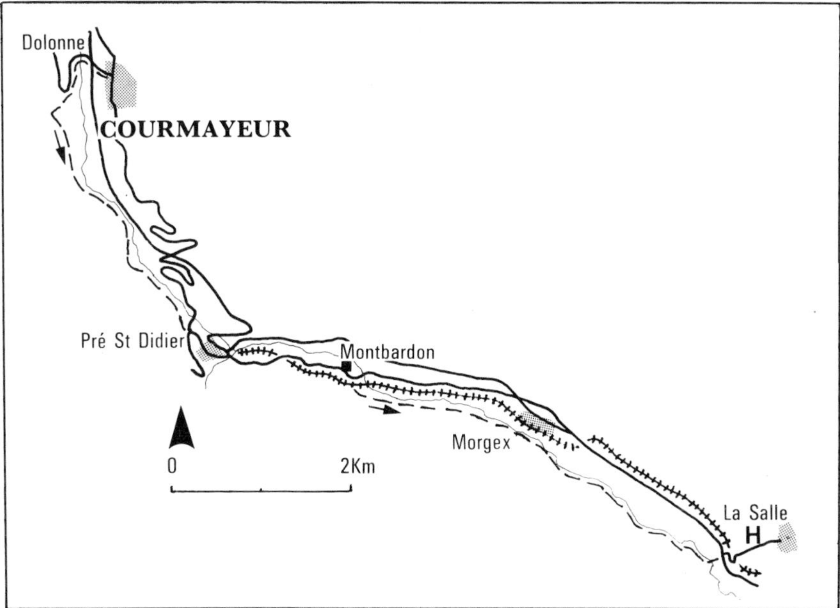

Cross beneath the main road below Courmayeur and walk up the road to Dolonne as far as the sharp bend before the village. Turn left on a path which follows the Dora Baltea river downstream to Pré St Didier. Walk through the village to the main road which is followed (again downstream) to the farm of Montbardon. Turn right over the railway on a path to Morgex village, beyond which another path leads to the main road again near la Salle where there is a convenient bus stop.

Take great care while walking along the stretch of main road from Pré St Didier.

ROUTE 4

Pian Chécroui Cable Car, Pra Neirons, Lago Chécroui, Lago del Miage, Val Veni

11km (7 miles). 4 hours. Moderate.
A walk with the best views of Mont Blanc and its steepest glacier.

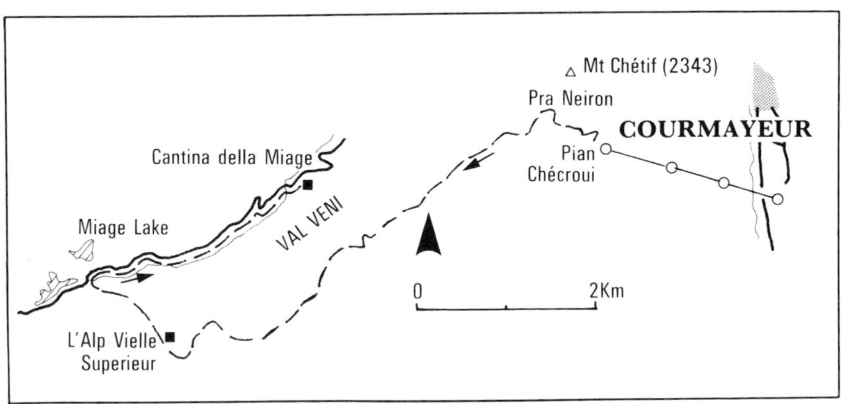

Take the cable car from Courmayeur to Pian Chécroui then walk on to Pra Neiron and turn left and cross Col Chécroui. Continue to Lago Chécroui climbing gradually all the way to the lake and beyond as far as the farmstead at l'Alp Vielle Superieur. Turn right and a steep downhill walk leads to the roadway in Val Veni above Lago del Miage. Turn right along the road to Cantina della Miage.

This walk is a must for mountain photographers and Lago Chécroui makes an excellent foreground for a shot of the Miage glacier.

Courmayeur

ROUTE 5

La Thuile (1,447m), Dora di Verney Valley, Col di Chavannes (2,603m), Col de la Seigne (2,541m), Val Veni

23km (14¼ miles). 8/9 hours. Moderate/Difficult.
Hard mountain walking through an alpine valley and over two high passes.

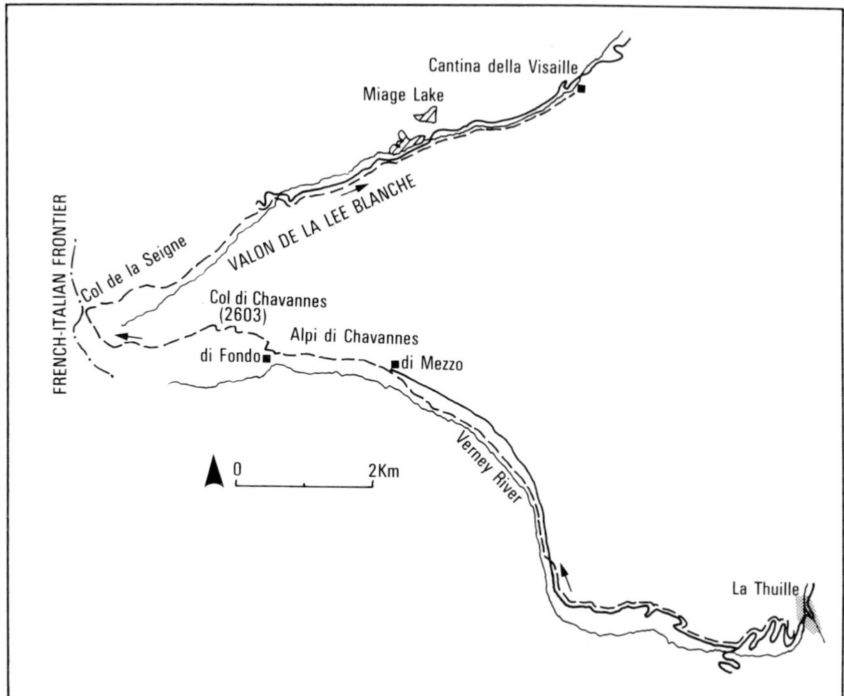

Take the bus to la Thuile and walk up the Little St Bernard road as far as the Verney river. Turn right at the bridge along a track which climbs the Verney Valley to the old hill farm settlements of Alpi di Chavannes, di Mezzo and di Fondo. Climb steeply to the Col di Chavannes and follow the contours round the upper Val Veni (Vallon de la Lée Blanche) to the French/Italian frontier at the Col de la Seigne. Turn right downhill past the ruined Italian frontier post and join the road as far as the restaurant of Cantina della Visaille where there is a bus stop.

A hard mountain walk, but the effort involved in the climb to the Col di Chavannes is well rewarded by the views of Mont Blanc across Val Veni.

ROUTE 6

Dolonne (1,205m), Arpette, Alp d'Arp, Col d'Arp (2,570m), Vallone di Youla, La Balme (1,309m)

12km (7½ miles). 7/8 hours. Moderate/Difficult.
An 'off the beaten track' hill walk.

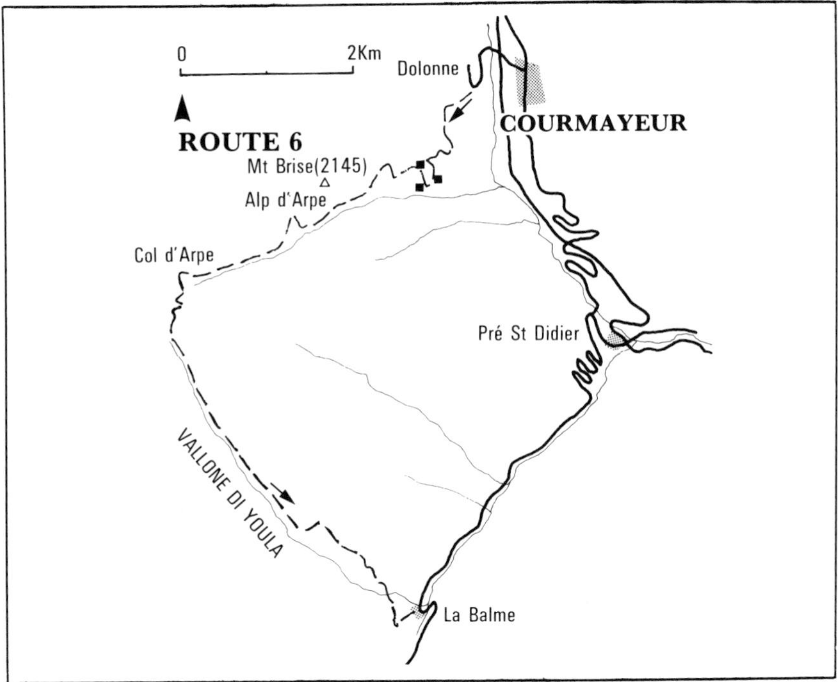

From the bend in the road before Dolonne turn left downhill as far as the stream. At the stream turn right and climb up through the forest opposite to a group of farm buildings. Turn right again, continuing uphill beneath Monte Brise, past Alp d'Arp to the Col d'Arp. Turn sharply to the right and downhill into Vallone di Youla. Where the valley widens near its mouth, ignore the first track to the right, but by some old farm buildings take the next track on the right and a steep walk downhill through alpine meadows and along the edge of a forest leads to la Balme, where the bus to Courmayeur can be caught.

ROUTE 7

Villair (1,327m), Testa della Trouche (2,584m), Val Sapin

15km ($9\frac{1}{4}$ miles). 8/9 hours. Difficult.
A truly high level walk amidst dramatic scenery, but care must be exercised on the descent from Col Sapin.

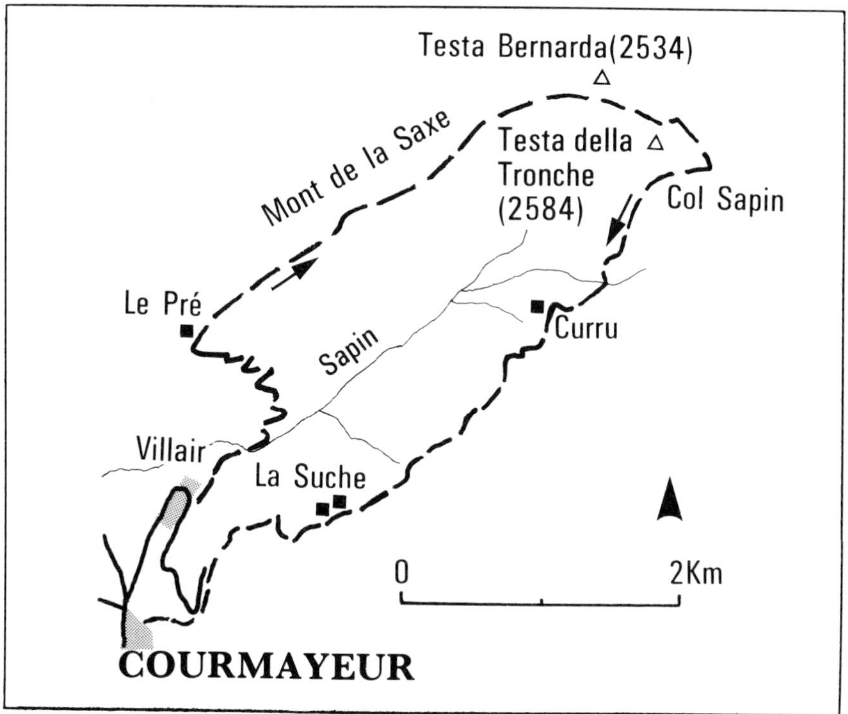

Walk northwards and uphill from Courmayeur to Villair then towards the River Sapin. Cross the river and follow a well marked path which climbs through sparse forest on a zig-zag route to the hill farms of le Pré. Turn right at the farmsteads and gradually climb uphill beneath the ridge of Mont de la Saxe to a wide col where the path divides. Turn right across the summit of Testa Bernarda and Testa della Trouche. Turn right at another path junction and climb a little way to Col Sapin. The route is a steep downhill slope beyond the col, so take care. Follow the path downhill to the hill farms of Curru and eventually enter a forest. Continue through la Suche and turn right at a 'T' junction, then still downhill until another junction is reached. Turn left here and along an improving track into Courmayeur.

The section of the walk from Testa Bernarda to Curru is an excellent area for alpine flower hunting (but please, photographs only, do not pick any flowers as it only kills the plants).

CORVARA

Val Badia

Recommended Map:
Kompass Carta Turistica (1:50,000) Sheet 55 (Cortina D'Ampezzo)

HOW TO GET THERE

Road: (1) South from Innsbruck over the Brenner Pass by the Austro/Italian autostrada (E6) to Waidbruck, then eastwards through Val Gardena and its pass to Corvara. (2) North from the Milan/Venice autostrada (E13) to Verona and E6 via Trento to Waidbruck, then as for the southerly route.
Rail: Nearest station: Bruneck (Brunico). Mainline connections via the Innsbruck/Verona line, change at Fortezza (33km bus connection).
Bus: Cortina/Bruneck Services.
Air: International airports at Milan or Munich (rail connections).
Language: German or Italian.

THE AREA

Even though Corvara, like Belluno, is a centre within the Dolomite Alps, unlike Belluno it is situated in their very heart and so is in complete contrast. While Belluno's Valleys have begun to open out into the Venetian plain here they are secretive and for centuries were inaccessible for much of the year. A glance at the map shows the spaghetti-like meanderings of modern roads which climb seemingly impossible precipices. This early inaccessibility left a roman legion in the area long after the fall of the Roman Empire and the people of Val Badia became their descendants. They speak a special language more closely linked to Roman Latin than modern Italian, known as 'Ladinisch'. The people of Val Badia speak three main languages: first Ladinisch, second German and third Italian, although the latter is their official language. They are very proud to be a unique enclave of what was, until World War I, part of the South Tyrol. Most of the town and village place names have both German and Italian spellings, eg Kurvar and Gadertal are the German version of Corvara and Val Badia respectively.

During World War I the region saw some terrible fighting for the command of fortified passes and summits which held the key to routes into Northern Italy. All around are still easily recognisable remains of

THINGS TO DO AND PLACES TO VISIT AROUND CORVARA

Alpine flowers
The best areas are between Col Alto and Pralongia and south of the Gardena Pass road.

Fishing
Trout fishing in most rivers and also a stocked lake which belongs to the Hotel Sompunt near Pedratsches (8km north of Corvara). Check locally for permits and regulations.

Bowling Alleys
Hotels Posta Zirm and La Perla.

Bathing
Outdoor: Salvansee (Pescosta).
Indoor: (Hallenbad): Sporthotel (Sompunt).

World War I Forts within easy access
Falzarego Pass, Col di Lana, Pordoi Pass (German War Memorial and cemetery).

Cabin, Gondola, and Chairlifts in the area
Corvara-Col Alto (chair).
Corvara-Boe Hut (cabin).
Colfosco-Pradat hut (chair).
Stem (la Villa)- Piz la Villa (gondola).
Pedratsches-Heiligkreuz hut (gondola).
St Kassien-Piz Sorega (chair).
Wolkenstein-Gardena Pass (cabin and chair).
Sella Pass-Demetz hut (gondola).
Pordoi Pass-Sass Pordoi (cabin).
Arabba-Belvedere (cabin).
Hotel Ciapela-Marmolada (cabin).

forts carved out of the living rock, such as those above the Falzarego Pass on the road from Corvara to Cortina. While not affected so drastically in World War II there are still reminders in the shape of platoon numbers painted on the doors of some of the older farm buildings. These were where retreating German army units were billeted when Hitler planned to use them in a last ditch stand with what was left of his armies further north in Bavaria.

Today the region is much happier and has become prosperous through the development of tourism and winter skiing. This is an area of great beauty where the dramatic and often stark peaks make a backcloth for beautiful flower filled meadows. Anyone with even the most passing interest in alpine flowers will be entranced by the sheer quantity and types found in this area. Animal life abounds, chamois are common on the high peaks as well as that delightful clown the marmot.

So special is the area that the range of peaks a little to the north of Corvara, the Puez Group, have been designated a National Park.

At one time Corvara was a place where one rested after crossing the Gardena or Campolongo passes, or in winter waited for them to reopen after snow. Today the town is more sophisticated and fortunately it remains unspoilt. There are still old farm houses, but now modern hotels sit beside a road which once rang beneath the hooves of post horses. Nightlife in a subdued way can be found in quiet bars and local entertainment is mostly homemade with an occasional discotheque or film shows of local interest.

Public transport is good with frequent bus services along most of the major roads. Chairlifts are numerous and while primarily intended for winter use, most are available in summer.

For the motorist Corvara is an ideal centre for exploring the northern Dolomites, but a word of caution. Distances between valleys are often much greater than a first glance at a map might indicate. Always look at the height of the passes and compare them with the start or finish heights, this should then give some indication of the climbing involved. Always allow plenty of time for a journey. Remember to give priority to larger vehicles on mountain roads, listen for their warning signals as they will invariably need to swing wide against oncoming traffic on tight bends. Another point to remember is that rain in the valleys early or late in the season often means mist or even snow on the passes.

FURTHER INFORMATION

Interesting towns nearby

Cortina
Via Falzarego Pass. Fashionable Ski resort. Shops.

Pieve di Cadore
Birthplace of the artist Titian.

Bruneck (Brunico)
Railway station. Shops.

St Christina
Wood carving school.

Camp Sites

Riverside between Corvara and Kollfuschg (Colfosco).
Sompunt (near Pedratsches).

Golf
Opposite camp site below Kollfuschg (Colfosco).

Accommodation
Mostly hotels and pensions in Corvara, with some privately let villas and apartments. Enquiries should be made to the tourist office.

Tourist Office
Azienda Autonoma Soggiorno, Corvara/Val Badia.

Bus Stop
Opposite Hotel Posta Zirm (check times locally).

THE WALKS

Spelling of place names mentioned below are given in the German form as used on the Kompass map. Where they differ greatly from the Italian version, the latter is given in brackets.

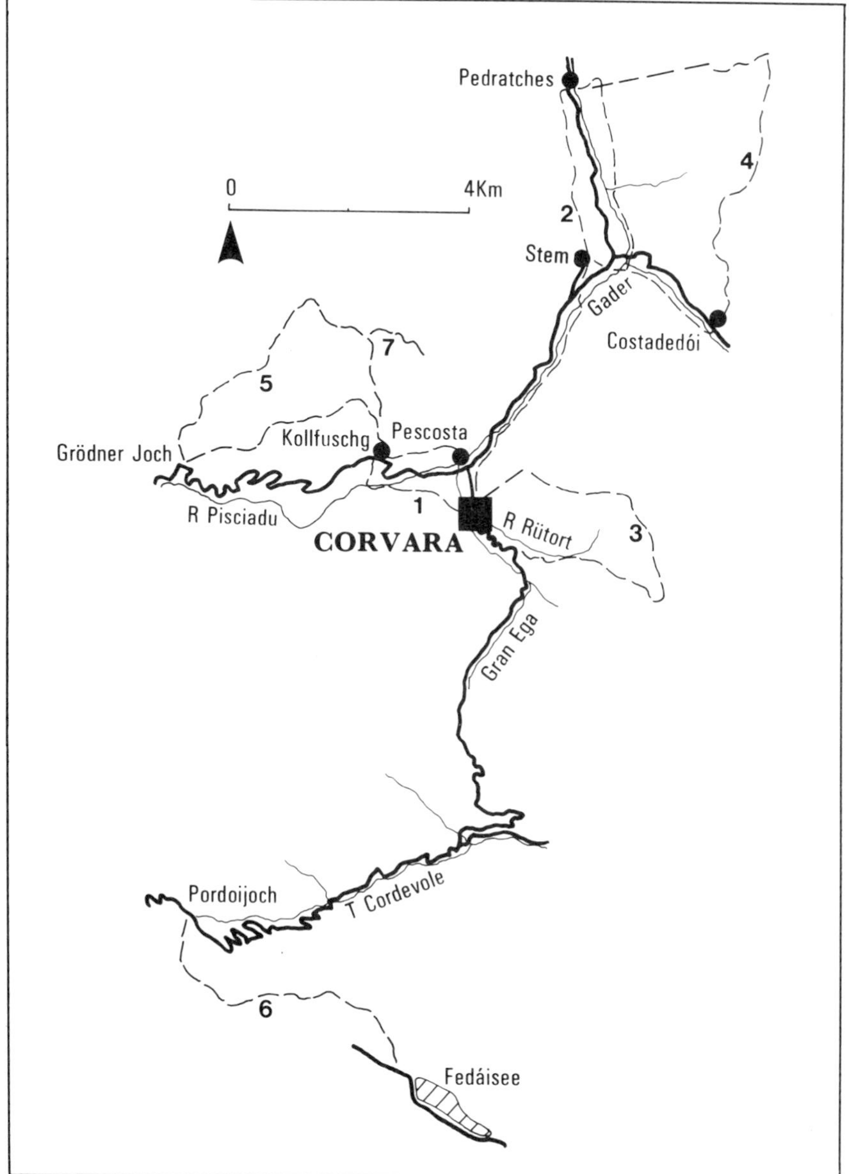

ROUTE 1

Corvara Golf Course, Kollfuschg (Colfosco), Pescosta

5km (3 miles). 1½ hours. Easy.
A pleasant stroll to ease away the strains of a long car journey.

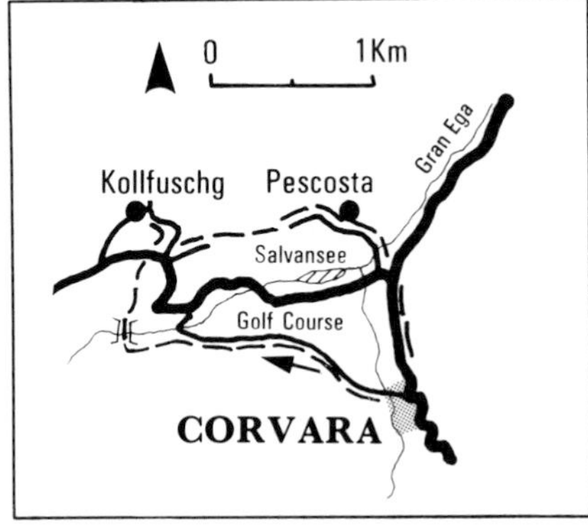

From the centre of Corvara follow the track by way of the golf course and camp site as far as the river. Turn left upstream for about ½km and at a footbridge turn right across the river and climb uphill then over the main road to Kollfuschg. After exploring the village return to the main road where a track to the left leads to Pescosta and the road back to Corvara.

Despite modern development Kollfuschg and Pescosta still retain a number of interesting old farm buildings.

ROUTE 2

Val Badia, Stem (la Villa), Pedratsches

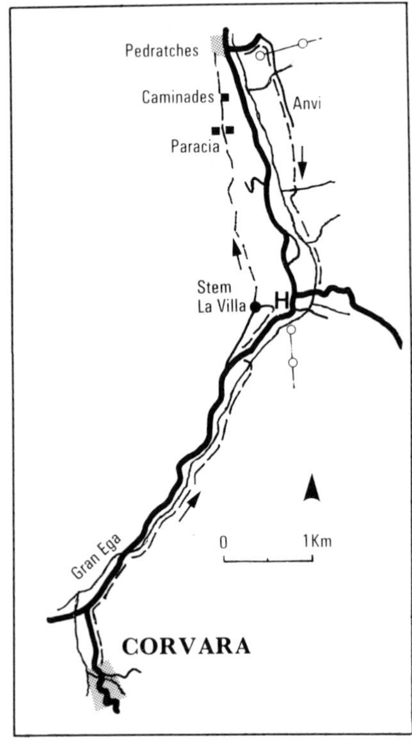

11km (7 miles). 3/4 hours. Easy.

Follow the Bruneck road northwards until it crosses the river. At the bridge turn right along a forest track and eventually rejoin the road below Stem (la Villa). Turn left into the village and walk as far as the central square. Turn right out of the square along a path through woods and meadows, passing Hotel Sompunt, continue through the hamlets of Paracia and Caminades to Pedratsches. Walk up the St Leonhard road almost as far as the centre of the village and turn right beneath the gondola lift and follow the track to Anvi. Beyond Anvi take the lower of three paths on the right and gradually descend to the river. Follow the river upstream to the main road where there is a regular bus service back to Corvara.

ROUTE 3

Col Alto chair lift, Pralongia Hut, Neger Hut

8km (5 miles). 3/4 hours. Easy/Moderate.
High alpine meadows with spectacular views of distant peaks.

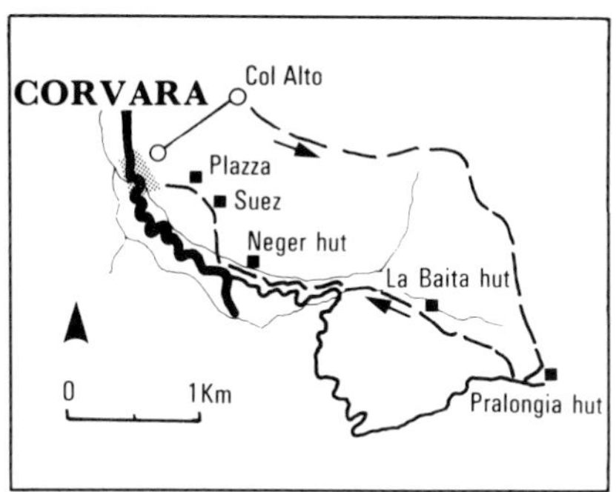

Take the Col Alto chairlift from behind the Posta Zirm Hotel and at the top follow path 23 (signposted) across an undulating grassy hillside to the Pralongia Hut. From the hut descend about 100m by a jeep track and turn right along path 24 to la Baita Hut and then the Neger Hut. Continue downhill to the Corvara road. Do not walk along the road but follow a path on the right to Suez and Plazza, then enter Corvara by a track which leads to the rear of the church.

ROUTE 4

Pedratsches, Heligkreuz Hut, Medes Wald, Costadedoi, Stem (la Villa)

8km (5 miles). 4 hours. Moderate.
High level forest walking with close views of the Kreuzkofel Peaks.

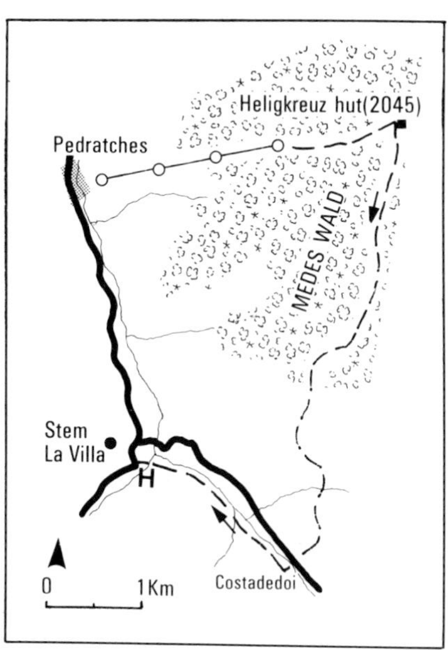

From Pedratsches take the gondola lift and walk along path 1 to the Heligkreuz Hut (the path is marked by the Stations of the Cross). At the hut follow path 15 (signposted) to the right through the forest and high meadows of the Medes Wald to Costadedoi. Cross the main road to join path 11 to Stem and catch a bus to Corvara.

The little chapel by the Heligkreuz Hut is interesting and has alleged relics of the Cross as part of the altar decoration.

ROUTE 5

Pescosta (1,574m), Pradat Hut, Ciampaijoch (Forcella di Ciampai) (2,388m), Crespeina Hochflache, Crespeinajoch (2,528), Cirjoch, Clark Hut, Grödner Joch (Passo Gardena), Forcelles Hut, Kollfuschg (Colfosco)

18km ($11\frac{1}{2}$ miles). 7/8 hours. Moderate/Difficult.
High level walking at its best across four mountain passes.

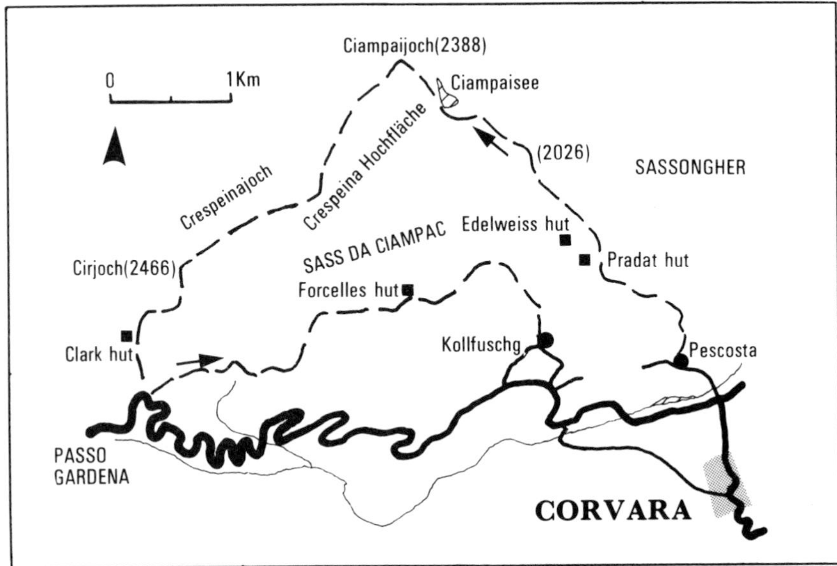

Beyond Pescosta a path climbs steeply but easily below the dominant cliffs of Sassongher to the Pradat Hut. Continue, passing the Edelweiss hut on the left then climbing gradually to point 2,026 on path 4. The angle of ascent eases a little as far as the lake of Ciampaisee. The path now steepens again before reaching the pass of Ciampaijoch (2,388m). Turn left on path 2 and cross a moonlike landscape in the high cauldron of the Crespeina Hochfläche. Climb steeply to Crespeinajoch (2,528m), then downhill steeply to the final pass at Cirjoch (2,466m). A short downhill section still on path 2 leads to the Clark Hut and the pass of the Grödner Joch, or Passo Gardena to give it its better known Italian name. *Anyone wishing to finish the walk here can catch a bus back to Corvara.* The route continues north-westwards on a path which follows the contours across the hillside beneath Sass da Ciampac to the Forcelles Hut and down to Kollfuschg and the road to Corvara.

An ideal first introduction to the stark grandure of the hidden recesses of the Dolomites, the climbing is steep in places, but if taken steadily should be well within the capabilities of any reasonably fit hill walker.

ROUTE 6

The Bindelweg (Vial del Pan), Pordoijoch, Sasso-Beccie Hut, Fedäiasee, Viletta Maria Hut

10km (6 miles). 4 hours. Moderate.
A classic high level route.

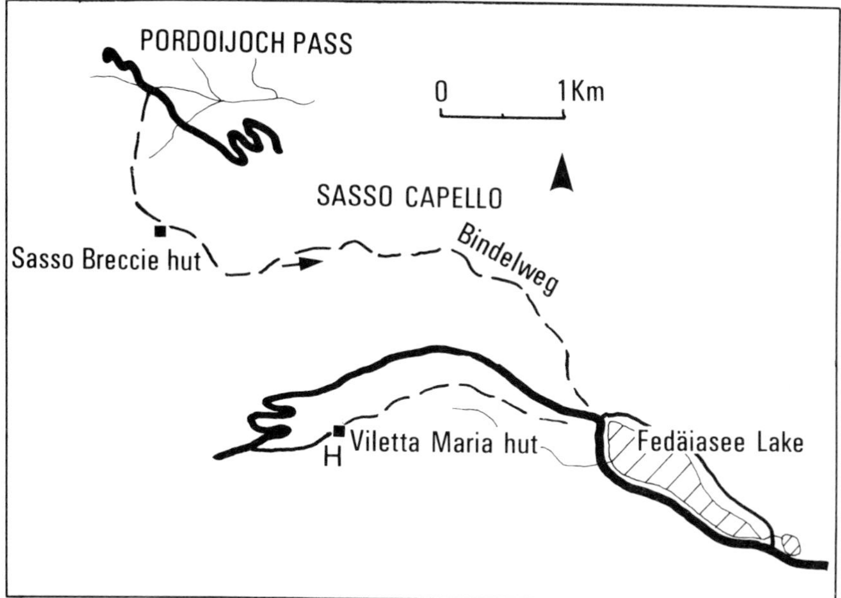

This route is easy to follow and starts at the top of the Pordoi Pass. The Bindelweg path is well waymarked as path 60 and climbs steadily from the pass to the Breccie hut. The path then follows the contours beneath the ridge of Sasso Capello before descending steeply to the manmade lake of Fedäiasee. A right turn at the dam leads to the Viletta Maria hut where there is a bus terminus. Return to the Pordoijoch by bus via Canazei.

The highlights of this route are the magnificent views of the glaciers of the Marmolada (3,340m) on the opposite side of the valley.

ROUTE 7

Sassongher (2,665m)

12km ($7\frac{1}{2}$ miles). 8 hours. Difficult. A mountain climb involving some exposed scrambling near to the summit.

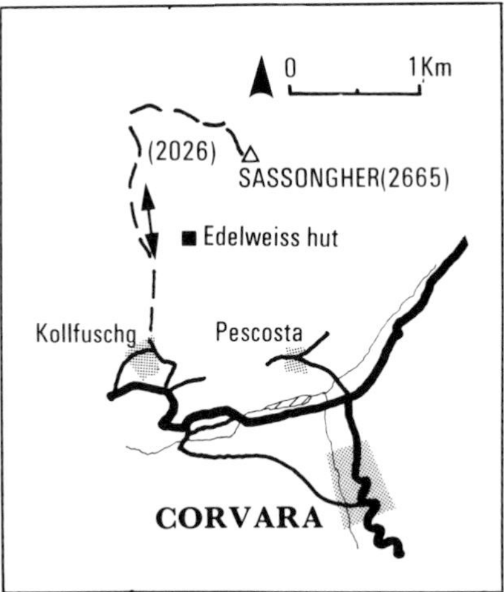

No one who stays in Corvara can fail to be impressed by the tower of Sassongher which seems to dominate every aspect of Val Badia.

There is an exposed section near to the summit which is protected by a wire rope. *It is however a place only for those with a good head for heights.*

Follow path 7 from Kollfuschg to the fork beyond point 2,026 and turn right towards the north-west ridge of Sassonger. At the ridge turn right along a well marked, but steep path which leads to a rock wall which is climbed aided by a fixed wire rope leading to easier ground below the summit. Return the same way.

The sense of achievement on reaching the summit must not dispell the need for care on the way down.

Forestry work beneath the peak of Heiligkreuz

BELLUNO

Piave

Recommended Map:
Kompass Carta Turistica (1:50,000) Sheet 77 Alpi Bellunesi

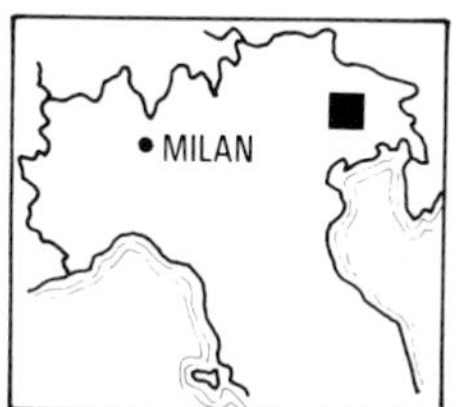

HOW TO GET THERE

Road: (1) South from Innsbruck by way of the Brenner Pass to Trento. Road 47 to Primolano and then Road 50 via Feltre to Belluno. (2) Leave the Milan/Venice autostrada (E13) at Padova and join Road 47 north to Primolano and 50 to Belluno.
Rail: Main line from Milan or Venice via Treviso.
Air: International airports at Milan and Venice (rail connections as above).
Language: Italian.

THE AREA

The smiling face of the Piave valley clearly marks the southern boundary of the fantastic limestone towers of the Dolomitic Alps, and the beautiful city of Belluno makes a delightful base from which to explore the nearby peaks and valleys.

With its close proximity to the Adriatic coast (Venice is little more than 1½ hours drive away), Belluno makes an interesting alternative when included as part of a seaside holiday. For centuries Belluno has been the administrative centre of the upper Piave and its stately Venetian styled palaces are well protected from the ravages of modern traffic by a well placed bypass. Agriculture is the main industry; Belluno marks the northern limit of the vineyards which grow the grapes of the Piave vintages, a range of pleasant medium quality red and white wines. This is also a cheese making region and an interesting diversion into the old part of the city will give due reward to the palate of the tourist prepared to experience the many and varied flavours on offer. Other culinary delights can be found down little side streets below the ancient city gates, such as a shop where you can watch pasta being made in a bewildering array of shapes.

During World War I German and Austrian armies managed to break through the fortified passes and peaks further north and drove the Italian armies down through the Piave to eventually threaten the industrial north of Italy. The retreat from Udine in the east to the Piave is graphically described in Ernest Hemingway's *A Farewell to*

Evening at the 7th Alpini

Arms. Hemingway was a volunteer ambulance driver at that time and the novel clearly reflects the horror of that war in this beautiful region.

The choice of Belluno as an attractive mountain holiday centre is threefold. Its closeness to the Adriatic and its links with the prosperity of the Renaissance have already been mentioned. The third and most

THINGS TO DO AND PLACES TO VISIT AROUND BELLUNO

Old City
Off the Piazzo Martiri. Renaissance and Venetian architecture. Market. Shops.

Museum
Old city. Roman and Renaissance exhibits.

Trout fishing
Rivers Ardo and Piave. Enquire locally at the tourist office for permits. Lago di Santa Croce. Permits available at nearby hotels.

Lake bathing and boating
Lago di Santa Croce.

Tennis
Piazza Piloni.
Fisterre.
Borgo Pra public park, east of main town area.
Alpe in Fiore.

Bathing
Public swimming pool (open air), Borgo Pra park.

Alpine Garden
Monte Faverghera. Collection of European and Oriental mountain plants.

important feature in a guide on mountain walking is the fact that a number of walks are from one of the Italian Alpine Club's huts, the Rifugio 7th Alpini. This hut, built by the 7th Alpine Regiment is an ideal introduction to the special life in alpine huts. Accommodation is very simple, varying from small private rooms to crowded dormitories or lagers. Food is basic but wholesome, and prices are reasonable. Above all is the special international atmosphere of friendship only found in the mountains. Obviously, Italian is the main language spoken in the hut, but German is readily understood, although you can easily get by with sign language. Members of any of the European Alpine Clubs get preferential terms while staying at this and other huts, but it is not essential to be a member if you intend only staying the odd night or so as the surcharge is small.

By using the Rifugio 7th Alpini the visitor can view at close quarters the fantastic walls of Monte Schiara. Those with sufficient mountain experience and a good head for heights might even attempt some of the climbs aided by *via ferrata*, a system or iron ladders and fixed wire ropes across the most difficult sections. Although the *via ferrata* offers safe passage over the most dangerous parts of the rock face, it must be stressed that only experienced climbers should attempt these routes. However, the humble hill walker adequately equipped with proper boots and windproof clothing, can enjoy a very close proximity to these climbs by using the 7th Alpini and the routes described in this text are highly recommended.

Rifugio 7th Alpini is the last stage southwards of the high level route across the Dolomites known as the Alta Via No 1. This is one of several high level routes across this dramatic mountain range and starts at Lake Braies near Dobiacco. The route takes at least 8-10 days, although it is usual to take longer to fit in climbs off route. The symbol for the route is a blue triangle. Other footpaths in the area are, in the main, clearly waymarked with red and white paint on rocks and trees. Path numbers corresponding to those on the Kompass map are shown at intervals, usually in black on the white band of the waymark. In this way route finding is easy, but care should still be given in following a particular route, especially at junctions with other tracks, or where the path is indistinctly defined on the ground.

Other walks described in this section of the guide use Belluno as a base and explore the valleys and lower peaks on either side of the Ardo, a stream which starts beneath Monte Schiara and joins the River Piave at Belluno. South of the city and reached by a road which climbs through vineyards is the easily climbed Monte Faverghera, where the view to the north is of the whole astonishing range of the Dolomites, while to the south stretches the Venetian plain and the Adriatic coast.

The use of public transport when following the walks in this section is minimal, but nevertheless it is worth knowing that the regional bus system is excellent and many comparatively remote villages are well serviced. Armed with this knowledge and a map the visitor could perhaps be easily encouraged to explore further routes other then those described.

FURTHER INFORMATION

Interesting towns nearby

Venice
Road 51 via Vittorio Veneto then 10 to Mestre and Venice.

Padova
Road 47 south.

Verona
As above then autostrada west.

Renaissance cities which were part of the Venetian Republic.

Pieve di Cadore
Birthplace of the artist Titian.

Lake Garda
Eastern Italian Lake District. Leave the Venice/Milan autostada at Verona to join the route 11.

Camp Sites
Park camping Nevegal.
Casera CTG Ronce.

Chair Lift
Nevegal-Monte Faverghera.

Accommodation
Belluno offers a wide range of accommodation from rented apartments to high class hotels. Details obtainable from the tourist office.

Tourist Office
Centro Touristico,
Piazza Martiri,
Belluno.

Bus Depot
By the railway station 150m north-west of city centre.

A farm above the Ardo

THE WALKS

While no walk actually starts or finishes in Belluno, it is assumed that the visitor will be staying there or nearby and will be either using a car or public transport to get to and from the routes. Also, due to the nature of the area, no walk can exactly be described as 'low level', but as with the rest of this guide, the walks are set out with the easiest first.

Path numbers mentioned in the description relate to numbers on the Kompass map. The same numbers are usually indicated on signposts at the start of the walk and occasionally painted on rocks or trees at intervals along the path.

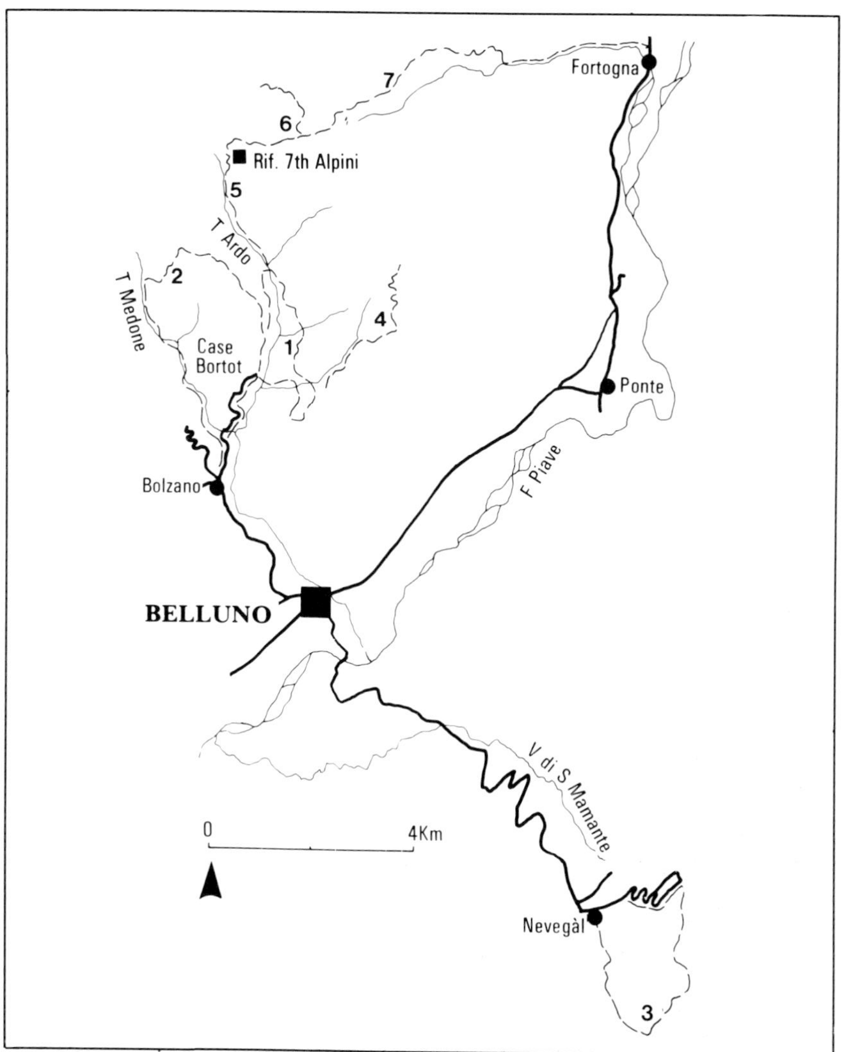

ROUTE 1

Bolzano di Belluno, Case Bortot, Ardo Valley, Mariano, Ponte Mortis

12km (7½ miles). 3/4 hours. Easy. A good introduction to the area. Mostly valley walking. Paths 501 and 519.

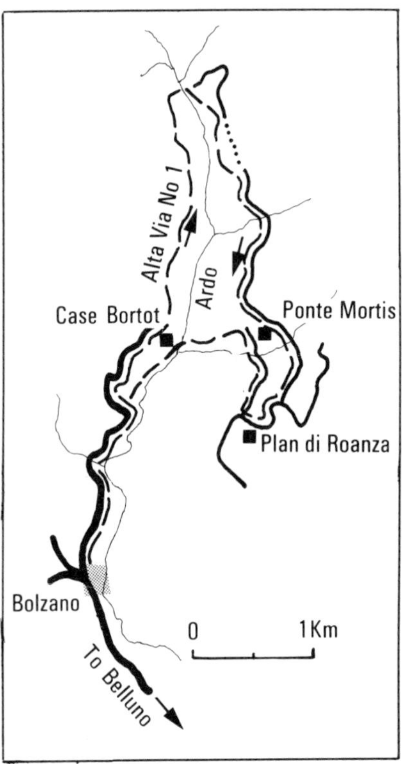

Either take the bus to Bolzano di Belluno and walk along the road to the restaurant of Case Bortot, or leave your car at the latter. The road continues northwards as a track which gradually becomes an easy to follow footpath marked with both the Alta Via No 1 blue and white triangle (this is the high level Dolomite route to Lake Braies) and the red and white stripes of path number 501. Follow 501 until it descends to and crosses the Ardo river, where another path numbered 519, turns away sharply to the right. Take this and follow the contours across the hillside until it joins the Monte Serva road at Pian di Roanza. Turn right along the road and after about a half kilometre turn right again as far as a group of farm buildings where a left turn leads down to Ponte Mortis and eventually the Bolzano road.

A variant to this walk turns left at Pra Podin and joins the Monte Serva road by the restaurant of Casera pra Furlon.

This is a pleasant introductory walk with views of the Monte Schiara Massif at the head of the Ardo valley. Salamanders, both golden and alpine, are common and will often be seen in the early morning, especially after wet weather. Woodland alpine flowers such as cyclamen bloom in their season.

ROUTE 2

Ponte de Gargadon, Medone river, Forcella Monpiana, Case Bortot

11km (7 miles). 4 hours. Moderate.
Path 506

An interesting walk along a deep river valley, through forest to a particularly fine viewpoint at Forcella Monpiana.

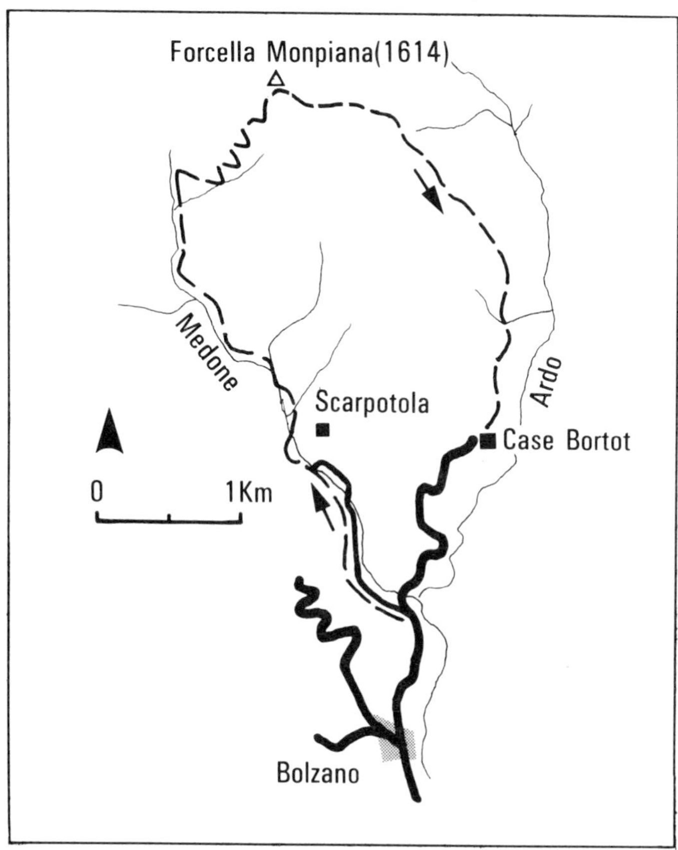

Leave the Bolzano/Case Bortot road immediately before the Gargadon bridge across the Medone river by a farm track on the left, which climbs gently up the south side of the valley. Leave the track before it crosses the river and continue uphill a little further to eventually cross the river opposite the farmstead of Scarpotala. Beyond the route begins to climb steeply, but on a well engineered path as far as the Col of Forcella Monpiana (1,614m). Turn right and downhill through forest to join path 501, where a right turn leads to the restaurant of Case Bortot and the road to Bolzano and Belluno.

The view from the Forcella Monpiana col is the highlight of this walk.

ROUTE 3

Nevegal and Monte Faverghera (1,611m)

5km (3 miles). 2/3 hours.
Easy to moderate.
An easy mountain climb with plenty of good refreshment stops.

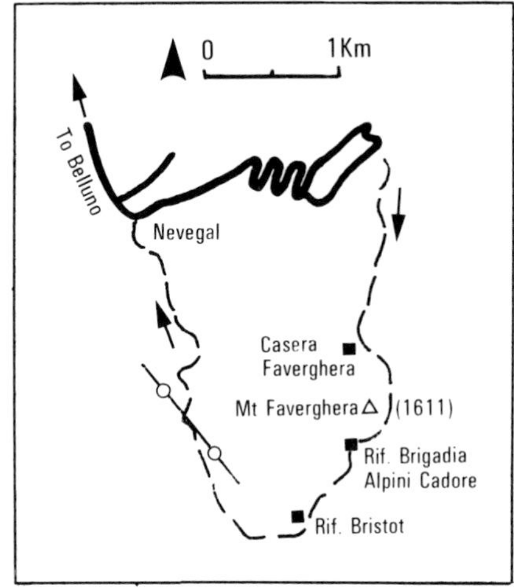

Take the Caleipo road south from Belluno as far as Nevegal (there is a bus route at least for part of this road — check locally), and walk from the road end to the alpine garden at Casera Faverghera. Continue across the summit of Monte Faverghera to the Rifugio Brigada Alpini Cadore and onwards to Rifugio Bristot. Descend to the right beneath the chair lift and back to Nevegal.

The highlight of this walk for flower lovers is the Alpine Garden, but the views north of the Dolomites and south towards Venice will appeal to all.

ROUTE 4

Monte Serva (2,133m)

8km (5 miles). 4/5 hours. Moderate.
Path 517
A moderate climb of 1,233m without any unduly difficult or rocky gradients.

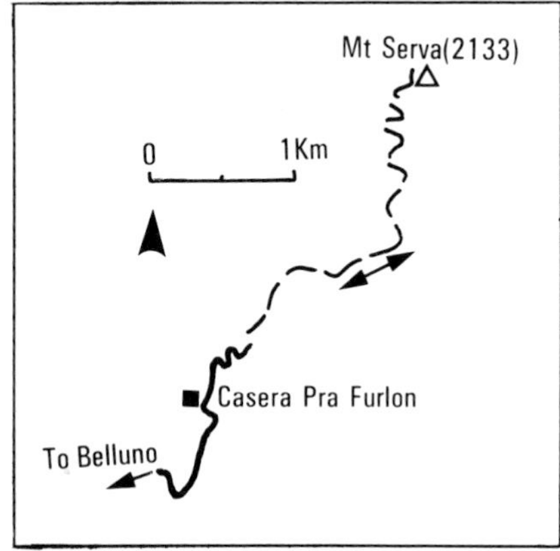

Drive along the Sopracroda road to the restaurant at Casera Pra Furlon and simply follow the path 517 to the summit of Monte Serva returning by the same route.

This is probably the easiest of all Dolomite peaks in the area and yet a first time 'mountaineer' should bear in mind the fact that it is, like all Dolomite peaks, a steep climb. Taken steadily however it is a most pleasant introduction to high level walking.

The next three walks are based on the CAI hut of the 7th Alpini. Beds and food are available without prior booking. The hut may be crowded and as no one is turned away sleeping accommodation could be primitive.

ROUTE 5

Case Bertot to Rifugio 7th Alpini (1,491m)

5km (3 miles). 2/3 hours.
Easy to moderate.
Path 501
A harder walk than it looks at first glance and one to be taken steadily.

From Case Bertot simply follow path 501 and the Alta Via No 1 signs along the valley of the Ardo, through pine forest, crossing the stream three times and then a steep climb to the hut by a series of zig-zags.

The Rifugio 7th Alpini is dramatically situated beneath the south face of Monte Schiara. Three via ferrata routes climb this face — the Sperti, Zacchi and Marmol — all are for experts only.

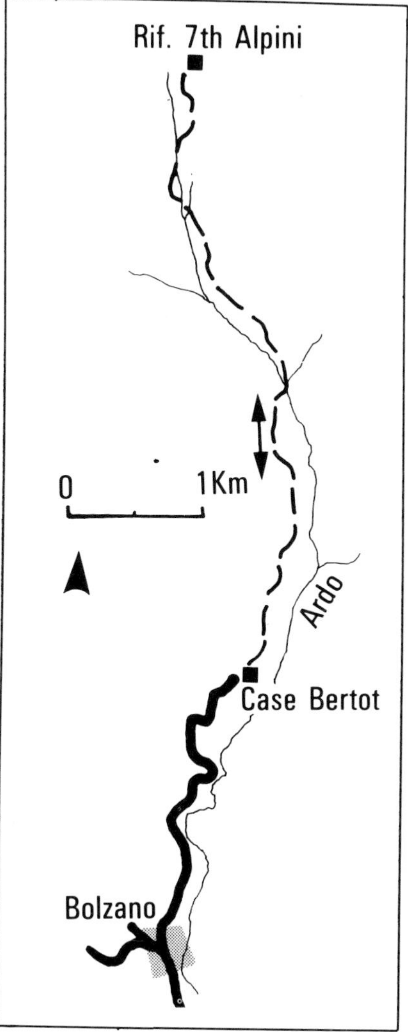

ROUTE 6

Rifugio 7th Alpini, Monte Pelf (2,502m)

5km (3 miles). 4/5 hours.
Moderate to difficult.
Paths 505 and 511

This is a stiff climb and the summit ridge is narrow, but should be within the capabilities of most fit walkers.

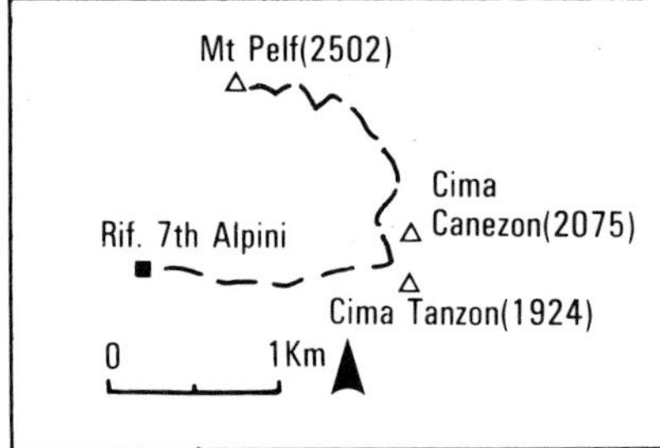

Follow path 505 (signposts begin at the hut), eastwards to half way beyond the col of Forcella Pis Pilon and the unnamed col between Cimas Canevon and Tanzon. Turn left at a sign and follow path 511 to the narrow summit ridge of Monte Pelf. The path is indistinct in places so look out for red markers painted on the rocks.

The view from the summit is beyond compare; Monte Schiara is the immediate neighbour and then a whole complex of summits appear to the north. Time spent in trying to identify, from the map, all the summits in view is a rewarding pastime.

ROUTE 7

Rifugio 7th Alpini to Fortogna

12km ($7\frac{1}{2}$ miles). 4/5 hours. Moderate.
Path 505

A pleasant way to return from the high mountains.

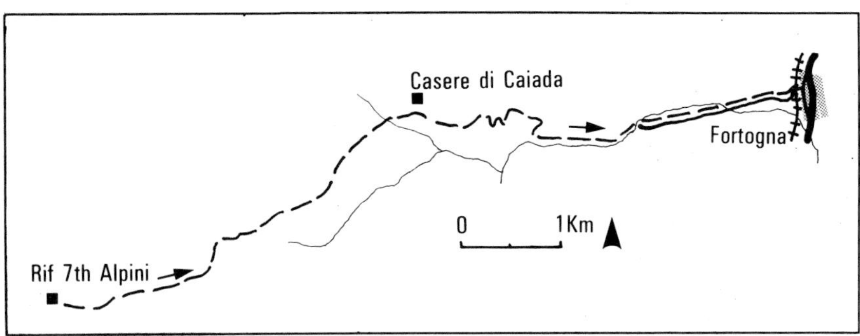

From the hut follow path 505 eastwards across Forcella Pis Pilon and the next col. Walk downhill through forest to the hill farmsteads of Casere di Caiada, then steeply down into the valley of the River Desedan on an improving track which leads to the village of Fortogna, where there is a choice of either train or bus back to Belluno.

Take care on the steep zig-zag path below Casere di Caiada which can be slippery in wet weather.